TEN THOUSAND APOLOGIES

Also by Adelle Stripe

Black Teeth and a Brilliant Smile

TEN THOUSAND APOLOGIES

Fat White Family and the Miracle of Failure

Adelle Stripe
and Lias Saoudi

WHITE RABBIT

First published in Great Britain in 2022 by White Rabbit,
an imprint of The Orion Publishing Group Ltd
Carmelite House, 50 Victoria Embankment
London EC4Y 0DZ

An Hachette UK Company

10 9 8 7 6 5 4 3 2 1

A CIP catalogue record for this book is
available from the British Library.

ISBN (Hardback) 978 1 4746 1784 0
ISBN (eBook) 978 1 4746 1786 4
ISBN (Audio) 978 1 4746 1787 1

Printed and bound in Great Britain by
Clays, Ltd, Elcograf, S.p.A

www.whiterabbitbooks.co.uk
www.orionbooks.co.uk

For Melkhir (Jida)

This is a fictional biography and an alternative version of historic events.

It is a portrait of a chaotic, intoxicated and unruly cast, many of whom remember the same event in a completely different way. The characters known as Fat White Family have been fabricated, reimagined and embellished. Fact has been used to create fiction.

This is their ecstatic truth and exists purely within the realm of speculation.

CONTENTS

CONTENTS

PROLOGUE

After a few uneventful days of sweating and coughing alone in his bedroom on the top floor of his father's semi-detached in suburban Cambridge, events took a serious turn for the worse. The previous days had been stress-free, and as the outside world started to crumble, being back in his room, asleep in a single bed, seemed like as safe a place as any. Trays of homecooked meals were delivered outside his door by his stepmother, who spent hours of each day preparing Algerian cuisine for the household. Tagines, couscous and fresh vegetables, mint tea and honey-soaked pastries. Within hours of arriving the burden had started to lift.

It was three o'clock in the afternoon, and he could hear his father talking loudly on the telephone as he worked in the room directly below, his voice booming through the ceiling, recounting the situation of his resident sons to the eldest, who lived in Manchester and had recently moved back to England after being thrown out of China penniless, his beloved French bulldogs left behind. His brother's apartment had been raided by the CCP, and they had parted ways on a sour note due to his vociferous criticism of their somewhat heavy-handed approach to human rights. Still, at least he was alive, and could now ring his father for a regular summit on the state of his younger brothers, who had been similarly banished from Algeria on the last flight home as the emerging plague took hold.

As he sat in his room, listening to his father, he heard him say, 'If after two weeks they haven't sorted themselves out, they're out on their arse. I'm not responsible for them anymore.' There was a long pause, and then his father shouted again, 'The

1

youngest doesn't know any better, but the other one . . . he has to do something. Yes, he *should* get the £92-a-week dole because this is bloody ridiculous!'

At that moment his heart began to sink as he recalled all of the far and distant lands he was supposed to have reached that year, the sold-out audiences, the euphoric road trips through Asia, festivals in Australia, then a month in Ireland, a garret in Paris and, of course, a season in the mountains of Kabylia, visiting his one-hundred-year-old grandmother and the extended family, who would celebrate the return of their prodigal grandson. He had not predicted that the entire year of touring would be cancelled, with the complete loss of his income. Nor had he envisaged that it would perhaps be he alone who would bring the contagion into Algeria, carrying it on Air France's flight from London, where he had spent a night smoking jazz cigarettes passed from the nicotine-stained fingertips of his louche saxophone player. After all of this, to end up back at his father's house was a bitter pill.

For the most part he tolerated his father, and they were able to communicate on a certain level across the cultural divide, but the conversation he heard downstairs that afternoon triggered an unpredictable response.

Surrounded by red mist, he ran downstairs, shouting at the top of his voice, 'I have spent years trying to drag this band out of the mire! At least your industry is unscathed! What about me? The band paid fifteen thousand in tax last year and the government won't give me a fucking thing! It's alright for you, raking in the shekels, sat in your office, complaining . . .'

Then his father blew up.

'Well, you should bloody *do something* instead of sitting on your arse upstairs,' he yelled. 'What *is* it that you *do* exactly?'

A feverish rage erupted, and the blood raced up through his neck as he screamed at his father for his lack of respect or empathy, then a torrent of expletives cascaded from his lips for several minutes as he transformed into his teenage self and bellowed at him for his shitty behaviour towards women, especially each of his wives, and his limp-minded obsession with cash.

'You will die alone if you continue this way!' he yelled at his father. 'As we know, old dogs do not learn new tricks!'

In the heat of the moment the telephone rang again. His father put his elder brother on loudspeaker, and the argument between him, the eternally compromised middle son, and his irate begetter escalated to fever pitch. There was a scream, then a thrash at the wall, and then a diabolical two-way outpouring of the particular brand of spiteful verbal abuse that could only emanate from within the cradle of their family.

Hearing the cacophony, his younger brother ran down the stairs, trying his best to calm the eruption by pushing his arms between the two of them, before chasing his brother down the road as he stormed out of the house, his face burning bright with the anger of an adolescent bombast he could not control.

After the storm had passed, the two brothers walked through the sleepy suburbs towards the tranquil acres of Grantchester.

'What was that all about?' the younger muttered to himself. 'Nothing. This whole situation is sending everyone nuts. The world is sick. It's fucked, man. At least I don't feel like the odd one out anymore . . .'

The middle brother paced along the road in painful silence, stretching his long grasshopper legs at a pace the youngest could barely keep up with.

As the sun started to dip behind the rooftops, they stopped for an hour, drank lukewarm bottles of Desperados by the Cam and listened to the gentle hiss of a poplar tree. When he returned home with a Chinese takeaway later that evening, he put £80 in cash on the kitchen table and slowly walked up to his room to check Facebook, where, on the family thread, his father had written a missive detailing his son's failures as a man as he saw them.

'How can he not have a roof over his head at his age?' he wrote. 'He has wasted his life and is nothing but a failure. Why can't he be more like his older brother, who has at least rented a flat!'

Upon reading this, he could no longer contain his fury, and decided to leave the very next morning. But not before responding on the thread that his father was nothing more than an emotional abortion of a man. He then misspelled the word 'Adios!' and left the group. With gritted teeth he began to pack, throwing crusty boxers into a carrier bag.

At dawn, he awoke from a dream in which his mother was suffocating from fluid on the lungs. As he opened his eyes he felt a sinking feeling in his stomach, knowing that he would have to leave under the cover of darkness and head back to the city, to become homeless again at the tender age of thirty-four.

On the train he received a text from his father saying, 'If you leave today then this family is finished, so why don't you come back and paint the fence?'

Staring at the screen in the palm of his hand, he wished he'd said goodbye to him in person, and immediately regretted the previous night's drama. Just like his progenitor, he was too proud to concede defeat. It was simply the latest in a long line of family arguments; no surprise, then, that this one had escalated beyond the point of no return. If anything happened to either of them in the next few months it would be a source of irredeemable, lifelong pain. A sadness welled inside him as he read the news headline on his phone predicting forty thousand deaths before summer was out. According to reports, London was the heart of the contagion.

He stepped off the train at King's Cross, looked to his left and right and saw that he was one of only three passengers to have boarded that day. The station was almost deserted and the plaza at 9 a.m. was empty, aside from pigeons with deformed feet pecking at a discreet mound of vomit and two homeless men sitting by the foyer with their hands held out for baksheesh.

The apocalypse has been and gone and only this toothless gang of junkies have survived, he thought to himself. *Maybe these were our civilisation's most upstanding citizens, the ones best prepared for the onslaught of doom, the only ones to have made it through alive . . .*

He made his way down to the empty Victoria line. The posters for films, festivals and cultural events now seemed ridiculous in their technicolour self-confidence. He sat in a desolate carriage heading towards Brixton, put his head in his hands and coughed up an anxious wad of dark phlegm into his mouth that tasted of a month-old fat pan. Despite everything, it felt good to be back in the dirt.

Front Garden Like a Prayer of Grass

Leaving the clogged A roads, Bashir stared at the shadowy streets as he made his way up Wakefield Road in his beat-up Datsun towards the centre of town. He was taken aback by the lack of colour. In Huddersfield, everything was black. The houses, the mills, the shops, the pavements. Coal dust clung to the brickwork, and in a region almost entirely powered by coal, its sediment was a defining feature of this Pennine landscape; if it was on the outside of buildings, or layering dust on windowsills, it was most certainly lining the lungs of its inhabitants.

He switched on the radio, tuning in to hear the first division football commentary, and then stopped the dial at a local station playing hits by the Commodores, Gary Glitter and Demis Roussos. Outside, girls with long hair and short skirts walked along the road beside him as lorries splashed rain puddles against their legs; they were whiter than any he had ever seen, almost pale blue in parts. He wondered if there was any sunlight in this part of Yorkshire at all.

Bashir wound down the window to clear the windscreen of condensation and started to sing along in the newly acquired language he'd mostly picked up from watching soap operas on a television set with a coat-hanger aerial at his digs in Norwich. His host family, in their own quiet way, represented a new life to him; it was a place of liberation, and even the strange English food, which mostly consisted of bland sausages, powdered mash, tinned peas, gravy and white bread with margarine on a side plate, was an exotic offering in all of its 1970s dowdiness.

He had arrived that winter from a lycée on the north coast of Greater Kabylia. A smart boy, and precocious, he was selected as one of three hundred in eastern Algeria to join the elite college. Bashir had been sent from his Berber village in the Djurdjura mountain range with a scholarship, determined to leave the post-civil war chaos of his country, but quickly found his own native tongue was outlawed by the authorities. Any students caught speaking Kabyle were reprimanded, and the FLN's government had decided to replace French with Arabic, which was a confusing situation for Bashir, who now had to speak three languages fluently to survive. When one of his schoolfriends was 'disappeared' by secret police for hiding a book in his locker written in the forbidden vernacular, Bashir quickly took it as a sign to leave the country at the first opportunity.

He spent a month in Algiers learning English, before transferring to the sleepy Anglian city of Norwich. When a letter arrived informing him that he'd be spending the next three years studying in a town called Huddersfield, he was puzzled but accepted the offer as one of five students from North Africa that year. He knew nothing of the place aside from Bill Shankly, who once managed Huddersfield Town, and that, according to his sponsor at the Algerian Oil Company, ICI had a factory there, a fact that he recalled as he drove into the town, making a mental note of jobs he might apply for when the moment arrived.

Only two months previously he had walked through passport control at Heathrow with a brown briefcase given to him by his father, Kaci, beaming with happiness and relief at the opportunity laid out in front of him. When he caught sight of his first English toilets upon landing in the terminal that day, he stared with amazement. They were the cleanest he had ever seen. As he pissed into the ceramic urinals he smiled at his friend beside him, both of them incredulous at the facilities; it was as if they were entering a portal into another dimension.

The townscape Bashir faced from his bedroom window each morning was a dismal one. Chimneys pumped out smoke from the rooftops, which mixed with dense diesel fumes to form an ashen fog that hung over the town; a Northern peasouper that never cleared. Peering out from his student hall, the buildings and rain provided a dingy contrast to the dry, sunlit environment of Maillot, the small town where he came from. Olive groves, cherry orchards, cork trees and date palms were a distant memory, and each day he yearned for the warmth and light, believing his blood was slowly turning to ice the longer he spent in the bleak industrial landscape of West Riding.

Although visually the mills, factories and terrace houses were unfamiliar, the people of Yorkshire reminded him of those he grew up with. Even with its dour appearance and chuntering attitude there was an element of its character that connected with those from Kabylia. Stoic, stubborn and separatist. Both regions militant in their political convictions. On weekends he drove around villages and drank warm beer in places with peculiar names that he struggled to pronounce: Netherthong, Slaithwaite, Mytholmroyd. In snugs and smoky pool rooms he conversed with the miserable old tykes who inhabited them. It was almost as if he was back in his own Kabylian heartland. In those upland watering holes, people were warm and cordial, and he never felt threatened. They taught him how to speak Yorkshire-Algerian, often laughing at his attempts to communicate in their rich local dialect. He had finally found a place that felt like home.

By the time Christmas arrived, he started to frequent Huddersfield's bars and nightclubs, in particular a debauched tavern called Johnny's. Surrounded by hard-drinking Yorkshiremen, who were sometimes dressed as Droogs, Turkish belly-dancers,

Native Americans or Playboy Bunnies, it quickly became a place where he could dance all night, talk to girls, drink until dawn and lose himself.

It was on a night out at Johnny's that Bashir first bumped into a girl called Michelle, who often spent her weekends dancing in the town's nightclubs before clocking on for her early shift at a textile mill. They met under a mirrorball one night, as women danced around their handbags to 'Dreadlock Holiday'. He bought her a glass of Babycham, and she kissed the dashing Algerian, running her fingers through his thick, curly hair, laughing at his dancing and silly jokes. Being with him was the perfect escape from the clatter of the looms.

You don't consider how much of an anomaly you're dealing with. It's your mum and dad, after all. It's not until much later on in life that you realise your family is clumsily straddling two, largely irreconcilable worlds.

My mum's fondness for otherdom, for the exotic, for the dark-skinned, handsome young stranger at the bar with the Afro and the crappy English doesn't need much explaining: northern boredom. That being said, since she moved back to Yorkshire from Northern Ireland a year ago, back to Scarborough and the country of her childhood after thirty years in exile, she's been brimming with anecdotes about how this miracle actually came to pass.

I seldom get my mother on her own. I've always had to scrap for her attention with three other, more belligerent males. But on one occasion shortly after Christmas last year I did, and she started spilling the beans over a couple of tumblers of gin and Diet Coke. During the summer holidays, as a child, she used to stand on Scarborough's North Bay, which was now five minutes from her house, and gaze out across the North Sea, believing that on the other side of it lay Africa. She told me that on a clear day, if she squinted her eyes just right, she could make out palm trees and little black fellows marching around beneath them with pale soles on the bottoms of their dark-skinned feet. From that point on in her life, Mum told me, she wanted to have black babies. That was her dream. 'I suppose Algeria is halfway there,' I told her . . .

☪

Michelle was the girl-next-door: luminous eyes, long dark hair and bangs, plump cheeks like ripened apples. Like many of the town's female residents, she had a stubborn spirit born from tough lives endured over centuries. These were women who often birthed nine children and lost a handful more. Many worked in the textile industry and were half-deaf from mill machinery. Generations of women fed and nursed their own geriatric parents, kept house, scrubbed the front step each day, boil-washed sheets and nets to an acceptable public standard and, when the request arrived, were expected to lay out the dead.

Michelle's family were from the village of Skelmanthorpe and her father worked at Woolley Colliery. Like many working-class lads in South Yorkshire at the time, he was offered a job in the mining industry at fifteen and immediately joined its ranks. His parents were active members of the Communist Party in Barnsley, as was he. After meeting his wife in Hoyland, they moved into a council house but were evicted due to rent arrears. Michelle, as the eldest, assumed responsibility over her siblings as they grew up, but recalls sitting in a café as a child with her belongings in bags around her, the whole family made homeless. Rather than sleep on the streets, they moved into a small terrace in the village at Station Terrace, where their grandparents lived. There were seven family members squashed into a two-up, two-down. Her parents had a volatile relationship but continued to have more children. Their house was so typically Yorkshire that it was used as a location to film *Oh No It's Selwyn Froggitt*, the ITV comedy about the donkey-jacket-wearing council labourer, Working Men's Club secretary and all-round public nuisance.

When Michelle was thirteen years old, talk of a strike started to bubble at home. Her father usually received a weekly pay packet, but for six weeks he had to support five children and his wife as he stood on the picket line. There was barely any government assistance, and in the village people shared cups of sugar, leftover flour and washing powder to survive.

Across the country, factories were run by coal; food production ceased, as did the textile industry, even candles were in short supply. For families like Michelle's, there was an extra sting. Open fires started at dawn and burned until midnight. Without coal they started to freeze. Window frames rotted from lashings of wind and rainfall, and ice formed inside on nithering winter mornings. The fight to stay warm was relentless.

During the Strike, the ton of coal that was delivered each month from the National Coal Board to its workers ceased without warning. For her father, it was catastrophic. Not only were his family going hungry; there was scant heat to warm them. Each day, he took his catapult into the fields and fired it at rabbits who shot out from beneath hedges on Strike Lane. For eight weeks they lived on rabbit stew, a nutritious hot meal riddled with tiny bones that had to be picked out of their teeth.

Just beyond their sandstone house was a coal screen from Emley Moor Colliery, where waste coal was dumped in slagheaps. It was the last pit in Yorkshire where miners lay on their sides to extract coal. From the mineshaft it was sent to Skelmanthorpe by conveyer belt, where it was washed, sorted and discarded before bagging. What was left became the only source of heat the family could find.

Lit by floodlights, and overseen by NCB security, the screen of waste coal became a nightly visit for the family. The neighbourhood children scrambled across it, throwing coal into bags and pockets before running off into the night. What was collected would often explode in the fireplace, spitting and detonating before fizzling out. Michelle's father was caught with a shovel one night and reprimanded, and for the next week they went cold. His persistence eventually paid off when he discovered an open seam of bituminous coal with a friend on the outskirts of the village. Together, they dug it out with a pickaxe, using the same methods monks had used in the fourteenth century. It was a lifesaver, a gift from God in their darkest hour.

The Strike of 1974 was punishing for the community. Michelle and her siblings circled each scrap of food like hyenas; one tin of beans fed five, with milk used to loosen the sauce. They shovelled thin pancakes into their ravenous mouths, and on Sundays their grandmother used a tin of stewing steak with pastry to make one small pie that was split between them on a saucer. A weekly packet of biscuits was the only sugar they ate. The children were so poor that cardboard lined their shoes. This Dickensian scene was being experienced by families across the region; poverty and hunger were commonplace, although the men still found enough money to go to the pub on Friday nights, a hard fact that had not escaped their wives. Drinking beer was non-negotiable, after all.

Throughout this time, Michelle's father was insistent that she received an education. Playing truant was never acceptable to him. He encouraged her to read the dictionary each day, as if her life depended on her ability to master words. Despite her teenage protestations, Michelle would drag herself to school where she took classes in Home Economics and Needlework, the usual lessons delivered to Northern working-class girls in training to be housewives or textile mill workers. Not much more was expected of them, although her father always had faith that his daughters would achieve more.

On weekends Michelle worked in a dairy, filling milk bottles and washing glass, fixing tops and scrubbing fridges to bring money in for the house. Lunchtime breaks were spent sitting on a stone wall in the dense moorland mist, eating warm Mucky Fat sandwiches. The farmer also gave her fifteen-year-old brother a winter job chopping firewood to sell from the front gate of his farm. Thrilled to be earning cash, he started chopping logs gathered from distant woodland on the back of a tractor. One day, tragically, his welly slipped and he fell straight into the circular saw. Its vicious mechanical jaws took the bottom of his arm off. Hearing his cries, the farmer's wife ran out to the bloody scene, made a makeshift tourniquet, picked his arm off the ground and put it in the pantry's deep freezer. By the time he arrived at Huddersfield Royal Infirmary, gangrene had set in; surgeons had to cut the arm back to the shoulder socket to save his life. Only a stump remained.

The community rallied round the family and held hog roasts to raise money to send her brother to Switzerland and get a bionic arm. Even though it was a kind gesture, the last thing her brother wanted was a robotic arm. His real object of desire was an automatic Capri. The NHS sent hooks and false limbs through the post, and he stuck the grotesque pink rubber appendages in the garden; poking out of the grass, they resembled zombies that were coming back from the dead. It was the only front lawn for miles around with such a peculiar decoration.

☪

After leaving school, like many other local girls Michelle started work at Samuel Tweed & Co at Whitley Willows Mill. The company made fabrics for floor rugs, scarves and stoles, and had introduced mohair onto the shop floor by the time Michelle started work. Outside the building was a mill pond where black swans floated across the water. Each day Michelle walked through

15

town to work in the mending shed. She repaired glitches in patterns, and re-stitched loose threads.

Her first rented room was in a basic cottage of soot-blackened stone on the outskirts of town, with stippled walls and low ceilings. At the top of the landing was an open shower with no door. It was a huge improvement on the cramped conditions she had experienced at home; finally having her own room was a luxury. Within a few months of moving in, Michelle started dating a young man, Ali, who she met in a bar by the Packhorse Centre, and for six months they had a romance until one day he travelled to Newcastle and never came back. Ali was a student at Huddersfield Polytechnic, but it was one of his friends, Bashir, who began to show her some attention in the weeks following Ali's departure. She was quite smitten with Bashir, who was the life and soul of the party. In contrast, he viewed their relationship as a welcome distraction from his studies, but one that held little long-term significance.

By winter 1979 she had fallen pregnant, which was an unexpected and unwelcome piece of news for Bashir, who was suddenly torn between two places. Back home in Kabylia, there were expectations and arrangements between families that started at a young age. In Berber culture, life is to be preserved and protected. Children are a responsibility that cannot be shunned. For months he was a broken man, unable to comprehend the way forward, paralysed by the hopes of his parents and the impending birth of his first child. He locked himself away in the library for the following months, hoping that study would offer a solution, or at the very least a temporary escape.

In Huddersfield at that time, being pregnant and unmarried at eighteen was a social taboo; young women were sent to homes or schools for unmarried mothers where their baby would be born in secret, away from the community and the shame it had brought. Newborns were removed from their mothers after birth and adopted; some were put into children's homes. Throughout her first trimester, Michelle worked each day in the mill but suffered from such severe morning sickness that she could barely spend time on the shop floor without throwing up from the constant nausea. She delayed the necessary conversation with her family, and when she finally told her mother, she was adamant that Michelle terminate the pregnancy. Her father was far more sympathetic and told his daughter, 'If you want to keep it, I will help and support you in any way I can. I'll even adopt it if that's what you need me to do. I am here for you.'

Michelle was touched by her father's concern and knew that he would always protect her. After she lost her job from disabling morning sickness, he collected her from the cottage and drove her back home to live with him. By this point, her mother had left him for a Mauritian lover, so by default Michelle became mother to the whole family.

The council eventually housed her on the Sheepridge Estate so she would have a place to bring up her child. It was a damaging period and on one occasion, while pregnant, she was violently attacked on the street for no reason at all.

When she finally went into labour, her empty howls filled the corridors as severe nurses admonished her for being unmarried in the birth suite. A friend who was also a single mother bought a cheap ring before she went into the hospital and was treated much more sympathetically, a small detail that could have made a huge difference at the time. She had not anticipated the judgemental attitudes of the hospital staff, or their lack of interest in the pain she was suffering.

A few hours after Michelle had delivered her son, a social worker visited her holding a folder of adoption papers. It was suggested that she should sign him away, 'for the best', as he was mixed race and more importantly, she didn't have a husband. Michelle was furious at the audacity, that the authorities would try and tear her son from her arms only hours after the birth, when she was in her most vulnerable state. Although she

17

was still sore and bruised, Michelle took no time in telling them where to shove it. She yelled, 'Fuck off – he's my baby and I'm keeping him', and threatened to throw the social worker out of the window before the Sister pulled her from the ward.

For the first few days the baby was called Benjamin, before Michelle misheard another Scottish name on a Fairy Liquid television advert on the ward and renamed him Tamlan, after Tamlin, meaning 'Little Tom'. One of Bashir's friends, Freddo, rang him when he heard that Michelle was still in the Princess Royal Maternity Home, to tell him she had delivered a son. Bashir suddenly felt an overwhelming sense of responsibility as a father. He finally came to visit carrying a small bunch of yellow carnations as a peace offering under one arm.

In contrast to the attitudes of the local authority, having a mixed race and 'illegitimate' child was accepted by Michelle's family, who saw no problem with baby Tam's Algerian heritage. Back in the village of Skelmanthorpe, however, views were different. A few months after his birth, a drinker was talking to Michelle's uncle in the pub, and shouted, 'I've seen her baby in town, and he's not that black!' as he slurped on his pint of Timothy Taylor. Her uncle was furious and stoved the drinker's face in until it was beaten to a pulp, a violent act that Michelle was secretly proud of when the news finally reached her.

Moonlight on the Prison Roof

The first indication the Saoudis had of the new addition to their family was via a phone call from Bashir at the airport. Down a crackling line, they were instructed to collect his wife and son from Algiers and take them to the village. His brothers, Sheriff and Abder, drove through Bouïra and out of Kabylia towards the capital where Michelle and Tam would be waiting for them, fresh from the flight. It was the first time Michelle had travelled on a plane; dragging the pushchair and luggage through departures at Manchester Airport, she was overcome by a profuse sense of fear. During take-off, it felt as though her stomach would fall through the floor. Her hands shook so hard it was impossible to hold a drink, and she closed the window blind as waves of panic washed over her.

Tam was nine months old and sat quietly throughout the journey to Algiers. Arabic music played on the flight tannoy as they disembarked the aircraft. Michelle was met with a wall of heat the like of which she'd never known before, and an arid breeze brushed across her pale skin. The damp, cloying, sooty air of Northern England suddenly seemed a lifetime away.

Driving through the rowdy, palm-lined avenues of Dar El Beïda, Khemis El-Khechna and down to Larbatache, the flat roofs and chimneys were silhouetted by television aerials and giant storks' nests. The birds flew over the car and up into the burnt amber sky, where the light was beginning to dip on the horizon. It took four hours, with Michelle worrying throughout the whole journey about her now non-existent suitcase that had failed to show up at customs.

It was Bashir's finals, and for the first eight weeks he stayed in a simple back-to-back on the Avenue at Mold Green, a house he had bought with his savings. He had worked all year driving a forklift at ICI, in a bookmaker's shop, and pulling pints to buy the terrace for £2,800. So that he could concentrate on his finals, Bashir sent his new family to Algeria, but had not told his father about the situation in advance. His father, Kaci, was shocked when a young white woman from Yorkshire turned up at his door at dusk, but immediately welcomed them into the house. He could not help but be overwhelmed with love for his grandson, who rolled about on the floormats gurgling and laughing in front of him that day. To celebrate their arrival the family killed a sheep and prepared a feast in Michelle's honour.

Outside their traditional Algerian house (where all windows faced into the central courtyard area, rather than out) children ran barefoot and made whooping noises to greet her. She was exhausted and lost without any knowledge of the language. On her bed, a folded cotton kaftan was left for her to wear, and as she stepped out into the courtyard wearing her new clothes, with Tam in her arms, a field of unfamiliar faces smiled back at her. They ate tagines of mutton stew flavoured with ras el hanout, shakshouka, merguez and baqlawa pastries washed down with glasses of tea, and later that night Michelle collapsed on the mattress, overcome by the new situation she found herself in. Outside, the party continued throughout the night, into the next day, and on for another week. Extended members of the family stayed at the house, and each morning their children would wake Michelle at 6 a.m., knocking on her door, wanting to play and say hello.

One morning, she was woken by the sound of shrieks and excitable children in the outhouse, where dates and figs were stored in large ceramic pots. Bashir's mother, Milkher, was shouting, 'Ezerem! Ezerem!', and Abder ran out to push Michelle back into the house. A large, venomous Lataste's viper had been found coiled up in one of the pots. Moments later, a shotgun rang out, and then there was a knock at Michelle's bedroom door. The children greeted her with the dead snake draped across their arms; its head was blown off, and its distinctive zig-zag pattern glistened in the light.

The noise of the house was a culture shock, and unlike anything Michelle had ever experienced, even with her five brothers and sisters in her own family home. The women rose at 4 a.m. and began to babble at the tops of their voices. Eventually it became a sound she was accustomed to, an essential sensory element of Algerian mountain life. It was only when Michelle announced that she was going shopping that it became apparent how restricted her life was about to become. It was forbidden for women to shop alone; she would not be allowed to walk through the streets of Maillot without a chaperone.

21

Whatever she needed would be brought to her, and the only physical freedom she would experience was granted by Kaci, who felt empathy for her situation. At dusk, he allowed her to walk outside the compound with Abder, who carried Tam as she stretched her legs in the lane that ran behind the house. Unlike many in Maillot, Kaci had lived in Paris after the new post-independence government had threatened him over his administrative job working for the French authorities, so he had some understanding of European culture and the freedoms of the West. It was during Michelle's visit that she first heard rumours about Kaci's earlier life from an English-speaking neighbour, only indicated by the number 51240 tattooed on his arm and hidden just beneath his shirt.

☪

Above the TV at my dad's house hangs a painting of my grandparents. It's one of those oil paintings based on a photo you commission online from somewhere in China, the kind of painting whose only power lies in its remarkable ability to strip its subject of all vitality. It brings to mind a scene in Huysmans' À rebours, where the quintessential decadent, Des Esseintes, decides he is sick of fake flowers, that what he's actually after are real flowers that look fake . . .

No member of the Saoudi clan cuts a more totemic figure than Kaci. His shadow hangs over all that bear the name. My father idolises his dad to the point of obsession. For years he has been on my case about writing a book about his story, despite having already written a book about the subject himself. To be fair it is a cracking story. The man survived twenty years on Devil's Island. For a murder he didn't commit. His innocence was a detail I frequently left out during my younger years when recounting the tale. That I was the grandson of a convicted murderer, that I had the blood of a killer pumping through my veins, I believed to be somehow more alluring on campus at UCL. That he did the hardest time imaginable for taking out one of his colonial overlords all the better.

The cousins he was sent there with, the ones actually responsible for the crime, perished quickly. A life sentence in French Guiana was something very few people survived. The accountant they murdered was in the process of giving my grandad a leg up. A bright boy, the Frenchman had taken him on as his assistant. He was talented with languages and numbers. The favouritism embittered his cousins, who then took matters into their own hands and shot the man. The authorities wasted no time. Soon all three were in the dock. Unable to pin it on any of them individually, they demanded information that would warrant a more concrete conviction. If my grandfather pointed the finger, they would spare him life in the colony and behead those responsible. Not much of a choice then. He kept quiet, and all three were shipped out not long after.

He watched the young men he was sent there with drop like flies in the malarial cauldron. Torn away from all things knowable in 1933, by the time he finally returned home he could no longer even speak his own language. He never bade an escape via the shark-and-alligator-infested waters like the famous Papillon, who was incarcerated there in the same period, and instead it was his wits and his French that kept him alive.

23

He learned to make himself useful and fast, despite the frequent beatings and arbitrary stints in solitary confinement. They turned his body into a conduit for the excess sadism of the French state, his mind into a cathedral of humiliations.

I've never heard my dad utter a bad word about my grandfather. He's recounted to me some of the incredibly harsh ways in which he was disciplined by the man, but never anything bitter. As far as I can tell Bashir was heir apparent to Kaci. Like his dad before him he was an incredibly bright and dedicated student. My uncle Abder, however, paints a somewhat different picture. Abder, unlike my dad, was devoid of all ambition. Even to this day he still lives with his mum, in the same house he grew up in. One of the laziest men alive he may well be, but he's open and warm in a way his other brothers are not. When I went to live with him in my early twenties, I asked him about Kaci. Did prison fuck him up? It must have fucked him up?

'Of course,' he replied, raising his index finger to the side of his head, rotating it around to indicate derangement. 'He could be very extreme, very extreme . . . I love my father, but also I was scared of this man.'

☪

Built amid several olive groves, the Saoudi house was surrounded by a landscape laden with fruit trees. Beneath the family's land was a dried-out riverbed that led to a track to the town. In Maillot, many shared their surname, including a café, pharmacy and school named after the extended family.

When Bashir was a small child, he heard stories of French colonial rule; how their army rampaged through the region and seized its land, resulting in the eventual mass famine of its citizens during the Second World War. Elders spoke of the Setif massacre, when the war of independence was triggered by a riot caused by French gendarmerie opening fire on protesters demanding their freedom from colonial rule on VE Day. After the gruesome retribution against French settlers, the military carried out mass executions of rural communities suspected of involvement. Thousands of villagers were subjected to scorched earth; burned, starved and bombed out of existence. Soldiers swarmed onto the land, and random shootings, stories of brutality in other villages and murdered livestock left a climate of terror and deep trauma in the region. Bashir often heard uncles and grandparents in their yard recall stories of the French. Stories which could be erased from books, or forbidden in public, but there was no rule to prevent colonial truth being spoken behind closed doors.

Bashir's mother was so traumatised by the experience it left her dependent on Valium for the rest of her life. She experienced seizures and would often faint. In an attempt to revive her, the family would place a sharpened knife in one of her hands and wave strong perfume under her nose.

By the time Michelle moved to Maillot in 1981, many of the old traditions were still prominent. She awoke to the sound of the muezzin at dawn. Her days were spent harvesting fruit, washing, cooking and watching Algerian soap operas not too dissimilar to *Crossroads*. A rudimentary understanding of the Berber language began to connect, and by the time Bashir arrived from Huddersfield, she had learned the names for food, how to converse in a basic fashion and some of the local greetings.

Although she had a deep affection for her new family, the organic food and the landscape, some other aspects of Algerian life were harder to acclimatise to. Life in the compound could be demanding; running water was temperamental and using the squat toilet was a challenging experience to begin with. It was always the women who collected water from the wadi; between them they used gallon tanks, carrying them up steep banks of the hillside to boil over the stove. In contrast to West Riding, where there was enough rainfall to supply most of the North from its reservoirs, Maillot, in its Northeast African position, was susceptible to painful, arid seasons with little water to draw from the well.

In the depths of summer, when Michelle was invited to a wedding, the female members of the household were packed into a van and driven across the desert. She was given customary gold jewellery and robes to wear, but when she arrived at the banquet, the room was full of women, sitting with the veiled bride, who was instructed to look depressed for three days leading up to the ceremony; it was a ritual obligation for her not to smile. The bride had not yet met the man she was going to marry, and was undoubtedly anxious about her husband, who had been arranged through the family.

Belly dancers and female singers provided entertainment, and the women danced together wearing off-shoulder embroidered dresses, red fouta scarves and filigree Tasfift headdresses set with amber or coral, adorned with silver coins. After her wedding, the bride would be taken to Algiers where her new life would begin. But before that, on the morning after her wedding night, it was custom for the groom's family to remove the conjugal mattress, check it for blood, and display the stain outside on public view to prove her virginity. An intact hymen would seal the marriage, but without blood on the mattress, the bride would be sent back to her own family, disgraced and shamed, her wedding annulled. It was the ultimate form of public humiliation; one that Michelle was grateful for not having experienced. Her wedding at Huddersfield Registry Office, with sausage rolls and pints of warm bitter to celebrate, was pale by comparison.

☪

My grandmother on my mother's side in Skelmanthorpe died young, in her early fifties. My memories of her are faint, the approximation of several early childhood encounters at best. When I think of her now, all I recall is a cloud of cigarette smoke and skin the texture of cracked leather. Apparently she died screwing the lodger. I don't know why this fills me with pride, but it does. My grandfather was a surly miner with an impeccably drab northern wit, who I knew slightly better.

Although I met my Algerian grandfather when I was a little boy, I have no recollection of our encounter. Less familiar, or rather a total mystery to me until recently, is the story of his wife, my only surviving grandparent. I have always known her simply as Jida, the Berber word for Grandma.

We've never really been able to have a conversation in person: she is illiterate and, unlike most Algerians, doesn't speak French, only Kabyle. My French is sub-pidgin and nobody in Maillot speaks good English. The only person in my life who speaks Kabyle and English is my father, so without him around it's almost impossible to communicate through speech. I visited Jida in the mountains a couple of years ago on my own. She'd hobble into my room every afternoon and sit silently on the bed while I was playing guitar or listening to music. She had a peculiar fondness for the Taxi Driver *soundtrack and a song I'd written about womanising called 'Waterfall'.*

She was married at the age of twelve and had her first child at thirteen. For the next fourteen years Jida lived with her first husband and bore five children. Four died in a plague that swept the village, including her husband. Locals called it the illness of Chorfa, which some believed was a curse. When she married Kaci at twenty-eight, he had just returned from Devil's Island. Together they had five children, with my father being the middle son.

Unless the Muslim way of life is something with which you have become intimately acquainted, I don't believe you can fully understand the meaning of the word 'patriarchy'. The root of so many problems in my life stems from the huge gulf between the gender politics of Islam and those of the West. For women like my grandmother, the mattress ritual was something she was accustomed to; morality was embedded in the female body, a territory owned and preserved by men; that was practically beyond question. I can't imagine the bamboozlement of my mum at the time. She'd never been much further away from home than Scarborough, and suddenly she found herself stranded in the high Atlas having to adhere to this ancient code, a relative prisoner, with no exit strategy whatsoever. To Western ears it may sound like nothing more than hellish, archaic repression, which of course on many levels it is, but there is a harmony and a purity to the culture there that is totally dead over here. That is as beyond question as the obviously sexist iniquity of the social structure.

Upon returning to Algeria as a young man – when I was in my early twenties and all I could think about was sex, when every action, from drug abuse to starting a band, had sexual conquest at its heart – I started to realise the price that we in the West were actually paying for leaving the old ways behind. That our world, with its pagan insistence on sensual gratification screaming out at you from the surface of every magazine, every film, every billboard, had in many ways driven me insane. It had turned me into nothing more than the summation of my physical impulses. That's not to say I've ever been on the cusp of pulling a Yusuf Islam or anything; I'd consistently revert to form within a week of landing back in the UK, but for a brief moment would always be full of a very real disgust for our way of life.

In lots of ways the world of women and the world of men have very little to do with each other in our corner of North Africa; the homestead is the dominion of women, between whom there was a mutually nurturing solidarity that was rather novel to my eyes. Family is still the underlying social structure; that institution hasn't been left to corrode by the wayside of individualist consumer culture. The generations commingle and support each other the whole way through life. They certainly don't leave each other to rot in nursing homes. Men may have their trials and tribulations beyond the home, but within its boundaries they are frequently the objects of female ridicule, henpecked and rigorously controlled by their mothers, aunties, sisters and wives. The conflict between these two systems, between that of East and West, would eventually destroy my family. There are people who manage to transcend this gulf, but sadly my parents were not those people.

Today they struggle to talk about each other without slipping into a stream of profanity and denunciation. I'm guessing a great deal of that animosity was borne of the cultural chasm between the two peoples, which drew out like a blade over the course of their marriage. My dad never adopted the Western perspective. He couldn't adopt it. Bashir was always in Kabylia in his head, and he still is.

One More Faith Bursting into Flames

After their return from Algeria, Bashir was offered a job in computer programming and the family moved to Southampton. Michelle's second son was born in the coastal city's Princess Anne Hospital in 1986.

The baby was born in a transverse position, his spine on hers, with his shoulders blocking his way out of the uterus. On that cold March afternoon, as cherry blossom petals drifted in the spring breeze outside, doctors feared he would not survive the delivery. They informed Michelle there was a risk to her own life, with some mothers suffering fatal ruptures as the baby struggles in utero. When his head finally appeared it was misshapen, with one ear bent backwards from the rough ride. Michelle held him in her arms and stared at the writhing infant, who looked uncanny with his soft skull, pronounced dimples and thick black hair. Like all mothers, she swore that one day he was going to be something special. He would have a better life than the one she had experienced. The child would be named Lias.

A bright baby from the offset, Lias had an unusual appearance, with a long skinny frame and coal-black eyes. Physically, he was the opposite of Tam, who was chubby and lazy, and wouldn't walk or talk until he was two. Baby Tam sat on the rug all day, with no interest in playing, moving or making a noise. Michelle joked that she could leave him home alone, spend the afternoon shopping, and when she returned, he would still be sat in the same place, staring at the wall. He was the original baby Buddha, docile in the extreme. In contrast, Lias walked at ten months, and by the time he was a year old was making conversation.

Bashir's job took the family to the west coast of Ireland, and Lias spent his formative years running through fields near a modest pebbledash bungalow in Castlegar, on the borders of Galway and Connemara, situated by the lush green fringes of Menlo Park.

Upon their arrival, Tam found his feet with a group of friends, mostly the sons of local farmers. Their raucous behaviour and surreal sense of humour appealed to him, as did the free-range life. Tam would play in the hay bales with them, riding on tractors with their elder brothers, and spent his waking hours scaling stone walls, playing Cowboys and Indians. At eight years of age he now had complete freedom, and the crumbling castles that surrounded the area stimulated the imagination.

Tam's new friends from the village were ruddy-faced farm boys and an antidote to his annoying little brother, who at two years old had reached the age where he wanted to tag along but was often pushed aside. The rough and tumble of country life was perfectly suited to Tam's character; he drank creamy unpasteurised milk from a churn, mucked out pigpens and became a dab hand at hurling, Galway's sport of choice.

One afternoon he jumped in the car with his friend, who whispered to him in the backseat, 'Something's gonna go down, come with us.' The car was driven by his friend's father, who pumped out Wet Wet Wet from the car stereo, smoking roll-ups as they darted through back lanes. The car stopped at a Traveller site, where caravans were parked in a line by the side of a wall. Tam tried to open the car door but was told, 'Stay here, just watch, don't come out,' and he stared out of the window as a gang of farmers dragged women and children out of their caravans. The women screamed, 'T'era t'era t'era', and their children cried and then the Traveller men arrived and the farmers beat them with planks of wood. The sun started setting and Tam stared at his feet as he heard the cracking, crunching sound of teeth knocked out and the breaking of bones and the wailing of young girls sobbing for their daddies and heads being stamped upon and then the raining of petrol as the farmers doused each caravan and threw lighters onto the fuel. The fire rampaged through the site burning each last vardo to ash. After he arrived home, Michelle asked him if he'd had a good time playing that day. 'It was alright,' he said. 'Not much happened.' When he fell to sleep that night, in a bunk bed above his brother, the imprint of the caravans' raging flames was the only thing his mind could see.

☪

The isolated position of the family's rented bungalow was exacerbated by the lack of public transport, and Michelle spent her afternoons cycling to the shop many miles away, racing through the verdant landscape, with Lias sitting on the front basket seat wrapped tight in a cagoule. Rain emptied on the village each day, with storms rolling in from the tumultuous North Atlantic Ocean. As soon as he was old enough, Lias ditched the stabilisers and started to cycle on his own around the lanes. This was his first taste of freedom, yet it soon came to an abrupt halt when he was set upon by a group of boys who pushed the pint-pot Lias off his bike, spitting and kicking at him for a reason he couldn't understand. He returned home sniffling with a small cut to his left eyebrow, and Michelle threatened to *wring their bloody necks* if she ever got hold of them.

His infant classes at St Nicholas' Parochial School had an informal approach to education, with a focus on play. It was, however, a Catholic school, and the religious undertone gave Lias his first taste of rebellion. One afternoon in class, the teacher handed out a series of simple Bible questions for the children to answer and left to speak to a colleague in the adjacent classroom. Sensing an opportunity, Lias, who was only five at the time, crawled up onto the teacher's desk and started dancing in front of the whole class, who began to laugh. Egged on by the attention, he shook his rear end at his cheering classmates, and proceeded to drop his trousers, pulling a full moon and flashing his entire nether regions for the audience, up and down, from side to side, and then flailing himself about as the teacher's pens and notebooks were trampled beneath his feet. Suddenly, the room fell silent. Lias was shaking his bare bottom, facing the blackboard. He heard a cough, and turned around to see the teacher with her arms crossed and a beetroot face shouting, 'Get down from there, boy!'

He was dragged by the scruff of his neck, along the parquet floor corridor and straight to the headmaster's office, where he was reprimanded beneath the gaze of Jesus on the cross. A phone call was made to his father, with an irate threat of expulsion for his public indecency, and within an hour Bashir had driven to the school to collect his son. They drove in ominous silence back to the house as Lias anticipated what was coming next. He would be given the traditional Algerian punishment for his indiscretion. Within moments of walking through the door, and despite Michelle's protestations, Bashir delivered a cruel discipline to his youngest boy, who gritted his teeth until he almost bit his tongue. But even the solid hiding couldn't shake the exhibitionism out of him. One day Lias would have his revenge on his father, that much he knew.

☪

Brighton was first on the bill. Nathan, Saul and I popped a few ecstasy pills and went looking for a party post-gig. We ended up crashing a do at someone's house. Everything was fine until around five in the morning. By that time all trace of womankind had aborted the session, leaving behind them a festering amalgam of rejected male sexual energies. The vibe took a sudden shift. With nobody to show off in front of, our unwitting hosts turned on the unfamiliar in their midst. Before managing to hot-tail it out of there Nathan had been headbutted square in the temple by one of the 'lads' on account of his not being 'one of the lads'. Waking up in the Travelodge after around forty-two seconds' sleep later that morning it occurred to me that road life might not amount to everything it was cracked up to be.

By the time we hit Sheffield halfway through the tour I was quite certain I'd taken the wrong path in life and made an irreversible mockery of my own future. I found myself alone outside the Harley venue that afternoon staring up at our tour poster. We called it 'The Tour of Struggle'. Upon the poster little cartoon versions of the band were marching around in a white void. I remembered the excitement with which I'd reacted when first shown the image by Georgia Keeling, the artist responsible. I began remembering a life that had come before finding myself trapped in that void, as hollow-eyed as one of her freakish depictions. That we had seven more dates to fulfil and zero days off was a fact I simply couldn't compute. A few stray tears even ran down my face. I was reaching the apotheosis of my self-pity.

We'd visited Sheffield on one previous occasion as part of our first three-date jaunt up and down the country six months prior. Our erstwhile manager had linked up with students who ran a night in the back of the Barrel Inn on London Road. After the show, a local nutcase had helped himself to Adam's guitar and marched off with it down the street. He'd been at the bar for some time hurling random abuse at various punters, threatening people with bar stools. The landlord informed us he was a member of the 'BBC' or 'Bare Blades Crew', and we'd best not even look at him the wrong way, as he had more than a few screws loose. One fella marched out after him, collared a police officer on his way, then brought back the pilfered axe. The offending party was cautioned and marched off into the night seemingly oblivious to what had just happened, cursing everything and nothing as he went.

Much to our collective horror, after soundcheck at the Harley the exact same guy showed up. We were all sat munching our free burgers, whining about the shitty number of drinks tokens we'd been given, when he swaggered in, all eight and a half feet of him. He pulled up a chair directly opposite our table then pointed his finger straight at our drummer, Dan. 'Oi you . . . Come 'ere!' Like flies off shite we evaporated upstairs, leaving Dan alone with him. We couldn't work it out. Surely it was no coincidence? He must have some kind of vendetta. Maybe it's the lyrics? Maybe he's a radical feminist? Has anyone been trolling Sheffield United on the Facebook page?

We sat huddled together upstairs in the backstage room, washing away our fear with our single complimentary cider or ale. The staff had refused to serve us lager or Guinness. I confronted the landlord over both issues – the psychopath downstairs and the lack of Guinness – in an attempt to reinstate some feeling of authority over my destiny. The psycho, he informed us, would be dealt with by security. As for the Guinness, who did we think we were? 'You want Guinness you can pay for it,' he chuntered.

Sometime after this brief altercation I decided, in an act of unadulterated spite, that 'tonight is the night'. It was time to explore GG Allin country. It was time to go Bobby Sands. My loathing for the world outside and for the world within had reached a kind of parity; a venomous lucidity took hold. I saved my usual pre-gig bowel movement for the actual gig, took to the stage and then asked my audience the eternal question: 'Is there life beyond the neutral zone?' A roar went up as I unbuckled my belt, pulled down my suit trousers and began to squat. Forcing a stream of tar-black, speed-infused anxiety into my cupped hands, I spread this warpaint from within right across my face. Like some Native American dignitary having readied himself for a quest of flesh and honour, I proceeded to confront my flock head on and marched through the crowd like Moses crossing the Red Sea. Only one among them was bold enough to take the bounty. I stripped him of his belt as I mounted his shoulders, my faeces running down the back of his neck, and before the congregation I began whipping this brave steed with all my might, all the while exclaiming, 'Cream of the young! Cream of the young! Of the young! Of the young!'

I stumbled back towards my own band. Each of them was terrified, each of them cowered, except for Adam, whose famous ability to keep cool under pressure – to not even so much as notice said pressure – held fast. We began ramming our tongues down each other's throats, as was frequently our custom in those days. The scatological aspect of our romance that evening didn't dawn on Adam until sometime after the gig. As a fellow GG enthusiast, he was disgusted, yes, but honoured all the same. The rest of the tour sold like hot cakes after that.

☪

Within a year, the Saoudi clan moved from their pastoral back-waters and bought a new-build box house in the suburb of Knocknacarra, with poky rooms and paper-thin walls. Bashir frequently worked abroad, often learning new languages in computer coding. He spoke to machines for a living and could easily adapt to the latest programmes that emerged from Silicon Valley.

Although she adored her family, Michelle was lonely and often overwhelmed by the responsibility of motherhood. The constant churn of cooking, feeding, cleaning, washing and caring chipped away at her, and now that she lived on another island completely, her family in Yorkshire were too far away to call on.

When the weather cleared, she would walk her two sons along Black Rock Beach, staring out across the cool transparent blue of Salthill; on a clear day they could see the hills of the Burren. Beyond them, on the skyline, Galway hookers bobbed on the water, heading towards the lagoons where tasselweed, bog beans and cinquefoil flourished. Winter saw savage storms blowing in from the North Atlantic Ocean, battering and thrashing the Aran Islands in the waters that surrounded them.

Unlike his brothers, who were the sort of children who slept all night, ate their food, and entertained themselves in the garden, Michelle and Bashir's third son, Nathan, was a difficult child. Sleep was of no interest to him, and a bedraggled Michelle was woken by him six or seven times a night until he was three years old. He screamed and cried and wailed past the witching hour, all through the night, until the sun came up. It wasn't as though he was neglected, malnourished, or in any form of distress – Michelle was a devoted and attentive mother – yet he simply refused to sleep through the night. His cries would wake the boys, and often the neighbours.

The clinginess was another aspect of his personality, although not one that continued into his teenage years. He demanded to sit on his mother's knee for each meal, pulling at her until she gave him her full attention. It became so overwhelming that on some days she refused to sit next to him at all.

A beguiling child, he had distinctive thick black eyelashes and dark olive skin, and from a young age he was kind, caring and extremely affectionate. Yet his behaviour was often baffling and erratic. When the cat disappeared, after two days Michelle detected a pissy stench in her wardrobe, and when she opened it she found the cat had been locked in there by Nathan and abandoned.

☪

Together, the Saoudi brothers could be unbearable, with power dynamics switching between all three as they grew up. Tam, the gleefully irresponsible older brother, would egg Lias on, pushing him to take risks, resulting in Lias exploding with frustration into some argument or drama that would escalate for days. The mercurial Tam was naturally gregarious, had the gift of the gab and was always the court jester. He had a taste for danger which would frequently land the neurotic Lias in trouble, causing him to descend into a guilt-ridden state of confusion and alienation. Tam and Nathan often called their middle brother the Oracle, joking that he was just a brain and a voice, with no body. When Nathan became old enough, he would become a pacifier of sorts, soaking up residual tensions, then quickly swinging to antagonism if he believed either of his brothers were taking themselves too seriously. As adults, Nathan and Tam could be hoodlums, with Lias acting as the bridge between the two. But as a young child, Nathan was often the fall guy; his small height and position in the pack was too much of an opportunity for Tam and Lias not to take advantage of.

On one occasion, consumed by excitement and fizzy drinks, Tam swung Nathan in circles by his legs like a fairground ride in their small bedroom as Lias sat on the windowsill shouting at Tam to stop. Their brother was only two, and defenceless, but still screamed with laughter at the game. When Tam misjudged the swing, Nathan cracked his head open on the door, resulting in a fractured skull and Ninja Turtles bedsheets splattered in red. Nathan ran downstairs wailing, his face and clothes drenched in blood. His parents took him to hospital, where his head of thick black hair was stitched up and wrapped in a huge bandage.

At the very least the brothers knew they would be grounded for a month. No computer games, no pocket money, enforced washing up for the foreseeable. It was a deserved punishment. Their horseplay had finally landed them in serious trouble. Yet they were only re-enacting the physical behaviour they had seen amongst their friends in the schoolyard. Teasing, joking, thumping and bewildered scrapping was normal for boys; in fact, it was encouraged. All three boys responded to fraternal bullying by using their fists, albeit in comical fashion. Tam and Lias, Nathan and Tam, Nathan and Lias, the dynamic shifted between them as they used physical and verbal explosions in an attempt to assert their power and control, just like their father had done.

In the five hours before Bashir and Michelle returned home with their youngest son, Tam and Lias sat on the front step shaking with fear and discussing the hiding they would receive.

'The buckle or the strap?' Lias quivered.

Tam nervously chuckled as the word fell out of his mouth. 'Both.'

'Don't say that,' Lias said. 'I'm scared enough as it is.'

They both knew what was coming.

When the car pulled up the drive, the brothers scrambled into their bunk beds and pulled the duvets over their heads. The bedroom door opened, and the two boys pretended to sleep.

'I didn't do anything!' Lias squealed from beneath the covers as Bashir loomed over him, blocking the hallway light. Downstairs, he heard Nathan's slow crying and Michelle attempting to comfort him. Outside, the orange glow of the lamppost flickered in the dark silence of night.

☪

Algerian men are a fairly belligerent breed, and my father is no different. In fact, he is a prime example as far as I can see. The difference between him and almost all of the others is his eternal fish-out-of-water status;

torn between cultures, there is an inherent lack of resolution in the man. Certain conversations with my old man don't make any sense, it's as if you're attempting to weld Lego to Meccano; our emotional vocabularies simply do not correspond. He radiates pain; I flee from it. On the other hand, when I was attacked in the street aged fourteen in Scotland, I called him from a payphone after running away and within minutes he showed up. He frantically bundled out of his Honda Accord while unsheathing a scimitar that had been decorating the living room wall, begging me to lead him to my assailants so he could 'slit their fucking throats!' That might not be everyone's idea of good parenting, but it certainly made me feel protected at the time.

For sure, masculinity and stoicism need to be pried apart somewhat. And there's nothing quite so obnoxious and self-defeating as attempting to walk through this life as if empathy were something worthy of ridicule. But, if you're a little North African, chances are you've had the stoicism beaten into you. To cry and whimper in front of others is the highest shame. And if you get started on enough times growing up, picked out as vulnerable and set upon by groups of lads, eventually you do everything you can to hide that vulnerability.

I don't refer to my father as a 'toxic male'. It doesn't seem quite fair. Although that's possibly how many a 'liberal' westerner who got to know him intimately enough would describe him . . . if he were white. Modernity has barely touched the world from which he sprang, where ancient traditions and rituals remain intact. My brothers and I have just made it all up as we go along, balancing out what we could learn about masculinity from the five-foot patriarch at home with what we could suss out from the cul-de-sac . . . and whatever happened to be on the telly. It's all just fragments. Coming of age, 'being a man' meant ingesting superhuman quantities of alcohol. It meant getting your end away. It meant learning to laugh at the darkest thing imaginable. Fitting in meant freezing over, otherwise you'd never be able to get on with anything, you'd just be curled up in a corner hiding, wishing that you'd been born someone else.

Ain't No Black in the Union Jack

The family moved to Ayr, on the west coast of Scotland, in 1993. The three sons had already experienced a transient life, one dictated by the revolving jobs of their father, who was increasingly frustrated by the pressures of providing for his family and wife. Detached from his home and culture in Algeria, Bashir had moved through different countries and jobs, in a constant state of transition. For the boys, their relationships with each other and Michelle were the only concrete fixture. Yet it was in Ayr that all three felt complete and happy. This was not the case for Michelle and Bashir, whose relationship started to sour in the years following their arrival in Scotland.

In Algerian society divorce is frowned upon; marriage is for life. Even though they had drifted apart from each other, Bashir would not accept the separation and refused to split from his wife. It was in his darkest moments that Bashir embarked upon a period of spiritual discovery and began to follow the teachings of the guru Sathya Sai Baba. A charismatic figure, Sai Baba had over thirty million followers, and his influence reached to the highest echelons of the Indian government. His followers believed him to be an avatar, a god in human form, and a miracle man who could heal the sick, spreading a message of love and servitude. His detractors believed him to be a predator and conman of epic proportions, who used sleight-of-hand tricks common in the Magic

Circle to turn jewellery into ash, pulling golden lingams from his mouth to amazed audiences desperate to believe in something.

Bashir was a devotee who travelled to Sai Baba's ashram in India to kiss his feet. Posters of Sai Baba wearing distinctive orange robes and Afro hair adorned the Saoudi household, and as Michelle and Bashir's separation became more likely, so Sai Baba's influence increased within the home. Any event, argument or stroke of luck became the guru's work and a source of constant mirth to Tam and Lias, who found their father's spiritual conversion hilarious. Bashir was consumed by his obsession, which culminated in a disastrous Christmas lunch, where he decided to attend a Sai Baba meeting instead of eating turkey and sprouts with his sons and his wife, who had spent five hours cooking that morning.

In Bashir's eyes, the arguments were a result of Sai Baba testing his devotion. For Michelle, it was the final straw. In the early days of January, she began to plan her exit, and took a job working in a care home. She saved each penny she earned, and eventually had enough money to put a deposit down on a small house in Maybole. After filling in the mortgage paperwork, she filed for divorce. At last, she was free to choose her own path.

☪

My stepfather, Leslie, lived in a detached bungalow covered in white pebbledash in an area called Knockmoyle in County Tyrone that backed onto a golf course. He was an accountant, a widower with three kids of his own, and as far as I could tell a decent man. The first time I met him was in the back garden of the house in Ayr while my dad was away on business. I came home from school one day and there he was, sprawled out on the grass drinking tins of Diamond White cider, a new beginning for my mother, the end of the beginning for me. I couldn't believe the accent he had on him. I grew up in Galway so was no stranger to a mick tongue, but this was something entirely different; it sounded as if he was forcing his vowels through a cheese grater, his castrato high pitch surreally juxtaposed with the butch, Gerry Adams-looking motherfucker sat in front of me. I didn't begrudge my mother moving on at all; although my childhood up until the divorce was largely a happy one, my folks' marriage now seemed to bring the pair nothing but misery. But no way in hell did I want to up sticks and leave for Ulster at the foot of my teenage years, a place the new couple had taken me and Nathan for a warm-up visit some time prior to the final split, spoiling us rotten with all kinds of fancy food and days out, trying to paper over the cracks of how shitty the area was.

Unlike Nathan, I was just about old enough to make up my mind as to which of my two parents I wanted to live with when crunch time finally arrived. I was confronted with the big question in the front room at my dad's house one spring afternoon. It was probably the strangest and ugliest moment of my childhood.

At that age you're just beginning to think about girls, you're just beginning to think about escaping the clutches of your progenitors. In my head it was a case of location, location, location. My pals and my life were in Scotland, so Scotland was where I would remain.

When my mother drove me back to the tiny little house where we were living, she was raw with sadness and fury, and began hurling my things into a bag so I could move in with my father. It quickly became apparent that this was a decision I had zero chance of following through on. I unpacked the crumpled-up T-shirts, folded them in half, and put them back into the wardrobe . . .

☾

In his thirteenth year, Lias made the decision to stay with his mother and younger brother and moved across the water to Cookstown, in County Tyrone. Just a few miles from the Irish border, their new home was a short drive from Lough Neagh, and beyond its shores, 30 miles east, was the city of Belfast. In ancient folklore, the lake was created by the pissing hole of a giant horse, or by the mythical hunter Finn McCool, who scooped up an enormous mound of earth and tossed it at a Scottish rival across the Irish Sea, forming the Isle of Man.

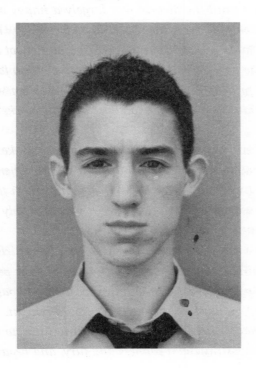

Lias and Nathan visited Bashir and Tam every few months by ferry, leaving the sinister grey murmur of Cookstown and heading across the choppy waters of the Irish Sea on the Seacat. They were too young to travel alone by air, and Lias was terrified of flying, so Michelle would drive them to the port at Belfast, before loading her sons onto the deck and waving goodbye. Each visit was quietly traumatic, the two boys surrounded by red-faced football fans travelling to Scotland for Celtic or Rangers matches, steaming drunk from discount lager before even reaching the shore. The green-shirted Celtic supporters were more considerate towards the two Saoudi brothers, at least attempting to curtail their behaviour onboard; the Rangers fans were feared by Lias and Nathan, who winced at the barbarity and aggression that spouted from their fists and mouths. The ferry's toilet floors were frequently covered with sliding pools of vomit that had tipped out of the bowls and then onto the lino as the boat dipped and rocked in the frantic winter storms of the Irish Sea. Lias would nip his nose to avoid the atrocious stench of ammonia and regurgitated lager that permeated each corner of the cabin.

Weekends with Bashir were a welcome respite from life in bandit country. For their father, however, knowing that another man had guardianship over his sons had almost broken him. He was visibly overjoyed each time he collected them at Stranraer. Upon arriving in Ayr, they would spend an hour at the video shop, collecting a pile of VHS tapes to watch that night. Bashir was barely capable of frying an egg in his current state of wifelessness, and only ate microwave meals in his newly single household. For his beloved sons he would pull out the stops and call the Indian takeaway to feed them. On Saturdays, he played football with the boys and took them ten-pin bowling for a treat. He was an attentive and involved father, one who made an effort each time they visited.

Sundays were always desperately sad; a funereal mood would descend in the car as Bashir drove his boys back to the ferry that awaited them on the horizon. Sometimes the pain was so severe he considered driving the estate car off the cliffs and into the sea. On their return journeys, the two boys would sit together with their heads down sailing away from the harbour, having just waved goodbye to Bashir, both experiencing an emotional agony that they could not express, as the sound of Loyalist anthems echoed through the cabins behind them.

Incensed at Michelle's remarriage, but equally distraught at losing his two youngest sons, Bashir found another wife from Algeria, and opened a café in Ayr that served Kabyle cuisine. His wife was in her early twenties, almost the same age as Tam, who had recently left home. It was, to begin with, an odd situation. His three sons were unaware of their father's new wife and were surprised to meet the young woman wandering around his garden one day, dressed in Kabylian clothes, unable to speak English.

'This is your new stepmum, say hello,' Bashir said.

Lias and Nathan looked at her with a puzzled expression as they realised he had brought her back from Algeria with a ring on her left hand and mostly without a whisper. There were some things about their father they would never truly understand.

☪

The only antidote to the violent absurdity of life is humour. There is no grimace so severe that it cannot be converted into laughter. This is a philosophy that, taken to its extremes, may land one in hot water. There are two moments from my late teens and early twenties that fill me with nervous dread when I think back to them now.

There was the time I got drunk and rode through New Cross in the passenger side of my first drummer's Vauxhall Nova with a replica automatic firearm in my lap, brandishing it at passers-by out of the window as we sped along. People would dive out of the way, hit the dirt and shriek with terror while my brother and I howled with laughter, the

*sound of our incredibly average first demo tape blaring out of the stereo
back at us the whole time.*

*The other was Saint Patrick's Day 2006 in Camden. Nathan and
I had decided to scrawl the abbreviations 'IRA' and 'UVF' onto our
young faces respectively, before hitting the Irish pubs loaded on Buckfast.
Within seconds of entering the first pub, the innocent celebration of all
things Celtic being enjoyed within was converted into an out-and-out
brawl. Pint glasses were hurled in our direction, then they were simply
hurled every which way. I remember fists landing into my upper back,
then a headlock, then darkness. Buckfast, when you drink enough of it,
renders you immune to life. The pale, sweat-through shock of violence
we'd painted across everybody's chops was dividend enough to keep our
bellies full of golden chuckles for days. Afterwards, we wiped that shit
off our faces tout suite and made our way to the next watering hole;
penniless, shameless . . . victorious. No surrender! We cackled endlessly,
deep into the mystic Fenian night.*

Unlike his older brothers, at the tender age of ten years old
Nathan was unable to comprehend the situation he found himself in. Leaving the relative freedom and safety of Ayr, on his
arrival in Cookstown regular platoons of British soldiers lined the
sleepy streets and patrolled front gardens, each one armed with
an assault rifle. He attempted to make friends with children on
the estate but was stared at for his looks and unusual surname.

His parents' separation had caused mental and physical distress, but he wasn't conscious of why it was happening. Every
hour he was desperate to pee, all day, and through the night,
but when he tried to go, the tap was dry. The agony lasted for
a whole year. Doctors diagnosed him with Pollakiuria, a urinary
condition with psychogenic triggers. Throughout his first year in
Cookstown, Nathan attempted to run away on various occasions,
the anxiety and distress of his parents' separation exacerbated by

the militaristic environment that surrounded him.

Soldiers patrolled the streets every day. Outside Leslie's house on a somnolent cul-de-sac of bungalows, three soldiers would stand on either side of the road, criss-crossed. The serenity of Cookstown's suburban estates was in stark contrast to what occurred beyond them. Clean cars and immaculate lawns lined the streets, living room windows were decorated with vertical blinds as if they were dentists' waiting rooms. The orange fuzz of concrete streetlamps lit up empty nest bedrooms with shelves of painted Airfix ships, magnolia covings and crocheted headrests. All pavements were clean aside from rogue dogshit, frequently abandoned or often ignored under the cloak of Ulster's dusk.

When Nathan took it upon himself to play with a toy gun with his new friend, he quickly discovered why it wasn't sensible to attempt a shoot-out game. The two boys rolled in the garden, climbing over fences, shouting, 'Bang bang, you're dead, boom boom' at each other. A group of soldiers walked around the corner, saw Nathan with the metallic pistol and barked at him to 'drop the gun'. With his face in the grass and both arms up, Nathan was overcome by fear as a group of soldiers surrounded him, pointing their guns towards his little head. It was evening, and night had closed in. The army wore night vision, and their red laser lights flashed on and off around him. For local children this was normal behaviour, but for Nathan and Lias it was a terrifying new world to navigate.

Driving to and from school, the boys would listen to radio reports of violence from around the province, such as the story of a Catholic joyrider in Belfast who'd been crucified by a Loyalist paramilitary 'neighbourhood watch' group; they'd nailed him to a wooden post with two rusty six-inch nails in the back of Seymour Hill estate, where he was found unconscious and bleeding.

Their stepfather Leslie was Protestant, and lived in the Unionist area of the neighbourhood, although after six months of living with Michelle she had dissolved any residual belief in God out of him. Lias was sent to Cookstown High School, wearing the Red Hand of Ulster on his blazer uniform, and there was still scant interaction between Protestant and Catholic children on the streets of the town. The two denominations would walk on separate sides of the High Street; the Catholic girls dressed in their superior green and black uniforms and wearing a heady combination of Silvikrin and Dewberry. It provoked uncontrollable levels of adolescent lust from the acne-ridden onlookers in their red-handed blazers.

On his first day at school, under a grey and miserable sky, Lias wished he could be anywhere but County Tyrone. It was the last place on earth for a teenager like him to live, and sitting in Home Economics, as the only boy of colour at the school, Lias fought to hold back the emotion that welled inside his big brown eyes.

His skin had the golden dark hue of a three-month trip to Algeria, and his head was still full to bursting with colour and strange North African light. He had travelled there with his father and brothers that summer, stopping at towns and cities along the way: London, Paris, Marseille and Rome. Much like Northern Ireland, Kabylia had been torn apart by terrorism in recent years. It was bandit country, and his young ears picked up on fragments of atrocities still taking place in the region, despite a recently brokered peace deal. It was all the adults seemed to talk about. There was even less to fight over in the Djurdjura mountains, just sheep, sunshine and siesta. Life moved at a dead pace. Like his new home of Tyrone, there were men with guns and checkpoints by the roadside. He wondered why these remote places and borderlands hummed with destruction and paranoia, when the large cosmopolitan cities they passed through were untouched by the borderland's violent undercurrent.

It was finally clear to him that he was made up of two worlds, a fact that became a great source of pride to his teenage self. He was now aware of what his name actually meant, and his sense of otherness had taken on a new meaning amongst the cacophony that surrounded him in the classroom that day. As his bottom lip started to quiver, he thought about all of his friends starting the second year of high school back in Scotland, his father slowly losing his mind, and his big brother, whose protection at school he'd always counted on, now 131 miles and a cold brown sea away. It took every bit of strength he had not to blub in front of all the loud, impossible strangers who stared at him and sniggered from behind their desks. Keeping the emotion in the back of his throat, he took a deep breath and tried to imagine the day he would leave the new hell he had found himself living in. There was no place more depressing than Cookstown that year, a fact he was certain of.

☪

I arrived in Cookstown in the summer of 1998, not long after the signing of the Good Friday Agreement, and only three days before the detonation of the Omagh bomb 26 miles up the road. Gun-wielding British Army squadrons used to make their way past our house several times a day. There were still roadblocks between the small towns, at the centre of which invariably lay a large, corrugated iron barracks. A soldier garrisoned in the middle of Cookstown trained his rifle on me the whole way up the High Street one Saturday afternoon while I was out buying CDs, I can only assume out of sheer boredom. I recall waiting for a haircut at John's barbershop on Irish Street with my mother not long after moving there. A policeman popped his head in and told everyone they'd best evacuate, there might be a device in or around the premises, then he disappeared. We got up to leave immediately, but most of the punters and the barber himself carried on as normal. Bomb scare fatigue had done away with the best of their anxieties. My stepfather had himself been on the periphery of three bomb blasts, two of them in Tyrone, to which he alluded with a devilish irreverence all too familiar in folks who grew up with the worst of the Troubles. I didn't realise until years later that this town of

49

roughly ten thousand people had been one of the worst-affected areas in the conflict. None of it made sense in my barely pubescent brain. There was nothing here save sheep, drizzle and alcoholism; people had been killing each other over what exactly?

The years leading up to my GCSEs were the toughest in Tyrone. After that the more thuggish youngsters intent on making my life a misery disappeared, off to claim their own proud little portions of decay. These kids were politicised to a comical degree, their schoolbooks adorned with anatomically proficient renderings of British Bulldogs clasping Union Jacks between their teeth, the initials LVF and UVF written across every imaginable surface: ties, blazer cuffs, pencil cases, school bags and Bibles. When Sinn Féin appointed Martin McGuinness education secretary of Northern Ireland in 1999 the entire school ground to a halt in mass protest. It was these same 'patriots' that led the charge. The school gates were suddenly a throng of fluttering red, white and blue; the immortal chant of 'Do you want a sausage supper, Bobby Sands?' rising up from the jubilant horde in occasional gusts – many a teacher appalled, many quietly keen, no doubt.

☪

Leslie's youngest son, Phillip, was the closest in age to Lias and Nathan. There was friction between the boys, who often squabbled for food, attention, or over the SEGA Mega Drive. The Saoudi brothers' acerbic approach to life was a puzzle to their new stepbrother, who failed to find Nathan's sense of humour funny. His Mother's Day card for Michelle included the lyrics to 'Simply the Best' and was signed from 'the world's greatest son', and her birthday card featured cut-outs of Phil Mitchell and Gary Barlow torn from *Take a Break*, all surrounded by rotating red swastikas rendered in felt tip pen. The Second World War was an obsession for the brothers, and throughout their time in Cookstown they read every single book they could find on the subject. Nathan excelled at history and would happily spend hours of each day watching *The World at War*. He first discovered the story of Hitler's bunker around the same time as he discovered masturbation and swung between these twin obsessions throughout the summer holidays, from one unfortunate mess to another.

It was in his deepest moment of teenage angst that Lias found a girlfriend, who he met after many embarrassed glances of longing at a local dance at the Royal Hotel's alcohol-free teenage disco. Stiff teenagers rocked from side to side in front of flashing lights, dancing to a slow number by Westlife, and Lias, who was shy and reserved, finally plucked up the courage to speak to Jeanette, a girl with black eyeliner and raven hair who was the daughter of a British Army soldier, a man who spent his days defusing IRA bombs. Lias had often caught a glimpse of her stalking the corridors at school, at which sightings his stomach would swell with terror, the maddening pangs of an unquantifiable desire kicking into life for the first time.

Like Lias, Jeanette was chronically shy, but obsessed by art, films, books and music. Her father had a vast record collection. A man of few words, his hobby was collecting vinyl that Lias would flick through each time he visited. Jeanette and her father were both obsessed with Bob Dylan. Between them, they owned Dylan's entire back catalogue, including the bootlegs. The nasal whine of Dylan's voice grated on Lias, and he would often become prickly after repeat rotations of 'All Along the Watchtower'. Then, one evening, as Lias was lying on her bed staring up at the big black swirl she had painted on her ceiling and Jeanette was combing Maybelline mascara onto her already laden eyelashes in the bathroom next door, 'Last Thoughts on Woody Guthrie', a poem about the nature of integrity, came on the stereo. In that moment Lias was changed forever. There was some hard truth loaded in the monologue, an epiphany of sorts, and whatever trick Dylan had just pulled on him, it was a trick Lias decided he had to learn. He bought his first guitar from the music shop in town the very next day.

Throughout their first summer of love, Jeanette's mother delivered bottles of Miller Lite to her bedroom and ordered pizza for them on Friday nights. Together, the young lovers would smoke petrol bar hash, fondle each other and watch Elvis movies. When they weren't listening to music, they spent their weekends hanging around the video shop, selecting films to watch on repeat.

As a child living in Scotland, Lias had been repulsed by the hideous characters of *Trainspotting*, the heroin addicts and desolation of Irvine Welsh's last gang of junkies, and was equally appalled by *Withnail and I*, whose decrepit existence and outlandish alcoholism was a million miles away from the repressed, socially conservative life of Ayr. By the time he had met Jeanette and was living in Cookstown, what had once repelled him suddenly took on a compelling exoticism. Their grotesque circumstances held a mysterious allure. Little did Lias know that in ten years' time he too would be living the life playing out on the screen in front of him.

By the age of sixteen Lias had isolated himself entirely, and had become obsessed with self-portraiture, spending each weekend rendering his own reflected image in charcoal, gouache and acrylics. Grotesque and precise, each portrait was an improvement on the last, and he began to create a figurative competence in his work. In the absence of any social life, he was studious, yet still retained a rebellious streak. Carrying a copy of Matthew Collings' *This is Modern Art*, Lias spent lunchtimes in the art classroom, hiding from other pupils and concentrating on his work. He achieved straight A's at A-Level, creating watercolour landscapes of the Northern Irish wilderness and repulsive, hyper-sexualised self-portraits in the style of his hero, Egon Schiele.

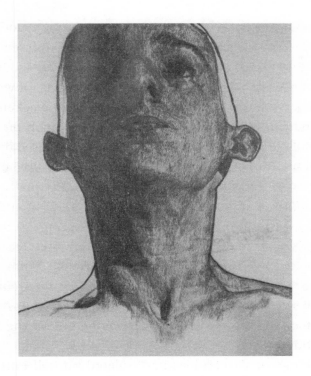

Inspired by Spike Lee's *Summer of Sam*, Lias felt a kinship with Adrien Brody, an actor with a large nose and wiry frame like his own, who played a New York punk in the CBGB scene. Each morning, he meticulously replicated Brody's absurd hairstyle from the film with sugar water and Michelle's Elnett cans, only to be pilloried at the school gates by his peers and excluded from class by infuriated staff.

Cookstown High School was a place to be tolerated, but as he progressed through the system, so did the bullying. He was surrounded by boorish and bigoted behaviour, often from oafish lads with severe haircuts and pink knuckles. He would hear them shouting his name, followed by 'Jew, Paki . . .' as he walked through the school gates, his eyes fixed firmly to the floor. As a British North African, he was called every insulting racial name the lads could think of, but the one that stuck the most was the

53

name they repeated as he tried to walk past them on his way home. 'Hey, sand nigger! Where you headin'?'

The more those words were used against him, the more familiar they became, until they lost all power as a weapon. Eventually, he became numb to it. Retribution was impossible, but as he hobbled home from a beating one night, his uniform torn and blood soaking through his shirt, he swore that one day he would use those words, taking each kick and bruise as a source for the well of his anger.

☪

As a teenager I was bullied and ostracised from the community I lived in. I was arrogant in the sense that I thought everyone around me in Cookstown was a troglodyte of the lowest order. I also had a deeply rooted sense of myself as intellectually superior and cultivated in a way that the youth who surrounded me could never be. These were the hard facts, as far as I was concerned. I constructed an escape plan very quickly. As the son of an Algerian whose father served life on a French penal colony, my own politics were by and large mapped out for me before I'd even bothered to think about them. It slowly occurred to me that most of the kids in County Tyrone, especially the working-class ones, had already become politically awake, or rather already had their side picked out for them at home. Even those lacking the slightest bit of discipline or focus when it came to their schooling were well versed in the Battle of the Boyne or the art of marching up and down a road rattling an orange snare drum.

I recall being asked if I liked the Sash at school one day. At the time there was a German trance-pop outfit called Sash! who'd had a massive hit with a track called 'Encore une fois', and what with me being into folk and rock 'n' roll from pretty much day dot, I told them I couldn't think less of Sash! I thought that Sash! was a load of bollocks. Needless to say, it took me some time to get my head around the beating I subsequently received; their violent passion for German trance was beyond me.

My girlfriend lived on the Monrush estate. It was a world away from the relative splendour of the cul-de-sac I called home, where Catholics and Protestants of a slightly more affluent hue lived comfortably side by side in their detached bungalows. Each of us had a little room to breathe, there were no flags, no painted curbsides, no murals; her overcrowded neck of the woods was dominated by Loyalist iconography of every kind. Long Live King Rat! the walls declared. To and from the local supermarket you were watched over by the balaclava-masked heroes of the struggle for continued Britishness, by paintings of curiously disembodied machine guns floating in a sea of bright orange and by innumerable shoddily proportioned red hands, beneath which you were constantly implored never to surrender. The youngsters regaled you with tall-sounding tales about the involvement of their families in the Troubles: 'My uncle Johnny crucified a taig up in Belfast! My da was in the Maze for kneecapping seven Fenians! My big brother and Billy Wright were like THIS!' Etc., etc.

It was common for locals to keep pictures of the Queen on their mantelpieces. Here at the bitter end of her Kingdom, she was everywhere. It began dawning on me just how far a little disposable income goes towards the easing of political tensions.

Even though she was my only friend in the world I broke up with Jeanette. She'd started dressing a bit goth, she was a wilful outsider, just like me, but I thought our being together only brought on more heat. Two freaks made twice the target. In trying to fit in, or at least avoid getting knocked about, I condemned myself to complete loneliness. I never plucked up the courage to explain to her why. Walking home from McDonald's one evening eating ice cream I'd been attacked by a gang of lads in front of her. They thumped me in the back of the head as per usual, called me a filthy little Jew-nosed nigger. The hiding itself wasn't all that severe, as hidings go. It was my reaction to it that haunted me; I would lay awake in bed at night reliving it over and over again, inserting fantasies of heroic, retributive violence on my part one minute, collapsing under the weight of the truth the next.

Nathan had endured similarly miserable trials in the province. He dealt with it by stabbing one of his assailants with a pencil one day.

55

He hospitalised the kid. After that they left him alone. I simply didn't have the stomach for it. My tactic was endless bargaining. I would attempt to talk my way out. There are few greater humiliations in life than that of looking back on yourself attempting to 'smooth things over' with people who have just spat in your face. It sent me tumbling into myself, down into a suicidal depression.

I once read a line about there being nothing quite like receiving a beating from an unremarkable human being. I remember it well because I parroted it for years in London when waxing lyrical about the tough times endured in the province. I now see that I was off the mark. The lads that picked on me were anything but unremarkable. The high tide of Empire had rolled back out to sea, leaving behind it these imperilled and stagnant little pools. They were clasping at a nationhood that no longer existed, condemned to a crumbling narrative that could no longer make sense of itself. Hounded by the unreality of their origins, they had chosen loathing over mediocrity. It was an ugly choice, but there was nothing unremarkable about it.

☪

It was around the age of fifteen that Nathan began to hang around with joyriders and the bad lads on the estates. Forever the outsider, his observation of sectarianism in County Tyrone was perhaps more astute than any of his friends, and as he rode in the back of souped-up Peugeot 106s, listening to the latest Dutch trance mix from Tiësto, smoking joints loaded with hydroponic skunk, he became incredulous at the opinions of his supposed peers.

Puberty was supposed to be when teenagers stopped being children and started to transform into an embryonic version of their adult selves. Up until that point, Nathan always believed his friends to have an innocence about them, an open-minded attitude, until the environment fully took hold of them. Tribalism was rife, and as soon as testosterone began to dominate their bodies all sense of fairness and willingness to mix dissolved, and they were swallowed up by the sectarian divide. For Nathan it was a moment of realisation, where the distinctive sense of his path being a different one began to formulate.

He worked hard at school, and had the same aptitude for Politics, English Literature and Art as his older brothers, but would spend evenings hanging around the bus park, eating chicken burgers and setting off fireworks with the wayward underlings of Dungannon. Although small in stature, Nathan was a tough fighter and could hold his own, throwing a fist when provoked, and often thumped his friends when they pushed him too far.

As his workload increased Nathan began skiving out of school, believing he didn't need formal education when it was easier to teach himself. His autodidactic method was the opposite to that of his older brother, who had fixed his gaze on leaving Northern Ireland as soon as was humanly possible.

After a weekend excursion to see Tam at Bretton Hall, an art college set in a lush green landscape near Wakefield where he was studying, Lias became intoxicated with the idea of applying for art school. Here was a world that revolved around nothing but self-expression and pleasure; it was the polar opposite of the Protestant misery of Cookstown. It would be another few years before he could make that world his home.

☪

Each afternoon Lias and Nathan would play football on the Eastvale estate, where they'd kick the ball around with the local boys until night closed in. Some of the lads began noticing the 'Portos' – migrant workers from East Timor referred to often as 'the Portuguese' – making their way into town on foot from the meat factory and started making monkey noises and screaming abuse with venom on their tongues. The immigrants ignored them and continued on their way, as Lias shook his head in embarrassment at the youngest of the gang, little Stephan, who hurled rocks at them from outside the shop and across the road.

'What the fuck are you doing?' Lias said. But the boy just kept on going, oblivious, smirking and sniggering at his friends. Their behaviour was set in stone from the earliest age.

Michelle had been stalked in Cookstown, so the family moved ten miles down the road to Dungannon, where Lias took a part-time job to help him save money for university. On the weekends he worked on the lines at the meat factory in town, which was the area's main employer. In the early hours he worked on buy-one-get-one-free supermarket orders. Standing in a giant freezer, dressed in a white hairnet and wellingtons, Lias sifted through pieces of flesh and arranged them in neat plateaux on polystyrene, before loading them onto a conveyor belt. His shifts were often soundtracked by the latest Ronan Keating smash hit that rattled from the factory radio, proving to him that time could actually stand still and almost collapse in on itself entirely, with the correct density of boredom. It was the closest he came to a near-death experience, and it was confounding to him that most of his colleagues on the production line had done that job full-time for years. A great many of the younger locals chose to leave at the earliest opportunity, searching for something more tenable, a career that paid more than £5 an hour and didn't involve the constant sound of buzz-saw slicing through bone. There was no greater incentive for Lias than the threat of a future at Dungannon Meats.

Hell Hath No Fury Like a Failed Artist

The Slade School of Fine Art in Bloomsbury was one of the most renowned art schools in the country, with alumni including such luminaries as Derek Jarman, Paula Rego and Wyndham Lewis. A voracious interest in contemporary art was a prerequisite, and at the interview, which comprised a panel of three, applicants were grilled on their own work, creative practice and ambition for the future. When in 2005 a letter arrived through the door in Dungannon offering Lias an interview, his heart jumped into his mouth. The standard of his work was deemed to be of exceptional quality, the brutal self-portraits and hinterland landscapes he had submitted caught the attention of a professor who believed there was a quality to his paintings that stood out.

Lias flew to Heathrow from Belfast in the spring of that year, wearing a pair of polished shoes, a suit jacket and red tie. He carried a plastic portfolio case through the streets, towards Euston and the imposing white Quad building on Gower Street that over-flowed with young and beautiful Londoners who were effortless in style and confidence. He had paid for a haircut before he left; it was a little too short around the sides, a standard army cut from a local barber who attempted to give him a sensible crop for the journey.

Pushing his fringe forward over his forehead, Lias rolled his shoulders uneasily in the badly fitting suit that he'd borrowed from his stepfather's closet. It was double-breasted, dishevelled and too short on the arm. He rolled up the sleeves and loosened his collar in an attempt to pull off the Shane MacGowan-circa-1984 look and stared down at his white socks and slip-ons. He wasn't quite sure what he was supposed to wear, but he knew for certain that everyone else walking into the interview that day had far more money and sophistication than he did. Dressed in Northern Irish high-street clobber, it was the first time he was truly aware of how much he stood out. Most days he threw on whatever was in the closet without giving it a second thought. His sartorial sense often resembled that of a turps-drinking street sleeper who had walked into a charity shop and put anything on that happened to be on the nearest rail, a dress sense that would continue throughout his life, and one day transcend onto the front cover of *New Musical Express*, complete with a Shaolin monk 'skullet' haircut and rancid gravy-stained stonewash jeans. Or perhaps his appearance on *The Late Show with David Letterman*, wearing a fisherman's vest with WARHAMMER 40K Tippexed on the back, screaming, 'Baby, is it raining in your mouth?'. Or even on the BBC's Glastonbury coverage, with a hole in his jeans so large the audience could see his ball sack, topped off with a pair of steamed-up nineties ski glasses and a five-day crystal-meth gurn that turned his face inside out.

When he walked into the seminar room, the academics shook his hand. It continued to tremble as he sat down. They explained how the Fine Art programme worked, and how it was already a great achievement for him to be there. 'Only the very best students are selected for the Slade,' they said.

When he removed his jacket the cotton of his white shirt stuck to his back. Beads of perspiration appeared on his forehead and started to trickle down the side of his cheeks, as if he were sweating tears from the corner of his eyes. He pulled a congealed tissue from his pocket and wiped at his face before clearing his throat and speaking in his hashed Irish/Scottish hybrid accent about his background, his approach to portraiture and views on the Young British Artists. He spoke with insight on narcissism, Schiele's tortured vision and the brutal paintings of Jenny Saville. Then Damien Hirst's *A Thousand Years*, and how its severed cow's head and the feeding flies that hatched from maggots and were fried on the Insect-O-Cutor told us everything we would ever need to know about the current state of the world. Lias parroted the budding entrepreneur's statement that he had rehearsed for a week beforehand: 'There has only ever been one idea, and it's the fear of death; art is about the fear of death.'

He spoke articulately about the Chapman brothers, and how he believed that their diorama, *Hell*, which consisted of thousands of miniature Nazi figures arranged in nine glass cases in the shape of a swastika, was a masterpiece. Even better were their sculptures of conjoined prick-nosed children.

Lias cleared his throat and said, 'If I could create anything on a par with those dismembered corpses hanging from trees then I'd sincerely feel I'd achieved something in life.'

The panel pushed him on each attempt at incendiary provocation, and for those twenty-five minutes it felt as though he had transformed into another person, as if he were acting, or ventriloquising the words of a much more intelligent being. Each insular and obsessive creative thought he had chewed over in the months leading up to this moment finally connected into a coherent and convincing explanation.

When he walked out of the room he knew that even if he didn't get a place he had somehow moved forward. The heated discussion between the panel over his work and ideas was a starting point, and the charged atmosphere of the building had already begun to infiltrate his brain. He was completely out of place, and for that reason alone, he believed it to be the only place he was destined to belong.

☪

When I finally arrived in London, I immediately set to work mythologis-
ing the time I'd spent in Ulster. It was an effortless process. The student
body at the Slade would believe almost anything I had to tell them about
the conflicted backwater from whence I'd sprung. My favourite 'embel-
lishment' was a description of the school run. According to me, one made
their way into Cookstown High School each day in a sort of armoured
bus, with great big metal grilles across all of the windows – essential given
the frequency of sectarian mob violence. My description of the hostilities
braved each day just to lay claim to a basic state education were an exact
derivative of the journey undertaken by Billy Elliot's scab father across
the picket line during the Miners' Strike. Everybody bought it.

Slightly less believable were my tales of racial discrimination. I alone
amounted to the ethnic minority at my high school, I informed my
new social circle. Other than myself, it was entirely white, and entirely
Protestant; the name Saoudi on the roll call was a neverending source
of ridicule. The sourest among the pupils came up with innumerable
terms of derision with which to lash me. My personal favourite had been
'Sir Nigger-lot' on account of its feudal undertones, which seemed
wholly appropriate somehow. This part of my story, unfortunately, I
hadn't had to make up.

☪

In late September, just as the leaves were starting to rust, Lias
arrived in London aching with anticipation for the new life ahead
of him. Unlike children brought up in the city who are offered
the wild choices of places to go, culture to consume or parties and
drugs to imbibe, for those raised in the backwaters entering city
life can be disquieting. For him, it was a thrilling experience, the
noise and the chaos, the sheer electricity of its pavements was
enough to keep him walking the streets for hours each day upon

his arrival. Even the black mucus coughed up from his lungs or blown from his nostrils held an exotic thrill. Through his own determination he had escaped the dreck surrounds of Northern Ireland, the bullying and violent small-mindedness that almost crushed the life out of him.

When Lias received the offer letter denoting the location of his student halls the deal was rendered sweeter still; he was destined for Ifor Evans Hall, in Camden Town, location of *Withnail and I*, which had by then become a revered text. The block was home to over five hundred students, a few hundred cockroaches and a small family of kitchen rodents at any given time. Nicknamed the 'Mouldy Gulag', it was a residence comprised of shared bathrooms, exposed pipes, chipped paintwork, mahogany doors, wired glass and single glazing. The building was an eyesore amidst the faded glamour of its surroundings, and the common rooms were filled with woodchip walls and shelves of abandoned books, business and IT manuals, and incomplete collections of Mills & Boon. Its exterior was covered by brown bricks and shamrock-green plastic panels. For the first year of his life at the Slade, Lias rented a single room on the second floor with a small bed, an MDF desk and collapsing wardrobe.

That first night, Lias walked out into the city puffing on Dunhills that his father had given him in two cartons to 'sell to other students and make money'. He had no idea which way was north or which was south, but following the road signs he eventually walked into Soho to drink alone in its pubs and bars, and to stare at the beautiful girls that ignored him.

Somewhat inebriated, Lias gazed up at the giant gold statue of Freddie Mercury that straddled the Dominion Theatre and took a deep lungful of the city's diesel fumes. He had already spent £38 on cocktails and was seeing doubles of each pedestrian. Wobbling along an alleyway, he paused and took a piss outside Bradley's Spanish Bar before a barmaid came outside and started tutting at his indiscretion, shouting, 'It's not a fackin' toilet ya know!'

The Tube was still a skittish proposition, and he had no idea which bus would take him back to Camden. As the rain started to pour, he huddled in the shop doorways of Goodge Street, pushing a rancid hot dog and onions bought from a street vendor into his mouth, before slowly staggering up the road towards Euston.

☪

When I first started at the Slade the tutors conducted a group exercise whereby the whole year would have to find a partner and, together, manifest a work of art out of nothing but a pile of randomly sized hunks of wood, a hammer and some nails. I paired off with a student called Jez, with whom I would become friends for the duration of my time at the college. He was an aloof and gently spoken south Londoner with a wry wit about him. I immediately pushed the idea of banging together a swastika and nailing it to the floor. Where my obsession with the symbolism of the Third Reich comes from is hard to define exactly, but most of the blame I place at my elder brother's door. Bouts of reactionary iconoclasm are easy enough to explain away: I was insecure, I wanted attention, and that symbol is one way you can always guarantee you'll get it. But it was there long before I arrived at the Slade. My brothers and I used to draw swastikas on everything. We found the Nazis hilarious, we found Hitler hilarious. It's their tendency towards arcane ritual and shitty mysticism in a bid to disguise that most base of impulses – race hate – that does it. There was nothing more amusing to me and my brothers than the Sieg Heil.

I had never been in as diverse a room of people as the one I'd been in at the Slade that day; I'd never met any black people, Japanese, Danish, Koreans or openly gay Bermudans, and I'd certainly never met any Israeli Jews, one of whom stormed out of the room at the sight of our 'art'. The tutors zoomed in on us and for the first time in my life I was being publicly challenged on the nature of art by people who'd read more about it than I had. They immediately tore holes in my argument. I had to think on my toes. I can't remember exactly what I said in my defence, but the incident coloured my entire time at the college. I was THAT student. I could sit here and tell you it was an attack on the bourgeois complacency of the entire establishment, but I didn't have a clue what that meant at the time. I was far too busy thinking about women to have bothered building any kind of critical defence for my impulsive provocations.

I was slowly waking up to the fact that I was now at the bottom of a new social order. A great many mistakes would have to be made before I could format my anger at this inevitability into something useful.

☪

Lias was a student who stood out from the very beginning. Restless in his awkwardness, and deliberate in his contrarian nature, he was the sort of Fine Art graduate who would arrive late, stumble up the stairs intoxicated, crash into a canvas, then collapse in a pile of rags, ranting, before group crit began. Or the type of rebellious student who was an archetypal firestarter, a hellion who would walk into a class naked and piss in a plant pot or make petrol-bomb installations. Each act was intentional but spontaneous, never entirely contrived. On the rare occasion when he did turn up to seminars or tutorials, he always presented original work, which his tutor believed had the raw, performative quality of Jean-Michel Basquiat or Antonin Artaud. The standard was invariably surprising, and frequently shocking to other members of the class. His troubled behaviour started to concern his tutors, who believed him capable of originality if only he'd apply himself more, with discipline and vigour.

His studio was on the top mezzanine floor of the Slade, and each wall was covered in drawings. Object paintings, and boards with nails and staples, were painted over in oil acrylic. Fellow students created studies on Eadweard Muybridge, paintings of dark underpasses, installations of bungee cords and bronze rabbit hearts, monoprints of infernos, origami faces, aporia textiles, human skulls crushed in a vice, embroidered baby dresses and leather shoes, rusting mechanical heads, Star of David compositions, neon bulb sculptures, diagrams of black holes, burned ceramics and purgatorial ladders.

Cocaine was the wanker powder of choice for his privileged classmates. Unlike them, Lias lacked a trust fund to pay for the habit, but still he attempted to keep up. It left him without money for oil paints, the effect of which was that he barely attended class for fear of embarrassment. On lunchbreaks he walked down to the Royal College of Surgeons to stare at displays in the Hunterian Museum of syphilitic skulls and the stolen bones of Charles Byrne the Irish giant. Sketches were made of human foetuses pickled in glass jars and the images of Henry Tonks, where the faces of horrendously disfigured Somme veterans were rendered in pastels, displaying a contortion of saliva, flesh and bone, before their eventual reconstruction through embryonic attempts at plastic surgery.

By his second year he had moved to Shoreditch, where he shared a flat with two other students. Drinking often started after breakfast. It was not uncommon for Lias to turn up late for lectures with his classmates after catching the 205 bus steaming drunk from the edge of Great Eastern Street. Before arriving in London, the only drugs he had experienced were small crumbles of weak Northern Irish hash and the occasional diet pill stolen from his friend's mother's bathroom cabinet. In London it only took a year before he had been introduced to LSD, which appeared in the form of a twitching medical student with a lisp who approached him and his friends in the Quad one day as they lay basking in the sun.

'Want some of this?' he said as he stuck his tongue out at them, revealing a small square of paper with an alien's face stamped on it.

Lias and his friend Alan started to laugh.

'Are you for real?' they said.

The student pulled his sunglasses up and sat next to them on the grass.

'Made them last night. In the lab up there. I'll do you a good price . . .'

He raised his eyebrows up and down and stuck his tongue out again like a lizard.

'Alright . . .' Lias said. 'How much?'

'Sheet only,' he replied. 'You'll have to buy twenty.'

Lias looked around and rolled onto one side, pulling his wallet out from his back pocket and raiding it for the last notes he had saved to buy food for the week. He handed over the cash and the student passed him a perforated sheet wrapped in a piece of clingfilm.

What followed was the best twelve hours of Lias's life, followed by the very worst.

He walked to St James's Park with Alan and together they swallowed a tab on the way there, then another when it didn't seem to work. After an hour there was still not much of an effect, so Lias chewed on a handful as they drank a bottle of beer beneath a tree and discussed the day's seminar.

'That was a fucking weird one,' he said. 'Never thought anatomy drawing would be like that. I mean, watching a body being cut up like that. A woman sawn in two. All those legs sliced open . . .'

'And the brain,' Alan replied. 'It was the cracking open of the head that did it for me. The sound of the drill and the slurp as the surgeon lifted it from the skull.'

'Never seen a dead body before,' Lias whispered. 'Got some decent drawings . . . maybe I'll go for the full *Screaming Pope* horror . . .'

A plastic bag floated in front of them in the breeze, and they lay beneath a rustling ash tree, hypnotised by the murmur of sodium streetlights above them. The ground started to move, and within minutes it felt as though Lias's head had exploded into shrapnel.

He remembered little of how he made it to Liverpool Street that night, other than the two of them yapping like hyenas at a bus stop. Then, hipsters dressed in vintage clothes at the Old Blue Last, which transformed into a seventeenth-century galleon that rocked violently from side to side.

When they eventually made it back to East London the next morning their flatmate Jamie had just woken up; he was showered and ready for class. It was a month since Lias had washed up and the pots had solidified in the sink. Jamie took one of the crusted bowls from the pile, rinsed off the matter and poured Rice Krispies into the bowl. He sat in the living room, attempting to eat his breakfast, as Lias became more irritating, pouncing around the sofa wearing a suit jacket with no shirt and swigging from a bottle of tequila as they listened to *Sgt. Pepper's Lonely Hearts Club Band* and made bird noises. To Lias, Jamie resembled a giant Viking, slowly filling the room. He was Odin with wings; a towering angel, each feather was iridescent and glistened in the morning light as he spooned cereal into his mouth.

Then, it turned nasty. Irritated by his flatmate, Jamie pulled faces at Lias, making short goblin grimaces every other minute, in between slurps on his tea. He denied he had done it yet kept repeating the move in the hope that Lias would go to bed and leave him alone for a minute or two. The demonic expressions turned ghoulish, until Lias started to scream as Jamie's face transformed into an oscillating well of ferocious teeth and bleeding violence. He howled manically, then ran out of the flat shouting, 'I've broken my mind . . .'

Jamie and Alan ran after him into the street on Arnold Circus and found him rolling on his belly in the middle of the road.

'Help! Help! You need to make it stop. I can't think anymore. My mind has gone.'

They pinned him down and pulled him from the road as he succumbed to a paranoid breakdown that would not cease for several days.

'It's alright,' Jamie said, 'I was just fucking with you.' And he held Lias close to his chest as he began to sob.

'How much did you take, anyway?' he asked.

'Seven,' Lias whimpered.

☪

North London's Irish pubs became a sanctuary for Lias, where he sank pints of daytime cider and hid from lectures. Contrary to the opinion he held of the Green Isle when he'd left months previously, it was in the watering holes of Camden, Kentish Town and Tufnell Park that he began to truly settle in. The Scottish accent was barely audible, and he quickly switched into the dialect of his stepfather and his scattershot Galway roots as soon as he walked through the doors.

It was in one of those spit and sawdust pubs that Lias made his stage debut. He had cut his teeth busking on the canal bridge in Camden, a spot selected as it was the place where the traffic was loudest, and most likely to drown out his attempts at folk and country songs acoompanied by a harmonica brace. Aided by Dutch courage he rallied around his fashionable new art-school friends, asking them to come and see him perform at an open mic night.

Throughout the week he had practised the same song, and the fantasy of becoming a singer-songwriter started to grow in his mind. Convinced of his own untapped genius, he picked Simon & Garfunkel's 'The Boxer' for his debut and was certain his rendition of this harmonically complex ditty would attract the attention of the same girls who ignored him most of the time, unless he made some outrageous statement in class.

When the night came, he carried his acoustic guitar down Camden High Street, passing teenage boys dressed in drainpipe jeans, red military coats and straw hats, past the pub where he sometimes saw a slotted Amy Winehouse stagger from the steps wearing her beehive wig, smoking two cigarettes at once, past the Barfly posters for Queens of Noize hung by the door, past Italian cyber goths with neon pipe-cleaner dreadlocks, shaved eyebrows and stretched earlobes, past canal bridges where plumes of skunk drifted from the tunnels, past irate taxi drivers and motorbike horns, and lines of traffic that crawled bumper-to-bumper up to the horizon, and walked towards the pub where his new life as a performer would begin.

When he reached the Old Eagle early, he was surprised to see his friends sitting at the tables at the front; each seat was taken, the pub thronged with familiar faces and a fog of smoke.

Lias put his name down on the door and ordered two tequilas before heading to the toilet cubicle to empty his dread-laden bowels in one hot volcanic eruption. Waves of fear washed through him until not one thing was left in his gut. He walked out into the pub and sat by the small stage, where the MC, an old bluesman, announced his name incorrectly.

Lias took a deep breath and stepped onto the platform.

He had assumed that once in front of an actual microphone and audience some mystical transformation would occur, that suddenly he would be able to channel the spirit of Robert Zimmerman out of sheer necessity. Reality and his dreams had become dangerously dislocated.

His left hand seized up on a G chord the minute he picked up the guitar. Lias had spent four hours a night running through the progression, but in the moment of truth, G was all his mind, body and soul could muster. It was as if his left hand had died, or decided entirely of its own volition at the very last minute it wanted nothing to do with Paul Simon, certainly not in public anyway.

The evening's alcohol consumption became irrelevant within seconds and he was abruptly stone-cold sober. Over the top of a clumsily strummed, monotonous G, he began dribbling out the lyrics.

His voice was absent of melody. The more he tried to force it out over the din of boos suddenly rolling around the room, the more offensive it became. Bright red and now drenched in sweat, he ploughed on regardless. He was left with no other choice.

By the time Lias began the second verse a grimacing Irishman by the bar started wailing, 'Please make it stop! This is fuckin' awful, man! Would y'all hear how bad this is?' His voice had a familiar twang, which gave Lias an excuse to stop playing and try to make friends with him from the stage.

'Where are you from, Northern Ireland?' Lias asked.

'Sure,' the man replied. 'Tyrone.'

'That's where I'm from!' he exclaimed, with a wretched grin on his face.

'Great,' the man said. 'You're still shite. Never sing again, do you hear me?'

Lias's shoulders dropped as he felt his soul dissolving in humiliation and embarrassment. He had always hoped that if his painting career didn't work out, at least he could perform, but this had proved to be an overly nourished nugget of adolescent fantasy; an aspiration that quickly dissipated as he saw his friends' faces in the audience, trying to hold back their guffaws.

The Tyrone man shook his head and made a cutting movement against his neck. Then the girls started to chuckle, and the MC walked back onto the stage, taking the microphone from the humiliated singer who stumbled from the stool with a deep crimson face. It was the first time Lias ever performed, and arguably the worst. No matter how bad he was in the future, this would always be the benchmark for lousy performances. In a drunken fervour, he swore he'd be back again next week. In reality, it would be another two years before he'd even pick up a guitar.

☾

In Northern Ireland I'd been convinced of my status as a prodigy. The problem was that back in Cookstown I had zero distraction. London throbbed with it. On every street corner there were misdemeanours to be indulged, there were impossibly attractive women everywhere, the buildings rolled up to the sky and the bars were constantly flooded with punters. There was live music, something I'd never seen before save for one Bob Dylan concert in Belfast. There were nightclubs and house parties, there were other like-minded young people also interested in art and music, and eventually, of course, there were drugs. College quickly took a back seat to my explorations of the city and a quest for female company, one that ended in rejection every single time for years. Why would some sophisticated middle-class young art luvvie from Shropshire ever think twice about River Island over here, with his maladjustment, sexual inexperience and class resentment he'd yet to learn how to conceal?

I knew from the moment I looked at some of the other guys on the first day at the Slade that I was done for. A lot of them were men, well-dressed men, and I was a stick-thin, clueless, scared shitless little boy that blew his student loan within three weeks of receiving it every time without fail. Things went from bad to worse when I started popping pills and snorting cocaine. I stopped turning up to class. I was usually too stoned or too hungover, too busy sat on my bed listening to the Pogues at an obnoxious volume, desperately trying to carve out a solid identity for myself in between fits of resentful masturbation to bother.

Patience Is Starting to Bruise

As his elder brothers had both left home, Nathan was the last son left in Dungannon. Tam had taken a job as a teacher in China, and was living in Hangzhou, where he taught English to secondary school students. Unlike his brothers, Nathan had no great interest in becoming an artist, but wanted to leave Northern Ireland and escape the boredom and sexlessness. He achieved good grades in English Literature and Politics and sat A-Levels for a year before being kicked out of sixth form college for 14 per cent attendance. Nathan had a rich interest in Marxism and wrote a convincing essay on its principles and the economic function of society, the bourgeoisie and proletariat, and capitalist society and class conflict in the works of Gramsci and Althusser. As a result of his effort, he was predicted three A grades and travelled to London to celebrate his eighteenth birthday in January. When he returned, the college board politely requested that he leave.

Carrying a small bag of clothes and a few books, he flew to Gatwick. Michelle gave him a brown envelope of cash from her savings and waved goodbye to her son, the last to fly the nest. The following day he started living on Lias's floor at his flat on Redchurch Street, curled up snail-like in an orange sleeping bag on the kitchen sofa for the winter.

The two brothers were finally reunited, and between his erratic forays into the Slade, Lias managed to secure a job at the Old Blue Last on Curtain Road, in the heart of Shoreditch. Situated on the corner of Great Eastern Street, facing west, the pub looked out towards the corporate tower blocks of the city, where the skyline was silhouetted with cranes beyond the boarded-up buildings that surrounded them. On Friday nights, the streets outside heaved with creative types, men in their forties with large turned-up jeans and Hoxton Fin haircuts riding children's bicycles, or Scandinavian fashion girls with platinum hair and baseball caps twinned with Edwardian wedding dresses. Some worked at internet start-up companies on Old Street, and talked loudly about venture capitalists on Bluetooth headsets, others were dressed in ugly shoes and oversized glasses, and spouted ridiculous statements about numbing exhibitions at White Cube out of their minds on the latest Colombian delivery. Lias served customers with mullet haircuts and glam rock outfits and listened to the bang bang bang of electroclash that permeated from the floor above. Always watching, but never joining in, he cleaned sticky tables and vomit-stained toilets, before heading to Charlie Wright's or Mother Bar to steal abandoned drinks from tables at 2 a.m. with Nathan, as a DJ dressed in a black PVC catsuit played 'Murder She Wrote' on seven-inch, the needle and crowd jumping on repeat.

☪

Some dreams are harder to kill than others. The dream of becoming a famous artist had begun to wane when the true nature of the art world became apparent to me. I had decided that it was one big clique, disgustingly exclusive, and besides, you couldn't combine it with spending time at the pub as easily as you could music.

Performing music meant strutting around in front of crowds of drunk women. The effects of music were instant and universal; they didn't belong solely to the upper and middle classes, whom I'd started to despise. You didn't need a degree to comprehend a tune, you just needed a bit of enthusiasm.

Art school felt like some sinister conspiracy to me; a feeling partly born out of my fear of rejection, fear of the dismissal of my self-appointed prodigy status, but also one born out of an undeniable feeling of class inferiority. The kids there were sophisticated in a way that I simply was not, and although I coveted their cultural wherewithal, I simultaneously sought to admonish it in the form of aggressively lewd and outlandish behaviour.

Somehow, I reckoned that by accentuating the aspects of myself I considered low-bred, instead of trying to hide, or indeed change them, I was fighting the good fight. A self-defeating philosophy if ever there was one but nonetheless one that lead me directly to punk. 'Lipstick Traces' by Greil Marcus became my handbook. This was the first book that took into account my anxieties about class and explained how you go about waging cultural war; from Dada to the Situationist International right up to the birth of punk and beyond, and in retrospect probably saved me from making a dire fool of myself for the rest of my life.

☪

It was in the flat on Redchurch Street, in London's oldest council estate, Arnold Circus, that the Saoudis started working on their first song, 'Warm Pork for Cold Pork'. They named their act the Sexy Offenders. The band only ever existed as a concept, but around that time Lias met a handsome girl called Mitzy, who was half-Turkish, half-Hungarian and looked strikingly like Lias, as if she were the female version of him. She was sophisticated and stylish, introducing him to Gaz's Rockin' Blues, cocaine and the wonders of oral sex.

Like many of the young and beautiful set who paraded around Shoreditch at that time, she was wealthy, and therefore out of Lias's league in every way. Despite being utterly besotted with her, he began taking her for granted within the space of six weeks. When she dumped him three months later due to his neglectful behaviour and ran off with a singer in a band, he was distraught. Mitzy delivered the message as they walked down Goodge Street one afternoon, at which point Lias started screaming like a baboon, in a rage that burned to such an extent he smashed his foot through a shop window in broad daylight.

A new kind of hell descended in the months that followed. His flatmate, Jamie, was an art student and a carpenter; he had built a temporary corridor and room within a room in their flat, granting Lias his own windowless chamber. Inside the compound was a single bed, a pile of clothes and a television set with a DVD player. For eight weeks Lias refused to leave the room, locking himself away, beating himself off to a copy of *Send it Down* so frequently that an emotional bond started to form with the girl from the opening scene. A compulsive favourite, he watched it over and over again in a repetitive act of onanistic insanity. Between viewings he called Mitzy relentlessly, until she blocked his calls, and her new boyfriend threatened to come and kick his head in, delivering a death threat when he refused to stop.

'I just don't understand what's wrong with you,' Nathan would say. 'Why are you so cut up? There are loads of women out there. It's not worth you getting so upset.'

'I'm upset because it hurts, Nathan. It's always blokes in bands.'

Lias put his head in his hands and sat on the edge of the bed, surrounded by sticky tissue paper and a gifted copy of *Pete Doherty: Last of the Rock Romantics*. Nathan walked into his room, flashed a grin and lit a cigarette in the doorway.

'You alright?'

'No,' Lias said. 'How does Jamie manage it? Look at him, man. Every time he steps foot out of the door he meets a glamour model, an It-girl or a sultry PhD student. Being pals with that bastard is like starving to death at a banquet.'

'Uh-huh. What you need to do is stop whining like a self-indulgent little prick.'

'It's just not fair. This celibacy thing, it's like my insides are getting burned out. I shouldn't be allowed out on the street. I can barely see straight. I can't continue like this. If I have to listen to him thrusting away one more time, I'm going to chop my own fucking head off.'

☪

To make the rent that September, Lias had squandered his student loan on a large pile of cocaine which he procured from a man with a dog. He had intended to sell it but hadn't managed to leave the room for three days since his acquisition. The delivery was kept in a glass bowl on the coffee table, and dwindled by the hour. Steaming after drinking whiskey and snorting the devil's dandruff for seventy-two hours straight, there was no realistic chance the drugs would ever be sold, as Lias had scant idea about how or where to sell his goods. The tableau that surrounded the flat's inhabitants consisted of a table covered in razor blades, scales and drug bags, overflowing ashtrays and three empty bottles of Jameson. They had been listening to Lias's latest obsession, the Fall, on repeat, and at full blast for at least two days and nights – in particular 'Totally Wired', a track that sounded better with each play as the session progressed.

At 6 a.m. there was a bang on the door. Nathan rushed to answer it, only to spy a line of police at the door through the keyhole. He ran into the front room shouting 'Hide it! Hide it! Hide it!' as Lias threw all of the drugs and paraphernalia into a holdall and rolled it under his bed.

'Morning officer,' Lias said, as he opened the door, wiping congealed powder from the corner of his nostrils. 'Is there anything wrong?'

The colour drained from his face as he imagined the jail term he would face for the substances they were about to uncover.

'We have a final noise abatement order from the council, which you can see here,' they said. 'There have been multiple complaints from tenants above and below this flat; these are people with families and children. They have been unable to sleep for three days due to the noise coming from your audio equipment.'

'Oh . . .'

Lias's heart swelled with relief as he realised what they were about to do.

'We are here to seize all of your audio equipment; even the laptop speakers have to go.'

After the ten policemen and council officers had cleared out the flat of their hi-fi, television speakers and transistor radio, the brothers let out a sigh of relief.

'Thank fuck for that,' said Nathan.

'Close call,' Lias replied.

'Shall we keep going then?'

After a brief disco nap they resumed festivities, pulled out the holdall and its contents, and decided that poetry would fill the void left by the racket of Mark E. Smith. Lias endeavoured to recite Samuel Taylor Coleridge's 'Kubla Khan' as Nathan heckled behind him, and then a ridiculous attempt at Sylvia Plath's 'Daddy'. The demented pair were interrupted again by a knock at the door, as Alexander Sebley stumbled into the flat. Dressed in tight jeans and lace-up boots, Sebley resembled Kurt Cobain, with long peroxide locks and triple denim with leather elbow pads. He was a tall, gentle and sensitive character who began a sorrowful rendition of W. B. Yeats's 'The Lake Isle of Innisfree' from the armchair, an act that immediately endeared him to Lias, who was captivated by his voice and pronunciation of 'bee-loud', delivered in the exquisite manner of an archive radio recording.

☪

Walking down Brick Lane one Sunday afternoon, through the cacophony of crowds that lined the cracked pavements, Sebley glimpsed a young man who bore a striking resemblance to the younger Saoudi brother and wondered if he was begging for change. As he worked through each passing group, some emptied their pockets for him. It wasn't until he made his way to the flat that he realised the man outside Beigel Bake *was* actually Nathan. He was surprised when he heard Nathan had managed to gain the affections of a nubile Parisian on the street that afternoon and had brought her back to the flat. Together they were smooching by an open window as MGMT's 'Electric Feel' blasted from the speakers and the smell of old takeaways and urine floated in from the alleyway outside.

Jamie's band, the Bridge, played at venues around New Cross, Shoreditch and Whitechapel in its peak Nathan Barley period. As headliners at the Rhythm Factory's Tuesday night show, the Bridge invited Lias and Nathan to support them in their shambolic three-piece form known as the Saudis. Sebley was in the audience that night and began watching with fascination. Nathan played drums and guitar, and Lias sang. A competent and professional guitarist, Robin, who wore a white vest and trilby, played alongside them. Sebley couldn't take his eyes off the car crash in front of him.

It was the first time Lias dropped his trousers onstage, a habit that would continue when he realised how much attention it brought him. Figuring that Iggy Pop had made a career out of it, and Jim Morrison was notorious for it, in the midst of one of the songs he started to peel his belt open, as the crowd started to whisper, and unzipped his pants beneath the spotlight, revealing his enormous bush, so much hair it resembled a black shock wig bought from a joke shop.

'Look, spiders! BEHOLD!' he yelped as his wiry pubes flashed at the crowd, a moment that was shattered when Nathan stopped playing altogether and shouted, 'You fucking dickhead!' before throwing a pint over his brother's face.

It was quite unlike anything Sebley had witnessed before. Weeks later, when they ran into him manning the door at a psy-trance party, they asked him if he'd like to join the band.

'But how do you know if I can even play?' he said.

☪

It was during the Saudis era that Lias and Nathan became friends with an eccentric local artist, Robert Rubbish, who was introduced to Lias one ribald afternoon at the Golden Heart in Spitalfields Market. The landlady was infamous for tolerating badly behaved artists that frequented her traditional boozer, so Lias was genuinely thrilled at the sight of the Rabelaisian Rubbish with his testicles laid out on the wooden floor, pouring a pint of cider over them in full view of the drinkers that day. He wore a tweed suit and was red-faced from his escapade; his sideburns glistened from the sweat.

'Now there's a man I can do business with,' Lias declared, as onlookers gasped around them.

In the following months, Rubbish spent languid afternoons with Lias and Nathan in Soho's Colony Room, where he was a member, and marvelled at the long line of weather-beaten queens who inhabited the place. They would buy round after round of drinks for Nathan, who, it turned out, inspired nostalgia for their Tangiers days due to his resemblance to the Moroccan rough trade of their formative years.

The three inebriated men staggered between the Colony Room and the basement of Trisha's bar, forming a friendship that would one day become a formality when Rubbish assumed the role of manager and pop Svengali. One day in the future Lias would be the star of his film, *A One-Eyed Man in the Kingdom of the Blind*, in which he played the Irish neo-noir detective Cormac O'Connell, a character based on Bergerac, who drank warm Bells single malt from his pocket each day and staggered around the island of Jersey before being consumed by a Wicker Man-esque pagan ritual and having sex with a doe-eyed, stocking-wearing starlet onscreen. The pig's head logo of Lias and Nathan's band would be designed by Rubbish, as would the sleeve of their debut LP, *Champagne Holocaust*, which vanished in mysterious circumstances. One day they would part company on bad terms, due to the inevitable carnage of the hype machine and a total collapse of loyalty, but for now, at the very least, they were firm friends, and it was here that the foundations of what would become Fat White Family began to form.

☪

Attending seminars and group crits at the Slade was the last thing on Lias's mind as the sexual odyssey of Shoreditch life started to consume him. Jamie continued to pick up the adoration of the most attractive girls in Bethnal Green, much to the chagrin of Lias. The Bridge weren't particularly offensive but were so appalling in Lias's eyes that he decided they needed to be trumped at all costs. Paintings, sculpture and performance were irrelevant at that point, and despite continued efforts from his tutors to get him to engage, Lias barely bothered to turn up to his studio at all. Acrylic paints hardened in their tubes, and dust gathered on cloths and canvases that hung from his easels.

Unopened letters from the Slade piled up by the front door; had he bothered to read them, they would state that he was on a final warning for non-attendance. Not that any of that mattered to him anymore. Art had abandoned him as the source of his inspiration, and he began to pour all of the focus and drive he was capable of into becoming a performer. Slick Londoners and their innate cultural capital became the new enemy, and from this moiling bitterness a new version of himself was born.

Long nights were spent working behind bars, and attempting to get gigs for the Saudis, which by that point comprised of the

Saoudi brothers, Sebley on guitar, Maxwell on bass and Mike on drums. Although rudimentary, the band rehearsed at Vampire in New Cross, and played around venues in the area, usually second or third on the bill. As was the current fashion, they played guerrilla gigs at any location that would tolerate the cacophony, and others that wouldn't, including HMV on Oxford Street, where Lias sang through a traffic cone at the bottom of the escalator, sporting an unwashed mullet, ripped suit jacket and drainpipe jeans, as Nathan bashed on a snare drum like an angry toddler, before they were all booted out by security.

After a show at Catch Bar on Kingsland Road, in the upstairs room with carmine walls and a sticky floor, police stopped Nathan outside and asked him if he was carrying any drugs.

'I've got two kilos of crack up my arse,' Nathan replied. 'Come and find it!'

The Saoudi brothers laughed at each other as a policeman opened the door to his van, at which point they started to run, faster and faster through the backstreets towards Hoxton, past the mechanics' workshops and lockups, the boarded-up shops, the strip joints and flashing lights, away from the van that started to chase them, and the siren wailing in bleak alleyways as their breath was snatched from their lungs.

The two stopped in a doorway to rest and smiled at each other, before coughing up nicotine phlegm onto the pavement.

'We should go and hide in Scottish Gary's,' Nathan said. 'They'll never find us in there.'

Lias brushed down his tight green and white Celtic football shirt and shrugged his shoulders.

'They'll be out looking for us,' he replied. 'There's no way we got away with that.'

Within seconds a torchlight flashed in his face and they heard the sound of walkie-talkies behind them. Handcuffed in the back of the caged van they howled, 'I fought the law and the LAW WON!' at the tops of their voices as they were driven through the streets back to Bethnal Green Police Station.

When they woke in the cells the next morning, Nathan didn't want to leave.

'I like it in here, can't I stay?' he said, as the receptionist gave him a caution for wasting police time.

☪

In the following weeks Lias and Nathan became friends with a local dealer, Reggie, and eventually moved into his small studio flat when they were ejected from Arnold Circus for non-payment of rent. That summer, the streets of East London were littered with free newspapers that told the news of a Wall Street Crash, the Lehman Brothers and America's sub-prime market. Headlines foretold its impact, and City traders in the area were starting to panic. This resulted in more reckless drinking around East London, and easy pickings for Reggie, who sold his wares to loud-mouthed suits in pint-pot strip joints and rodent-infested back alleys.

To stay warm in the winter months, Nathan spent long afternoons in the local bookmaker's shop, drinking hot chocolate for 50p, smoking roll-ups and scribbling lyrics on betting slips. It was a feral existence, and he found a new group of companions beneath the flashing screens of Irish dogtracks, steeplechases and the overbearing image of John McCririck in a deerstalker hat. The interior had the hum of a spaceship and the smell of fear and desperation hung in the air like peasouper smog.

He'd often drink in the Carpenter's Arms on Cheshire Street, or early doors at 6 a.m. on Columbia Road market, where flower traders set up their stalls, and inside the Royal Oak, where casualties would filter in from clubs and warehouse parties by the canalsides. The Royal was the sort of early hours establishment where all would be calm for a moment, the pub full of ecstasy comedown drinkers, before a deranged local would lean forward and bite off his friend's ear in full view of the customers.

It was outside one of these pubs on a bright sunny London morning that Reggie bumped into Nathan, and the two started drinking together. Reggie was the first Algerian Nathan had met in the city, and they quickly began to talk about the country they both originated from. The session lasted all day, and by evening they staggered back to Reggie's basement flat tucked away by the Royal London Hospital and a busy main road.

On hearing that Nathan was homeless after being kicked out of his girlfriend's flat for not changing his socks for two weeks, Reggie offered him a place to stay, which was generous considering it was a studio flat that he had been given since his release from prison. Within a few weeks, Nathan had found a mattress going cheap in a charity shop and rolled it on a stolen shopping trolley all the way to Reggie's flat through the streets of Whitechapel.

In exchange for board, Nathan's job was to bag up cocaine into small wraps made from stolen National Lottery slips, using digital scales, without taking any of it himself. Each morning, Reggie would rise at dawn and shout at Nathan to 'Make your bed, boy', such was the routine he had been forced into during his years in Holloway Prison. Despite the regime, Nathan was glad to have a roof over his head, and it was only a matter of weeks before Lias joined him, having been formally excommunicated from his academic career.

Lias was coming to terms with the reality of having no job or place to live. He moved into Reggie's to share the small mattress with Nathan in a damp corner of the gloomy room, top-to-tailing with his younger brother, the two booting and writhing each night under the same second-hand duvet, sharing Dutch ovens and rancid feet for four long months.

The pressure of living with each other in such conditions culminated in a fight one evening when Nathan threw a punch at Lias's face that broke his already damaged nose, leaving it with three enormous scars, as if he had been attacked by a tiger. Three days previously, Lias had been sacked from a local bar for playing Rod Stewart so loud it cleared the venue. He threw an almighty tantrum at the manager, who was still traumatised from the last Algerian who had worked in the venue's kitchen and macheted the wooden bar top over a wage dispute. Overwhelmed by fear she hid in the office, while Lias and Nathan proceeded to empty the bar's spirit shelf into their rucksacks.

For the next forty-eight hours they drank like kings, eventually downing a bottle of Courvoisier XO between them before heading to a Guillemots gig. After the show, Lias sank into a sofa where he chatted up a young woman and stared longingly into her eyes. Just as he leaned forward to make his move, Nathan leapt to his feet and wafted his bollocks straight into her face. Infuriated, Lias leapt at his brother, who retaliated in style. Needless to say, the woman disappeared quickly into the miserable East London night and was never seen again. The next morning the brothers woke up in bed together, covered in blood and surrounded by empty spirit bottles. They had no idea how they had made it home, but Lias's nose was clearly damaged beyond repair.

There was little joy to be had for all three of the flat's residents that year, yet they continued to write songs. In boozers the Krays once frequented, beneath Union Jacks and booming football screens, Reggie and Nathan would drink until last orders, at which point they would head into Shoreditch, occasionally brawling with City Boys or a gaggle of Essex lads dressed in T. M. Lewin shirts. A sport that earned the moniker 'going for a ruckus'.

The enduring generosity of Reggie's hospitality finally expired one fatal evening when Lias and Nathan came back to the flat after being up for two days at a squat party in Hackney. The bedraggled pair rolled through the door tripping on acid. To them, everything generated hilarity, but Reggie, who had been drinking for hours, was at the other end of the mood spectrum. As he morbidly reflected on his desperate situation, he recounted a litany of his previous bad choices. It was inevitable, he thought, that he would end up behind bars again. He began to tell the brothers about his bleak early life, and the misery and desperation of his family.

Lias nodded in silence, attempting a show of compassion at Reggie's crescendo of grief. Nathan, on the other hand, could only manage a certain amount of tragedy under the influence and started smiling. He stared at Lias, who tried to ignore him, but was well aware of his younger brother's total lack of restraint.

As Lias leaned over to Reggie to pat him on the back after his desperate monologue, Nathan shouted at the top of his voice, in the most comic baritone he could manage.

'NEXXXXXXXT!'

The two Saoudis burst into raucous laughter. Barely able to contain themselves, they rolled onto the mattress, choking with joy. Reggie's face dropped.

'That's not fucking funny,' Reggie said. 'Why are you laughing? Stop it. Stop it now!'

No matter which words fell from his mouth, their laughter increased. The more he complained, the more they howled.

'You pair of little cunts,' he hollered. 'No more. You are both OUT. Don't ever fucking step foot in here again.'

The brothers fought to gather their breath as Reggie's irate face exploded like a kaleidoscope through their hallucinations. He pulled out two binbags, filled up each one with their belongings, and threw them out of the front door.

Lias and Nathan stopped laughing as rain started to fall around them, drenching their clothes and faces.

'What the hell are we gonna do now?' said Nathan.

'We've really blown it this time,' his brother replied.

Sport Socks and a Warm Sweater

After three months of living in abandoned buildings, boarded-up schools and a derelict Victorian hospital, the Saoudi brothers left the fading landscape of Bow and crossed the Thames towards New Cross and Telegraph Hill. By this point they had become hardened squatters, sleeping under charity shop blankets and using camping gas to warm up tins of beans by candlelight. Nathan applied to Goldsmiths to study English Literature on a foundation course and was accepted. The now-disgraced Lias had been booted out of the Slade and was forced to sign on.

For the first part of winter, they moved into a squat on Pepys Road that had been broken into by an ex-soldier with a speciality for removing door panels and jacking electricity in exchange for ecstasy pills. During a session one night, Nathan tunnelled and punched his way through the toilet wall in an attempt to attack revellers who had locked themselves inside the lavatory with two wraps of powder. It left a large hole in the plaster that allowed him to spy on Lias during his private moments as an act of humiliation. Above the door Nathan wrote in marker pen a quote that he had adapted from *Mein Kampf*, signed by Adolf Hitler: 'Genius is something will-o'-the-wisp if not followed through with order, discipline and hard work.'

The squat was populated by a crew of semi-derelict headcases, including a ten-year-old street kid who hung around with Nathan all the time, and a young man with learning disabilities called Jamie Wrestle. Another friend, nicknamed 'Mikey the Pikey', was a regular visitor who appeared in the middle of the night to wake up whoever happened to be sleeping. Nathan kept a rotting duck carcass in his room that festered and mutated as the weeks went by, until a swarm of sleepy bluebottles hatched from its insides and drowsily made their way to the windowpane, blocking the sunlight until the latch was opened and they flew off into the London smog.

Penniless, and subsisting on microwave meals from his £46-a-week unemployment benefit, Lias was forced by the dole office to take a job at the Maritime Museum in Greenwich. Each morning he would wash over a bucket, don his uniform and stumble down Greenwich High Road to the site of the Meridian Line, where he was frequently placed in the museum's clock room, the quietest corner of the building dedicated to the history of timekeeping. As an invigilator, his role was to stand for hours at a time, offering leaflets or information to visitors who only ever wanted to know where the toilet was or where Nelson's blood-stained jacket from the Battle of Trafalgar was located. A CCTV camera watched his every move from overhead. No books or chairs were permitted for staff, and so each minute of the day was spent on his feet watching the slow *tick tick tick* of antique clocks, atomic clocks, grandmother clocks and cuckoo clocks. It was even worse on an MDMA comedown, which was frequently the state of affairs on Monday mornings. The clock room was more of a trial than Dungannon Meats, where at least he had the romance of physical Springsteen-esque blue-collar factory work to complain about as opposed to this arduous silence and the slow, perturbing passing of time.

☪

With no permanent place to live, the brothers opted to spend the summer of 2008 living in Algeria, reasoning that at least they would have a roof over their heads for a few sunny months. They travelled to Algiers by plane with Sebley and their two other bandmates, Maxwell and Mike.

For twelve weeks the five of them smoked in the olive groves, away from the chaos and dirt of London, a city full of psychic pollution, advertising and aggression to which, like many young people, they had all gravitated from far, far away. In the arid heat of the Kabylia mountains Lias, Nathan and Sebley started to write what would become the first Fat White Family songs, 'Touch the Leather', 'Teenage Toy' and 'Special Ape'.

Over the mountain lay the shrine of Matoub Lounès, a Kabyle singer and local Berber hero. His songs were written near Tizi Ouzou, the nearest large town. They listened to his songs blasting out of the car stereo as they made their way through the land-scape on treacherous roads. Each bend had sheer drops, some two hundred feet down, that were so notorious that bodies were rarely retrieved from accidents. The remains of skulls, ribcages and shattered femurs lined the slopes below the winding tarmac that snaked along routes into scree-ridden gorges.

Matoub's cheap cassettes were sold in markets across Algeria and France, and a fair number were stacked in Bashir's drawers at home. His album *Lettre ouvert aux* was often played in his car; the Saoudi brothers were fascinated by the bleeding crescent moon on its sleeve and would one day use it on their own artwork with Fat White Family. Like Lias and Nathan, Matoub was a natural troublemaker; when he changed the lyrics of the national hymn it was seen by the government as an act of vandalism.

As the car dropped through the Tikjda Pass, the Saoudis' uncle Abder recounted to his nephews how Matoub was wounded so severely for writing and singing his songs that he became wheelchair-bound.

'Didn't they shoot him up here?' Lias asked.

'His body was full of bullets. Terrible pain,' Abder shouted, as the car's high gear made an irritating noise. 'I remember . . . his body was crushed . . . you know he became addicted to morphine? He had one leg shorter than the other after it was reset. The doctors made a mess of him. Oh yes, and he was left wearing a shit bag . . . a colostomy, you know? This was before they shot him. He shouldn't have come back from France. Too many enemies.'

Lias and Nathan stared out of the window at the jagged cliffs and listened to their uncle, who shouted over the top of Matoub's voice as it pumped out of the speakers.

'Matoub wasn't worried about who he offended – he insulted everyone, including the bloody Islamists.'

This whole subject was of great interest to Abder, who felt a sense of pride when he listened to Matoub's music and started to sing along in Kabyle Berber with the windows wound down.

'He was like one of your English punks,' he said. 'A troublemaker.'

The summer of 2008 was an emotionally charged tour for the band. It became the point where a group of men in their early twenties who were happy to play to one man and his dog, third on the bill in a squalid New Cross pub, ended up playing to audiences of hundreds.

In Algeria there were moments of elation and fear; Kabyle people were generous and kind, but there were bombs going off and threats in the region, and on one night they were told not to go out on the streets at all. Throughout July, Sebley slept outside on a cast iron bed under a fig tree in the Saoudi courtyard, beneath the moonlight, dehydrated, slowly going insane, being woken by the call to prayer, and the sound of donkeys baying and bats flying overhead.

Subsisting on a diet of fruit picked from the family's groves, Saoudi Olive Oil (made in a small local factory) and couscous, the organic food added to the transformative effect of living in Algeria. Purity was suddenly within reach. Each day, Lias and

Nathan bought food from the market. Live chickens were slaughtered in front of them, their legs kicking long after the head had been removed, a scene uncommon to squeamish Western eyes. As an offering to the family a white baby goat was bought from the market, and was christened 'Sai Baba' after Bashir's guru. The kid followed them around all day like a dog, the band fed and watered it by hand in the parched afternoon light, and it became the Saudis' band mascot, their pet for the summer. Sai Baba slept in the yard, beside Sebley's bed, under the twinkling blanket of the night sky above, blissfully unaware of the fate that awaited him as the key ingredient of a family tagine.

In the streets outside, before iftar, they listened to a man chewing shisha by the gate, a mixture of tobacco and fig leaves rolled in paper nestled beneath the gumline. His stained teeth were the colour of desert sunsets and he carried a shotgun over one arm, his job being the guard for Chinese roadbuilders who lived in a compound on the barren freeway that was being constructed around the back of Jida Saoudi's house leading up to the village. The road had been under development for almost ten years and was still not completed.

Everyone in Maillot was a Saoudi cousin, and one afternoon, in broken French, they told Lias how they'd found work as security guards on large infrastructure projects elsewhere in the country. They explained how the government was bringing in hordes of migrant workers from China to build highways, so it was now their job to watch over the new labour force and raw materials armed with rifles.

As he listened to their account, Lias wondered how harsh life must be in China if a country like Algeria held some kind of economic allure.

'Do you get on with the Chinese? Are they fitting in over here? You got Chinese food yet?'

'Non!' they chanted in unison. 'Je déteste, je déteste le chinois! Regarde, Lias, regarde . . .'

Lias's cousin Boubker took to his feet excitedly and pointed a finger off into the middle distance, at an empty stretch of mountain scape, then clasped his arms around a machine gun made of thin air and shouted excitedly.

'Regarde le chinois Lias Kaci, regarde . . . BANG BANG BANG BANG BANG!'

☪

It was a few hours in a battered old minibus to the roadside brothel, and the mood in the vehicle was something akin to that inside the jet in the film Alive *just before it plunges into the Andes. There was no limit to the tomfoolery, the posturing or the schoolboy intrigue. I'd never visited a whorehouse before. Our drummer Mike had worked as a rent boy back in London, so he became the de facto leader on this particular adventure, the one confidently pushing things forward. The idea didn't really appeal to me, but I was curious. Perhaps it was Sebley's flirting with my cousins and letting them into the rehearsal barn, singing doo-wop songs to them, then taking their photographs and sharing his cigarettes that led my uncle Abder to conclude that this was the appropriate course of action, a cautionary measure even. Or maybe he just fancied a beer and a bit of time away from the wife. Whorehouses double up as drinking dens in Algeria, a rarity for the mountain folk.*

The establishment itself, like anywhere in Algeria that serves booze, was shrouded in dust, withered and miserably gaudy. The usual portraits of Matoub and Zidane adorned the walls. There were coloured lights, like Christmas lights, and an artificial palm tree over by the bar. Degraded Maghrebian vaporwave.

The minute we were introduced to the girls we were all exposed as the pathetic schoolboys we in fact were. Leaden silence strangled the room, each of us sheepishly staring into our beers, all but denying the idea had ever even crossed our minds. Our drummer, Mike, was particularly shameless in his U-turnage; having led us to this precipice, he was now the first to confirm his non-participation.

The others followed suit while the bemused prostitutes took their umbrage out on my poor old uncle, who was becoming more and more visibly embarrassed. I fell into a pair of dark eyes as the rest of the gang bade their retreat, swallowed up the rest of my ale, and made my decision. My uncle's honour was clearly at stake, and the way her long dark hair straddled her bare, coffee-coloured shoulders had started to make me feel off-balance.

I was led out of the main building into an adjacent bamboo shack, as terrified as I was excited. She closed the door behind us, sat me down on a single mattress, removed my trousers and began placing a condom on my now screamingly erect penis. She removed her denim boob tube, dropped her skirt and removed her panties, placing a tender hand on the back of my neck as she carried me down into her. I came instantly. A solitary stroke by the dusty roadside. She had the decency not to let out a laugh, but I could hear it in her eyes all the same.

Back in the van I told the boys it was brief, real brief, somewhere around the two-minute mark, which seemed a sufficient exaggeration at the time.

☪

During rehearsals, the band's amplifiers were plugged into unearthed power supplies in the barn where they practised. To avoid death by electrocution, the band stood motionless on blocks of polystyrene. They were a drum pedal short and spent weeks travelling around blacksmiths in small dusty towns on an arduous journey to get a new one made. Eventually, the drum was held by hand as they practised a cover of Buddy Holly's 'Fade Away', a staple for them that year. A Land Rover drove them along dusty tracks to meet a journalist from *Le Monde* in a coffee shop, and on the way they hit a stray dog from a pack that roamed the hillsides that surrounded the Saoudi residence. The band winced as the vehicle crushed its bones beneath the wheels. It was the most terrible of sounds.

Their Maillot show was a performance the band would continue to think about ten years later. Most of the audience had not witnessed anything like it in their lifetimes, and the band had never played to a crowd that size. The auditorium was full of men, because of the cultural view that it was dishonourable for women to attend bars or live concerts in that part of the country. Outside the queue shouted *Saudis! Saudis!* as they waited to enter. The local mayor was insistent that the town's visitors would play as his guests and initially started to build a stage for them outside the mosque, in the open air. The band quickly intervened, believing it to be potentially a problematic event, certainly outside a religious building. Even Lias knew he could not get away with his sordid lyrics in the presence of Allah. They were quickly rehoused in an old Soviet-style municipal cinema, and as there was no advertising, promoting the show was strictly word-of-mouth.

In the video footage, a crowd of six hundred locals stare up at the strange scene above and are transfixed – or slightly perturbed – by the music being performed. It was a night of extremes for the crowd and the band. They didn't know what punk rock was. And the Saudis didn't really know either. Testosterone filled the room with a murky fog of dense masculine energy. Singing in a foreign language to the audience, the band stumbled through their set as equipment started to break, feedback ringing from the amplifiers. But for the group, the short, chaotic gigs they played in Algeria would be the ones that came to define their onstage career. They were significant, in a way that playing to five thousand fans at Brixton Academy could never be.

By the time they reached the nearest city, Tizi Ouzou, the Saudis' live shows marked the first time punk or rock 'n' roll had been performed live in those places. Their next gig was smaller, but the sound improved. It was an important moment for them, a lightbulb going on. When they started playing their rudimentary versions of rock 'n' roll the kids screamed and jumped up and down and the stage began shaking beneath their feet. The band couldn't have anticipated the reaction they would receive. When the crowd emptied out the venue's seats had been torn out and were left scattered across the floor.

☪

The trip to Algeria transformed the Saudis, in terms of what they were capable of, and the potential their music had. They had left London feeling disgruntled and frustrated by the music scene, their living situation and lack of money, and returned to the city with fresh eyes. Yes, it was dirty and unclean, *haram* as the Algerians would call it, but being away from it, out in the sunshine with no distractions for three months, gave them a new perspective. If they hadn't quite grasped the advanced techniques of songwriting, they were at least confident of their ability to perform live.

It was at one of their bottom-of-the-bill gigs at the New Cross Inn in south-east London, where they were supporting a line-up of landfill indie bands currently in vogue, that Nathan first met Saul Adamczewski. He was sitting outside the pub smoking a joint, wearing a thick gold chain around his neck, his voice raised over the rabble of traffic. Nathan could see he was the centre of attention and bounded over to him in the London haze, asking if he had a lighter.

'Yeah,' Saul said. 'Keep it.'

Nathan cracked a smile as he stared into Saul's enormous cartoon eyes and touched the chain on his neck.

'Can I have this as well?' Nathan asked.

There was a pause, Saul blinked and then removed it, dropping the chain into the palm of his hand. Nathan's Irish accent and dark olive skin that had deepened after an extended period in Algeria were enough to convince Saul he was a gypsy, so therefore if he asked for the chain, he should give it to him without hesitation. Saul had learned enough on the streets of Peckham not to question those kinds of propositions.

'You want a drink?' Saul laughed.

Nathan said yes, and his new friend returned with two tequilas for them both, the beginning of a session that continued long into the next day, and then to the next week, when Nathan awoke in Saul's father's house by Warwick Gardens with a hangover worse than death.

Saul's band, the Metros, had been signed to 1965 Records by James Endeacott, a gregarious Yorkshireman with a head of 'Viking Gold' ringlets who was responsible for signing the Strokes and the Libertines. Still only eighteen, Saul was discovered through the various word-of-mouth Brixton networks, and the band were immediately signed as the next Arctic Monkeys. They often played underage festivals and developed their own rabid fanbase by standing outside girls' schools in the area handing out flyers to the best-looking girls before each show. It was a tactic that worked.

Originally called the Wanking Skankers, Saul and his friends wrote a batch of dodgy uptempo songs as a joke at the expense of some of the other local bands they had seen, who they deemed to be appalling in both taste and expression. They were too young to get drunk, so music became their main source of entertainment. A five-track demo was recorded in Honor Oak, and one song that featured the lyrics 'Education's overrated, and I'm the monster it created' became their first single. The group were quickly dispatched to Rockfield Studios in Wales to record their debut album. The recording sessions were a disaster. Unlike its previous residents such as Oasis, Queen or the Manic Street Preachers, the Metros thought the studio would look far better with its equipment smashed up and thrown from the barn into the rain outside, an act that would cost their label many thousands of pounds. In the midst of their album tour they were banned from a hotel chain for their appalling behaviour, leaving rooms trashed across the country. When the band were due to fly out to Japan, the tour was abandoned. Saul had failed to show up for the flight, having vanished to Crystal Palace Park to stare at concrete dinosaurs instead. His fear of flying was so extreme he could not face getting on a plane, even with thousands of fans awaiting him at the other end. A holiday with his friend in Cyprus ten years previously had terrified him to such an extent that he was traumatised. Eight-year-old Saul had boarded a Cessna plane from Istanbul with his friend's father, which hit a dramatic storm eight miles high, shaking the tiny plane like a pepperpot. When it landed Saul was violently sick; it was fear like he had never known. His friend's father tried to make up for it all week by offering Saul one euro for every baby iguana he could squash, but even the mass murder of the island's reptiles and a hundred notes in his pocket was not enough to convince him to ever get in a plane again.

Even in his teenage years, Saul saw music as the ultimate way of avoiding work. His songs of failed local criminals, shady boozers and Peckham life were inspired by Dexy's Midnight Runners, Ian Dury and Rancid. When the record deal finally arrived, Saul was catapulted from having pocket money to more cash than he could ever dream of. In the months after the band imploded, Saul was left working on a building site in Penge, penniless and addicted to drugs, after turning down an offer to clean offices at Columbia Records. The cataclysmic ups and downs of life in the British music industry had taken their toll on the young frontman, adding to the turmoil that had already been brewing in his teenage years.

Jerry Lee Lewis in a Headlock

Saul Henry Owen Adamczewski was born during a thunderstorm at King's Hospital in 1988, a birth that almost occurred in the broken lift shaft, his mother, Ruth, trying to hold back his head as he erupted into life. His father, Simon, pulled her into a men's geriatric ward, where he was delivered from behind a curtain as elderly men ate their porridge. He inherited his mother's eyes, azure and watery, and so distinctive that onlookers were hypnotised by their unusual size and beauty.

His elder brother, Joe, had a stammer and couldn't get a word in edgeways as Saul was such a talkative child. Saul had to learn to wait his turn with a star chart when he was still in the pushchair, though he struggled to carry that skill for listening and patience with others through into adulthood. As a little boy he was frequently anxious and would attempt to work out serious existential questions. Ruth spent many hours reassuring him, but she quickly discovered that music and drawing were two things that pacified and nurtured her youngest son. At night, he listened to the dark Celtic ballad of Christy Moore's 'The Dying Soldier' as his lullaby, the only song that could soothe him to sleep.

His parents separated when Saul was a baby, so he was raised by his mother, who he called by her first name, in a house full of music and paintings on Romola Road in Tulse Hill. Ruth's boyfriend played in a band and often made cassette tapes for her sons' entertainment. He would sneak Saul and Joe into his gigs at the Windmill in Brixton when they were still young, and the brothers would sit at the back, hiding under tables and eating crisps as the band played on the stage.

It was when he started school that Saul's behavioural problems really began. It was turbulent for him from the beginning. He was described as naughty with a high profile at Rosendale Primary – after pulling a water fountain from the wall he denied he had done it. Despite his disruptive behaviour, Saul was a bright child, left-handed, who initially wrote backwards. As the years progressed, so his discipline deteriorated, and he was referred to the local children's service following outbursts in the classroom. A fight with a learning support assistant in class triggered an investigation, and the boundaries were tightened around him. He believed their treatment of him to be unfair, as the teacher favoured girls over boys.

Each morning was challenging for Ruth, who would have to drag her son kicking and screaming to school, where he would often be admonished in the classroom, thrown out into the corridor or put in the corner of the room to work on his own. When he applied to go to Charter School with his friend Jak he wasn't offered a place and was sent instead to Kingsdale, a school known for its religious philosophy and rich racial diversity. Kingsdale was where Saul's problems escalated, and he progressed from being a troubled pupil into a full-blown special case. The school at that time had a large number of refugee children with emotional trauma, almost half had special educational needs, and the main languages were Yoruba, Twi, French and Spanish. When Saul arrived, he was immediately bullied for being white and posh, despite being raised by a single parent who was only a teaching assistant herself. In the first few weeks he was stabbed with a compass, threatened with a knife and robbed for his dinner money.

The upset continued at home. On weekends he would run away, stealing Ruth's Benson & Hedges, taking his giant watch clock off the wall and placing it in his rucksack, before hiding under a bush all weekend in Brockwell Park pretending to be Tom Sawyer as his frantic parents scoured south London looking for him. Saul was suspended for throwing sugar cubes at teachers and was constantly admonished for his confrontational and nihilistic views of the future. When he became overwhelmed or afraid it triggered outbursts of anger and Saul fell behind in class, until his engagement was so poor that he was placed in remedial learning.

After numerous meetings, the school referred Saul to a psychiatrist where he was diagnosed as clinically depressed, experiencing nightmares that caused him to wake up screaming most nights. The bullying became so intense at school he tried every excuse he could not to go back. Prescribed medication numbed him to his surroundings, and Saul's depression surged to such a severe extent that one day when Ruth came home from work, she found her son with a belt around his neck hanging from the kitchen door. On days when he was forced to attend, he would bash his head against the wall and punch objects, screaming *Just kill me!* in Ruth's face as he sobbed at the pain welling up from within.

When he returned to Kingsdale following his suspension, he sought protection from a racist gang who promised to look after him. They had shaved heads, wore Union Jack socks tucked into their tracksuit bottoms and walked around the schoolyard as if they were prison cons already. For a frightened and withdrawn Saul, he saw it as the only way he could function at school, and he rapidly descended into belligerent behaviour with the black African boys in Religious Education lessons, where he disputed the existence of God with the teacher, who was a fire and brimstone pastor at an evangelical church in the area. Creationism was taught in class, and Saul was admonished for blaspheming. The arguments about Christianity spilled out from the classroom into the streets outside, and quickly escalated into aggression between students. When he was finally expelled for racist language and violent conduct it came as some relief. Saul was put on the Special Educational Needs Register and given a Statement.

☪

Saul's tendency towards uncontrollable outbursts of rage coupled with an obsessive perfectionism where all things musical were concerned had only made itself apparent for the briefest of moments during our time in the Saudis. Once we moved into that grubby little flat together in Peckham and began working on what would eventually become the Fat White Family, however, everything took on a more serious hue. Bruised from his apparent fall from grace and exiled from the music industry, he was determined that this time there would be no mistakes. It was in the pursuit of the perfect version of a song called 'Auto Neutron' that this fact laid itself bare.

We had a drum kit set up in the living room, a couple of crummy little amps, a battered old PA and an ancient stand-up organ. For months that tune was worked and re-worked. It went on every day, all of us switching instruments at his behest, patiently awaiting the next manoeuvre he'd dreamt up in his head. You'd think you were finally free of it, then he'd insist on starting all over again. We'd got hold of a little Tascam four-track to make our first demo. Even though we were just sat around our shitty living room, it felt like the pressure was somehow on.

This was the driving force behind the group. This tendency of his, a kind of mania if you like, to treat what you were doing as if it mattered, as if it was the very measure of your value as a human being. I didn't have it in me to take myself that seriously, not in a musical capacity. I loved the idea of myself in a band, had a strong desire for public adoration, but this bare-bones songcraft stuff was beyond me. My vision didn't extend much further than the lyrical content.

It'd always been a challenge for me to sing the same thing twice. I'm not tone deaf, but borderline. I struggle with the psychology of singing, become hyper self-conscious. I have to find a way out of that trap in order to do whatever it is I'm singing any kind of justice. In a way Saul was the worst person in the world for me to couple up with, then. He'd elaborated what we were doing in his head very precisely. We had a different approach: where I'd spend all of my spare time going over and over a couplet in my skull until it was just right, he was busy dreaming up these things called 'harmonies'.

Having spent days unravelling the mystery of the Tascam, acquainting ourselves with its strange inner life, we set about weaving together the musical landscape of this first opus. It was going well, but in its going well I slowly filled up with anxiety. Soon I would have to deliver the backing vocals. Not during a live performance, where you can back off the mic, where everybody is a little too distracted by whatever it is that they're playing to properly notice you fucking it up, but isolated, with headphones on . . . scrutinised.

There I was, suddenly, cans on, the bass warmly, seductively ushering me forth towards the inexorable . . .

'Ahhh, ahhh, ooh, ooh . . .'

'No man, no man, not like that, not like that. Like this, like this . . .'

We'd go through it again together without the mic. I'd follow his vocal, get to a point where I was singing it confidently enough, then we'd give it another whirl. The moment I was plugged back in, the moment the little red light was on, it would all go completely to shit. We tried it without the other vocals in there, maybe it'd be easier. No dice. The moment we were rolling, my head filled up with visions of dread. What was I doing here? Why had I signed up for this? There were things in life I was actually quite good at, and I had betrayed those things, I had betrayed those things because like every other sexually frustrated young man with a drug problem who came of age during the Doherty era, being in a band looked like easy street. I was a disgrace, a sham, a poseur, and now I would suffer the full cost of my delusions . . .

'Oh, for fuck's sake man! "AAAHHH AAAHHH, OOOHHH OOOHHH", not fucking "AAAH AAAH, OOOHH OOHHH!!"'

Whatever patience Saul started out with had dried up. Having to go over this simple bit of a demo over and over and over again was breaking him. He was awash with frustration, could barely sit still because of it.

105

But although my shortcoming was beyond his comprehension, onwards we ploughed. We couldn't just stop. By this point I knew it was a lost cause. I couldn't make the take before being screamed at to make the take; now that I felt like a proper prick the game was up. Still I agreed to give it another go. I would get it any moment, I said, too embarrassed to call it a day but knowing full well this was now an impossibility.

I sat there with the headphones on again, every part of the tune now felt insulting, even the bongo track was laughing at me. I counted myself in and let rip one more time . . .

'Aaahhh aaahhh, ooohhh ooohhh . . .'

In one abominable flourish Saul spasmed up out of his chair, hurling a ride cymbal across the room in my general direction as he did so, narrowly missing my head and taking a decent chunk out of the wall with the impact.

'NO!! NO!! NO!! FOR FUCK'S SAKE!! "AHHHH AHHHH AHHH", NOT FUCKING "AHHH AHH AHHH"!! WHAT THE FUCK IS WRONG WITH YOU?!'

And so began our fruitful and fractious recording partnership . . .

☾

With no respect for authority, no remorse for his actions and a confrontational personality, it was only a matter of time before a teenage Saul would discover punk rock. Bright, inquisitive and articulate, he was able to hold his own with adults, but maintained a strong belief that *good people are no fun*. When he turned up for a meeting at the Maudsley to see a psychiatrist, Saul had a large Mohican, and it was noted that he had a particular and arresting sartorial style. He wore deck shoes, an army jacket over a shirt and tie, and jeans cut off above the knee. His tie was decorated with badges bought at Camden Market; one had a swastika with a cross through it, the other a hammer and sickle. The 'new look' had been adopted after his expulsion from Kingsdale; punk was his only saving grace. After some discussion about his behavioural problems at school, he was diagnosed with conduct disorder, a personality disorder that triggers explosive confrontation. The psychiatrist told him it also manifests as non-aggressive conduct, such as vandalism or arson, deceitfulness or theft, lying or conning others for personal gain, or violations of the rules. Saul's running away, playing truant and staying out all night were part of his mental health condition, not just teenage behaviour. As an adult, there would be a high risk of addiction and criminality, of suicide or violent and aggressive outbursts. But as his brain was still growing at thirteen, the problem he was diagnosed with was not set in stone. By managing his symptoms and undergoing therapy, and attending a school that allowed him to flourish, there was hope it would be under control by the time he reached adulthood.

Over the winter months Saul spent his days alone at home, under a black cloud, waiting for a school that would accept him. His father Simon arranged private tuition two days a week, which was beneficial but not a replacement for daily lessons. Out of desperation, his father sent him to live in Vienna with his Uncle Mickey, who was a child psychologist.

The Adamczewski family were originally milliners from Poland but moved to Heidelberg in the Franco-Prussian War, then settled in Vienna. It was a city where Simon had once lived in a commune in the 1970s, hiding a member of the Baader–Meinhof in his attic as political turmoil erupted in the UK. And before him, his own father, Bernhard, had lived in the city post-Second World War after returning from a prisoner-of-war camp, his life spared as a letter writer for the dead. Later he'd fled and become a shepherd in the Dolomites to escape the horror of his teenage conscription by the Waffen-SS as the Eagle's Nest started to implode. Saul's other grandfather, Ruth's father, lived in Israel, where he converted to Judaism and was circumcised at the age of forty. He made programmes on the Palestine conflict for the BBC, swinging between bouts of alcoholism, rehabilitation and relapse, an affliction that would continue to dog his errant grandson throughout his adult life.

When Saul arrived in Vienna for the summer, he was enlisted to attend the WUK, a free school run by a Viennese collective where students could decide what they wanted to learn, a programme designed specifically for them. Children who were interested in botany or sculpture would flourish. For Saul this meant playing guitar all day, every day. All students were considered equal; they even voted out their maths teacher when they deemed him to be incompetent. Saul, the latest addition, was believed to be such a troublemaker that he was eventually voted out of the school by the pupils. He had made friends with the pupils in the year above him who were cool, and collectively they were cruel to the others, teasing or winding people up. Saul accepted the vote that was meted out. Even at that age, he was aware of his shortcomings.

☪

There were key disparities between Lyndhurst Grove and where I'd grown up. The Adamczewski home didn't centre around the television, but rather the kitchen table. The only permissible distraction was the constant low volume hum of Radio 4. This meant everything was geared towards chat. Great when you were in the mood, sadistic if you were hungover. Everyone was always hungover.

My family had one or two dogs on the go at any given time, but the Adamczewski place was like Dr Doolittle's annexe. There were hamsters running on wheels on the kitchen worktop, cats galore and a giant Irish wolfhound with obvious behavioural problems stalking about the place.

I recall the sound of Saul's younger brother Sasha playing guitar and bellowing out tunes at the top of his lungs in some other room of the house, the kind of thing you just didn't do at my family home. Good or bad you would have been ridiculed by at least one of the family. His little sister, Vida, was sat at the table studying Chinese. She couldn't have been much older than ten.

I'd stumbled into their lives on a random night of the week, and they were about to tuck into squid salad followed by filet mignon. What with Saul's dad being a former restauranteur turned house-husband – a dedicated man with time on his hands – the food was never ordinary. We all sat down by candlelight, refilling our glasses with wine as the conversation ebbed and flowed eloquently across the spread before us. 'These folks are sorted,' I was thinking to myself when Frida, the wolfhound, took it upon herself to puncture the bourgeois idyll. Unable to contain her desire for the flesh set upon the table, she began shrieking up at her master like a banshee. Each howl brought forth some primordial anxiety, derailed gravity, making a mockery of your chain of thought. I couldn't understand why anyone would bother elaborating such finery, only to sully it completely with the presence of this monster. After she had been routinely ignored for a few moments, Saul's dad eventually grabbed a butter knife and gave her a quick, sharp jab in the ribs, bellowing as he did so, 'GET BACK IN YOUR BOX!' The animal screamed, then quickly retreated into a barely wolfhound-sized caged on the opposite side of the room. Once incarcerated, she would barely brave so much as a whimper. It seemed a cruel kind of justice, but fair, and – most importantly of all – effective.

Maybe our families weren't so dissimilar after all?

After her decree nisi, Ruth remarried. Her new husband was a social worker who'd heard of an establishment suited to Saul's needs. Between Ruth, Simon and his wife, they worked on an application to get Saul into the New School at West Heath. Situated in Sevenoaks, it was a boarding school of the last resort, a place for students expelled from every school in London, with the most severe emotional needs, paid for by the local authority. In a previous life it had been Princess Diana's school and was funded by Mohamed Al-Fayed after her death, as a way of preserving her memory. The site had five purpose-built bungalows named after its celebrity funders, including Wayne Sleep and Esther Rantzen, and boarding students were given their own room, with alarmed windows to prevent escape.

Saul was invited to an interview with the headmistress, who was immediately taken with him when he walked through the door with Ruth.

'What incredible blue eyes you have,' she said. 'One day you're going to be famous. I really want you at my school, Saul.'

It was the first time anyone in a position of authority had shown confidence in him as a person or treated him as an adult. It triggered an immediate change in him, and he agreed to become a boarder five days a week. Saul was given his own room, where he kept his guitar and pinned up posters and drawings above his bed.

During his first week at the school, he witnessed a boy throw a chair through the window and watched the glass shatter into a hundred pieces on the concrete outside. When the boy wasn't suspended, Saul took it upon himself to do the same thing and started throwing chairs through windows every week. The trend quickly caught on, until most of the windows in the school were boarded up.

On the streets of Sevenoaks, the residents of the New School would be called 'spastics' by young louts from the local school. Saul would lob bottles at them from over the road, confronting them and shouting back. His best friend, Julius, was a goth who wore make-up and cowered from confrontation. Over time, Saul came to realise he'd rather sit in his room with Julius, obsessing about the Libertines and talking until the early hours about the antics of Pete and Carl, than get their heads booted in on the streets outside.

Collectively, the residents were deeply troubled, and Saul nicknamed his new home the 'Funny Farm'. Most of the pupils were seriously disturbed; some were teenagers who had suffered such severe bullying that they could no longer be in mainstream education, others were bullies who doled out such stress and violence to their classmates that they had to be removed from school altogether. It created an uneasy dynamic in the classes, which comprised of three or four pupils, and the same number of teachers and assistants to control them. Some of the pupils were Travellers, others were mentally ill children of the aristocracy, and some of the girls Saul became friends with had been sexually abused, were drug users, or had been sold into prostitution at the age of fourteen.

There was a chaotic atmosphere in the corridors; the larger, stronger and more violent boys would explode in a flash. The school would go into lockdown, and Saul often spent his mornings clenched up like a tightened fist on his bed, with a pillow over his head to avoid the ringing sirens that echoed above him. In the kitchen, glass had to be hidden from the girls, who were often self-harmers and would steal shards from broken pop bottles, using them to shred lines into their forearms and bleed out on the carpet. Some acted with the sexual confidence of older women, and Saul would feel them up in the woods, drinking smuggled bottles of Mad Dog 20/20 beneath the shelter of an old oak tree and the flickering light of a crescent moon.

☪

In his fifteenth year, and despite his lack of engagement with formal learning, it was noted that Saul had a particular talent for art, drama and music. The school play that year was one perhaps sardonically suggested by a teacher. The production of *One Flew Over the Cuckoo's Nest* was rehearsed in the school hall, and the lead part of Randle McMurphy was played by Saul, who learned his lines perfectly; he truly believed that he was the McMurphy of the New School, the only sane pupil within its walls.

One teacher, Mr Lyons, allowed Saul to stay in his music lessons after class and spent hours of each day teaching basic musical scales to his young protégé and his gang of friends. A wave of young musicians started to flourish, despite their increasingly disruptive behaviour. Saul listened to Jimi Hendrix, Buzzcocks and the Pogues in class, and attempted to play some of the songs on guitar. He had an ear for pitch and tone, and could quickly pick up and learn new songs with an almost innate talent.

Each day, the teacher would pick a chart hit and the pupils would play together, patiently learning each part until they sounded competent. Lyons' own son, Dan, who was only thirteen, would sometimes come in and play the drums with them, collaborating with Saul on songs including Radiohead's 'Creep'. The Lyons' dinner table at home in the sleepy Kentish village of East Peckham was frequently dominated by the stress of teaching Saul, who was one of the most challenging boys. Yet he was also one of the most gifted. Dan formed a friendship with Saul that continued into his twenties, when he would become the drummer with Fat White Family.

When he wasn't studying music, Saul was in the art studio, making intricate sculptures or drawing vicious caricatures in the style of Robert Crumb. He was frequently excluded for days at a time for disruptive behaviour, and it still fell to Ruth to transport him to Tulse Hill station every Monday, then London Bridge, and on to Sevenoaks, where a taxi awaited him. He often absconded on the way to school, and his mother would stand sobbing on the platform, only to catch a sight of her son pressed up to the train window as the train pulled away, his face laughing and gurning through the glass.

One weekend, when he brought his girlfriend home from school, Ruth was called by her fuming foster parent, who said she had stolen all of the cash from their house and had to return immediately. His girlfriend had grown up in care and was sent to the New School where she quickly became smitten with Saul, who played 'Boys Don't Cry' to her through the bars of his bedroom window each night as she stared from the rose bushes outside. Their romance accelerated rapidly, and she became pregnant at the age of fifteen, when he was only sixteen. Simon was called into school to collect his son, and an appointment at the abortion clinic was quickly arranged.

☪

It wasn't surprising to his family that Saul became a musician. It was the only way to channel his fury and burgeoning creativity; his perfectionism resulted in a talent for arranging and performing live. He was the perfect frontman in many respects: a disaffected youth who had emerged from the tumble dryer of teenage street life with a pocket full of songs and experiences that would fuel his first foray onto the stage.

His first band, the Metros, was formed with a gang of friends from the Peckham area during weekends on leave from the New School. Although they had gained notoriety and a cult live following, after failing to recoup their substantial record deal they were quickly dropped.

It was in the final months of playing with the Metros that Saul noticed a certain Lias Saoudi in front of him in the audience at an East London show; he had arrived at the venue sporting a gold sequinned vest. Lias was distinctive, with his lanky physique and avian facial features. Much to Saul's chagrin, as he sang to the crowd he watched the object of his desire French kiss Lias, who had his tongue down her throat for most of the set. It was here the seeds of discontent were first sown.

After the gig, a girl who would (eventually) become Saul's girlfriend took a seat on Lias's lap, drinking a vodka cranberry through a straw and groping him between each slurp. Saul stood across the room at the bar, raging like a mad bull. When she finally left he stopped her in the corridor and said, 'How can you get off with him? Didn't you see he's got a nose like a massive cock? He looks like a prick!' Saul's future girlfriend shrugged her shoulders and smiled, replying that he had a special something about him and was interested in what she had to say, unlike most men she had met recently, including the one she was currently speaking to.

A few weeks later, at a house party in Brixton, Saul and a friend stood outside a block of maisonettes ringing the buzzer, but were denied entry. They decided to scale the outside of the building and shimmied up the balcony fronts until they reached the room with its windows open and music blaring out. Saul rolled over the top and crashed into the living room, splayed out on the carpet and knocked a plant pot over with his enormous feet and gangly legs. He heard a cough and looked up, only to see Lias sitting on the table in front of him, with arms crossed, as the rabble of the party played out behind him. He smiled at Saul and started to laugh.

'Well, that's quite an entrance,' he said. His voice had decided to land in a broad Scottish accent that night, rather than the Northern Irish twang where it usually resided.

'Yeah,' Saul replied. 'Have you got any Guinness?'

'There's some in the fridge.'

The two sat facing each other and Saul rolled a cigarette as Lias started to complain about the corporatisation of the streetscape in comparison to Algeria's simple life, indulgently moaning how they were all beholden to free market fundamentalism as he took another sip of Budweiser.

Lias was the most interesting person he had met in months; he was raw and funny and more intelligent than most of Saul's other friends in the south London music scene. Even though Saul thought his band, the Saudis, were a bit of a joke, there was an idiosyncratic element to his personality. He didn't look or sound like anybody else, and he wasn't trying to impress. Which in itself impressed Saul, who, as the lead singer of the Metros, had his fair share of hangers-on at the time. Nathan, meanwhile, couldn't put his guitar strap on properly and wore it like a necklace. They made a terrible din, but the Saudis had some of the best lyrics Saul had heard. When they eventually supported the Metros a few months later, Saul stood by the side of the stage with his mouth wide open. He was completely blown away by the performance. Saul knew from that moment that his own band was over, and in Lias Saoudi he had finally found his foil.

☪

Subsisting on the remainder of his record deal stipend in the months following the breakup of the Metros, Saul's days were spent drinking in the Hermit's Cave in Camberwell, where he played pool, listened to the jukebox and bought poor quality cocaine from local dealers. He was frequently arrested and cautioned by the same policeman as he stumbled home hammered, often with dregs of illegal substances poorly stashed in his inside pocket.

On Thursday afternoons, he'd walk down to Johansen's delicatessen to buy the finest food his money could afford, feeding his new friends, including the Saoudi brothers, then paying for their drinks and plying them with drugs. He was nothing if not generous and saw no better way to spend his previously hard-earned cash.

The Saoudis were on the verge of starvation, living on peanuts bought across the bar and stolen roasting joints, which were weighed as onions at the new-fangled self-service checkouts that swept through the capital at that time. Thankfully Saul had been educated in the fine art of cuisine by his father, who had owned a restaurant on Bellenden Road. As a result of Simon's culinary whip Saul had a refined palette, and not only knew how food should taste but also how to cook it to standard.

Saul's new drinking gang included Anna, Georgia and French Pascal, who played guitar for the Saudis. They developed their own private sense of the absurd, a language rich in ridicule and the outer limits of self-deprecation, one that could appear nonsensical to outsiders but created a bond between them inspired by the deranged situations of their early lives. Nathan stood out from the pub's regulars in his knee-length fur coat, long string of pearls, oversized sunglasses and pointed leather boots, and would often find himself at the receiving end of the landlord's humourless daughter, who barred him on numerous occasions. Members of the Hermit's Cave gang would snort Peckham blow in the toilets until Saul's money ran out on Saturday, after which point they would all starve until Thursday came around again. It inspired the first song Saul and Lias wrote together, a country jangle of sorts:

It's a Thursday night and I'm feeling alright.
It's the start of the weekend, it's the beginning of the rest of my life.
I wanna sex you up, I wanna hose you down,
spread a little bit of cheddar in another part of the town . . .

To save money, they took turns on a lukewarm bottle of Sailor Jerry passed around from beneath the table and carried it home after last orders, swilling at the rum until the early hours, then adding it to the pile of bottles gathering flies in the corner of the squat. To christen the moment, Lias designed matching 'Thursday Night' tattoos for him and Saul, based on the Sailor Jerry font, which were committed to the inside of their forearms in scruffy black ink at a shady tattoo parlour on Denmark Street, paid for by Saul as a birthday present. By the time the year was out, the Saudis' name had been banished to the dustbin, and a new temporary moniker stood in its place: Quran Quran.

☪

By the time I'd turned thirty, a pattern regarding how I relate to men had started to make itself apparent. Where men were concerned, I was what you might call a serial monogamist. My girlfriends have been extremely few and far between. In the last ten years I've had perhaps just one serious relationship; it ended in such a gruesomely protracted tit-for-tat war of sexual attrition that I pretty much gave up that game for good. I settled for status-enhancing mismatches and one-night stands instead. A long march to the beating heart of loneliness, then. On the other hand, there has never been a time when I haven't been seriously involved with a boy.

At Cookstown High School it was my girlfriend's cousin, Ashley, or 'Flash' as we called him. Ashley was a precursor to Saul in every way, so much so I wonder if my relationship with Saul wasn't an inevitable consequence of this earliest bromance. Something akin to Humbert Humbert's fixating on Lolita on account of his long-lost first love. Ashley had milky pale skin, big blue eyes and floppy blond hair. He was exactly my size and height, perhaps ever so slightly taller. Born to provocation from the womb, he was equipped with an acidic wit and more intelligence than he knew what to do with. We formed our own 'Yuppies Out!'-style pseudo-political faction, 'The Phantoms', while we were doing our A levels. Our mission was simple: to draw a penis upon every possible surface within the school, each one signed with a mysterious letter 'P'. When the inevitable came and we were hauled before the powers that be and threatened with expulsion, we set about writing page after page of defensive polemic regarding the essentiality of free expression and the power of forgiveness in a world turned sour.

Needless to say, we walked the charges.

Then there was Matthew, my first beau at college. Matthew used to lock himself in his room at our flatshare after an MDMA binge for days at a time. He'd pull his old cathode ray TV close enough to his bed on a chair to watch pornography with headphones plugged in. He was a man of detail. He introduced me to the Smiths and the Fall; bands I didn't quite understand yet. He used to go around the supermarkets sticking Boycott Israeli Goods tags on all of the avocados, which I also found confusing. He was a complete failure with women, so much so my own failures didn't seem so grotesque, for which I'm grateful to this day.

There was Jamie, my first and last alpha. He was broad-chested, broad-chinned and broadly appealing to the opposite sex, which drove me wild with jealousy. He was a fellow art student, a carpenter and a musician. And he could cook. I knew the minute I laid eyes on him at the Slade that my chances with women were null and void. He had confidence and competence. It was against this tender rock of a man that I would break myself in the years to come. My hungering for success as a musician was in no small way derived from my wanting to trump Jamie at something, at anything.

When I lived in Berlin years later, I fell in love with an effeminate goth named Shannon, from Australia. Like Saul he was into heroin, but unlike Saul the drug didn't turn him into Hitler, which seemed a boon at the time. I would always find little shot glasses of his blood in my rented room after he'd stayed there a while. He'd leave them there after shooting up while I was out buying beer or whatever, these sordid little tokens of his affection for me. We wandered the streets of the German capital for a whole summer, busking, boozing, snorting and laughing. He and his girlfriend used to dress like characters out of The Matrix, *which I ridiculed them for until my first rejection by the notorious Berghain door* staff. They were ushered in while I was politely led to one side, at which point he bade a hasty retreat. He opted instead to keep me company in some dive bar in Kotti while I nursed my wounds, leaving his girlfriend inside the club. After a particularly decadent evening at the Trinkteufel that followed, we both ended up making love to my flatmate. I'll never forget the spastic mix of pleasure and confusion that broke out across his face while trying to insert his MDMA-compromised penis into the opposing end of the woman. A primal grimace-cum-gurn etched forever onto the back of my retina.

When I showed up in Cambodia alone years later, after touring our second album, Songs for Our Mothers, I quickly partnered up with a strapping Lebanese–Nigerian motorcyclist. I found Ali, dark-skinned, muscular, Afro-headed and kind, skinny-dipping in the shallows off Otres beach on my first night in Sihanoukville. Lost in an ecstasy-fuelled haze of passionate adoration for each other, we rode his Yamaha up to Laos together, a country he told me was too beautiful not to see. I was on the back of his bike hurtling up dirt roads at 60 mph, clasping onto his abdomen for dear life as we embarked upon the first leg of a journey that would stretch on for well over a thousand miles.

We would talk endlessly about finding girls in the next town.

The girls never materialised.

Shapeshifter par excellence and mullet-haired musical impresario Alex 'Sax' White was next. My first public schoolboy, he made his way into my arms while Saul was out of the picture living his Parisian bourgeois fantasy in Le Marais. It was great to finally work out what all the fuss was about. It doesn't matter how low you sling it while accompanied by someone so well spoken and forensically empathetic, someone so unquestionably self-assured: you still feel like, somehow, you're doing 'the right thing'. We used to lie around in bed together all weekend semi-naked, scratching like crazy, discussing my inability to find love. I'd spend around 20 per cent of each evening on my knees in the toilet violently howling whatever sugary drink I was using to offset the gear back out into the world. Despicable scenes really, but it felt like quite the honeymoon period at the time.

Most recently, I became infatuated with the Irish novelist Rob Doyle. We'd been flirting with each other over Instagram for six months during lockdown before finally meeting in the flesh during the summer of 2020. Within forty-eight hours of our meeting, the Berlin drug squad had us spread up against a wall in broad daylight. I suppose there was an excess of mutual respect between us, too much build-up.

Unquestionably, though, the defining relationship – of my youth, at least – has been with Saul. A masochist at heart, what I was searching for was someone to feed me jugs of my own blood, and he was only too happy to oblige. No, no, that's unfair, although it felt like that years into the abyss, once he'd lost control of the drugs and became tyrannical. There was a natural affinity between us like no other, and an unspoken sense of that bond as something durable in the extreme; despite the respective shadiness of both of our characters, it was something you could have a bit of faith in. Secure in our love for one another, we were then at liberty to heap ridicule and scorn upon anyone or anything that didn't quite add up in the world.

☪

When 2010 began, Saul's recording career was effectively over, and he was forced to spend the spring working as a roofer with a friend of the family, Billy, who he had known since childhood and was once his babysitter. The wiry-framed Saul found physical labour hard going, and each close of shift left him in considerable pain after heaving wheelbarrows of tiles and bags of concrete around the site in Penge.

By night, he wrote songs as an antidote to the Metros, who he had come to loathe and disown by that point. Saul was uncomfortable playing the frontman, and after his foray as Jack the Lad in the Metros, turned his back completely on that period and dissolved into the underground. He would never write music to please record companies again, that much he knew. The money, hype and expectations heaped upon him when he was barely two years out of the New School, and still suffering from multiple behavioural problems, had triggered a resentment and bitterness towards the music industry that became permanent. He felt chewed up and spat out, and carried the burden of rejection with him each waking hour of the day.

After long shifts pushing wheelbarrows around and carrying tiles up stepladders, his old babysitter would invite Saul back to his house for a session to cheer him up. Loud music, drinking, drugging, more drinking, then harder drugs.

One day Billy said to Saul, 'You know we're going to do real drugs when we get back tonight. Have you ever done it before?'

'Yeah, yeah . . .' lied Saul. 'Of course I have.'

After that, Saul would go back to Billy's house every night after work. He would smoke a crack pipe then chase heroin off tinfoil, without realising his friend was ripping him off and smoking most of it for himself.

Its effect was numbing and it became a source of real comfort. Heroin switched off the noise and chaos in his head. There was no longer any rage or anxiety welling inside of him. Just a soft cushion that made daily life bearable and gave him intensely perverted dreams. Even better, he began to hear music in an entirely new way. Some days it made him so ill he vomited down the side of the house he was working on, sometimes from its rooftop, as his head began to spin from the small bag of brown powder he had smoked in the lavatory before he made the ascent.

☪

In an twist of squalid synchronicity, a flat came on the rental market in Brixton that was just about affordable. It was the cheapest in south London at the time, and Lias, Nathan, Sebley and Saul clubbed together to put down a deposit for a roof over their heads. Sebley forged the guarantor documents in Portsmouth, a role he was skilled at from multiple moves over the years. The residence was on Flaxman Road, near Loughborough Junction; just behind the row of fading Georgian houses was a railway line that rumbled and coughed throughout the night. Beyond that were the remains of a scrapyard that had been burned to the ground at the turn of the millennium, previously known as Brixton Breakers, the birthplace of the previous generation's YBAs.

Across the train tracks, a stone's throw from Lias's new bedroom, was a location that transcended the squalid; it was formerly run by a biker gang who crushed stolen cars by day, and by night was a site for drug dealing. Within its metal fence was a puppy farm, run by what the tabloids described as 'The Most Evil Man in Britain'. A fly-tipping site, it was overrun by rodents and feral Staffies. In the 1990s, this decrepit hellhole was also an art studio for Damien Hirst and Marcus Harvey, the place where sharks and calves and sheep were pushed through circular saws and dropped into glass tanks of formaldehyde. Before dawn, foxes broke into the studios, skittering across drying masterpieces by Richard Clegg before taking a large runny shit all over them. A miasmic fungus festered within its walls, propelling the artists to create work quickly, before their canvases were permanently ruined. The smell of death, decomposition and dogshit hung in the air and reached up into the windowsills of Flaxman Road.

As a teenager in Northern Ireland Lias had obsessed over those artworks, and now he was living within throwing distance of the site that spawned them. From his bedroom he looked out towards the corrugated rooftops and imagined the eleven-foot canvas of Myra Hindley's mugshot painted with casts of children's hands in black and white. The site took on a mythical significance in his mind.

The new residence immediately descended into the same condition as previous squats they'd inhabited. The filth was on a par with Withnail's sink; washing up was rarely done, a line of sludge on the sink welded cups to the drainer, rat excrement peppered each kitchen drawer, teabag splats stained the cupboard fronts, pans of three-day-old soup fermented on the hob, damp bath towels with the tang of groins and armpits were draped over door handles, and the scent of overflowing bins hung in the air. After their drinking sessions at the Hermit's Cave (an establishment they were all frequently barred from), Lias would bring back the waifs and strays to the flat for licentious parties that lasted for days.

When the toilet blocked it was abandoned, and Lias and Saul defecated in Tesco carrier bags before flinging them into next door's wheelie bin rather than fix the blockage. When Sebley finally bought a plunger and stuck his marigolds down the pan, it erupted into a fountain of green effluvium that bubbled and belched its way onto the bathroom walls. Flaxman would eventually be deemed so toxic, so uninhabitable and so shocking that a television company run by Saul's stepmother would pay to film a pilot inside of it, for a new series in the vein of *The Young*

Ones. No set dresser could ever create such a scene; the level of depravity was a work of art in itself.

Saul's friend from his New School days, Dan Lyons, turned up one drunken night and never left. He slept on the sofa after missing his train back to Twickenham, where he was an English student sharing a house with two rugger-buggers. He started to play drums with Saul again, eventually moving in and at one point becoming a fully fledged member of the band.

The latest addition to Flaxman was French Pascal, who moved into the flat for a short time. He played lead guitar for the Saudis and specialised in Van Halen licks and black metal shredding; he was an incredible guitarist trapped in completely the wrong band. Pascal had come to England armed only with a Fender Stratocaster and a pile of Burroughs books. The drugs and drinking became so intense that Pascal lost his mind one night after being called 'Froggy Man' thirty-six times. In an act of Gallic fury he defenestrated his single mattress out of the window into the pouring rain, and curled up on the floor next to Nathan's bed, sleeping on the floorboards amongst empty Mezcal bottles for the next three months until he almost died and had to move out. Nathan was Emperor Nero tucked up in his double bed with red wine crusted around his lips, and from then the anorexic Frenchman that slept at his feet became a rat-like corpse, emaciated and hollowed out from the living hell he had found himself in. 'In order to start again you have to have nothing,' he would often say, lost in a nihilistic reverie.

Saul was renowned for his inability to hold onto anything for longer than five minutes and always lost his keys. Even when Lias made a necklace out of shoelaces for him and tied them around his neck, the keys never stayed there for long. After arriving home early from the pub one night, he booted the front door down believing it would open immediately, like in the films, and shattered the door's glass. Within moments, he was besieged by the gay couple living upstairs. Armed with baseball bats, they proceeded to batter him until they realised it wasn't a burglar, just the ghoulish one who lived in the attic flat. Luckily, Saul had bumped a line of ketamine before he kicked the door down, and he didn't feel a thing from the beating, even when he rolled down the stairs outside and cracked his head on the pavement.

At Flaxman there were few boundaries and even fewer possessions. The art-school ethos infiltrated the squalor, but it was a choice to exist in that level of degradation. Nudity was embraced, and it wasn't uncommon to see flaccid members flashed in the living room or hairy testicles laid on the kitchen table. For Dan, who was uncomfortable with the lack of boundaries, it was a place to endure rather than enjoy.

The remaining band members frequently rehearsed in the living room, which was piled with ashtrays and empty beer cans, and a television with a broken volume control wrapped in a blanket. Their musical obsessions were the wine-bar funk of Joe Jackson, and Bruce Springsteen, in particular his 1978 album *Darkness on the Edge of Town*, a collection of immaculate, eternally thrusting stonewash that sounded like music from heaven under the influence of 'plant food' and cocaine cut with an unforgiving amount of baby laxative.

Together the residents would drink Guinness with their shirts off, snort Saul's last lines of stipend coke, and attempt to channel the spirit of the Boss. As part of his record deal, Saul had been gifted Bruce's back catalogue, which formed the soundtrack to their one long malodorous year trapped in the bowels of Loughborough Junction.

Collectively, they believed it to be a majestic period in their lives, when hangovers only lasted a day, and the existential loathing of adult life hadn't truly taken its toll. They spent many a night howling along to *Darkness . . .* in a state of idiotic revelry; what started as irony quickly became sacrosanct and manifested in AOR songs written at sunrise on the sticky living room floor. 'Straight Banana' and 'Tennant's Superman' to begin with, then

'Heart Shaped Bruce', their ode to the king of blue-collar America, based on a woman who was obsessed with the Boss and murdered her jealous husband:

> *I need a real man, with a lack of inhibition . . .*
> *I could love a postman, I could love a fireman,*
> *I could even love a binman*
> *but the only one I will ever truly love is the Boss, man.*

The more Bruce they channelled, the more the gigs dried up. Even with Saul onboard, the audience became smaller, and when his former record label's stipend eventually ran out, there was no money left for cocaine, either. It was time to leave Bruce behind and for the band to move on.

It Started with a Whimper and Then There Came a Bang

A wooden coffin was carried by pallbearers through Gower Street towards the site where Lias Saoudi would be laid to rest. Bashir, Saul, Sebley and Nathan were amongst the sombre-suited men who hung their heads and walked with the burden towards the congregation. Together, the gathering of friends and family sang Rod Stewart's 'Sailing' from their hymn sheets. His coffin was placed on a plinth. Nathan opened the lid and stared down at his brother's face, which was pale and serene for the first time in as many years. An Algerian flag waved in the breeze.

In the open casket, Lias was dressed in a silver suit, red polka dot shirt and a pair of his favourite sunglasses. A small bouquet of flowers was placed between his hands and the petals moved in the solemn wind that blew through the streets around them. After a moving speech by Bashir about a Berber horse that ran through the desert, the celebrant, Robert Rubbish, made a late entrance after an all-night session in Soho dressed in a black cassock and matching collar. When he opened the Bible in his hands to deliver the eulogy, he pulled up his robe to reveal a distinct lack of underwear beneath, bringing a bawdy element of surprise to the committal. After an hour of lying motionless under the influence of Valium, Lias was no longer able to contain himself and started to twitch. After the final prayer, the lid was placed on the coffin and he was carried to the accident and emergency department of UCH, where he was rightly rejected by hospital staff. It was not the first funeral that an art student had held at the Slade School of Fine Art, and it certainly wouldn't be the last.

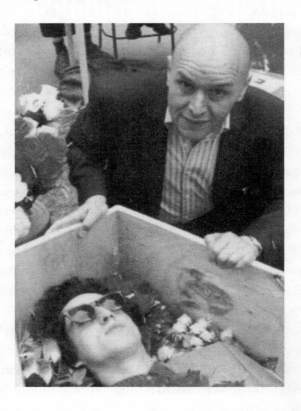

In order to pass his degree, the professor had allowed Lias to hold his graduation show two years after he was expelled in order to achieve his dissertation grade. He spent most of the summer planning for the event in which he would ritually dissolve his body in order to create a new and revised version of himself. A carpet of blue balloons surrounded the coffin with 'The Last Breath of Lias Saoudi' written in marker pen on the front. Afterwards, his friends sat around drinking snakebite at the wake, as his father shrugged his shoulders at the odd situation he had found himself in. There were some things about his son that he would never understand.

☪

In the weeks following the funeral, the residents of Flaxman Road clubbed together and decided to move back to Peckham, into a house large enough to contain their equipment and belongings, but cheap enough to afford if they all slept two to a room.

On the day they moved into their crumbling Victorian terrace on Sturdy Road, Lias and Nathan turned up at the front door, only to find that the occupant was refusing to move. He was an extreme hoarder, with floor-to-ceiling clutter lining each room and crusted egg embedded in his beard. The two brothers followed him into the house to be confronted by the sight of old pizza-box mountains, thousands of broken toys, used yoghurt pots, piles of clothes and carrier bags full of rotting food. Each internal door had a lock on the outside, and upstairs it was impossible to see where he slept.

'Do you need us to help you with this?' Lias asked.

The man sighed and shook his head.

'I don't know where to begin,' he replied. 'Can you give me a hand taking this to my mum's . . . she only lives a few streets away.'

Nathan brushed the dust from his trousers and propped the door open with a rusty fuel can.

'We have to be in by tonight but maybe we can cart some of it around? I know . . .'

He scratched his eyebrow and smiled at the man.

'We'll steal shopping trolleys from Tesco, bring them here, then we can wheel it. But you'll have to help us.'

'Thank you,' the man said. 'I'm embarrassed but it's all got on top of me.'

The brothers spent most of that day and the next carting the man's junk to his mother's house, before dumping piles of it in her front garden.

The tone for Sturdy Road was set from the beginning. Like Flaxman, it was a party pad, rehearsal room and general doss house for anyone who needed a floor to crash on. Lias and Saul would sometimes end up at the Nun's Head pub for Hank Dog's Easycome, a regular acoustic session that toured around various pubs in south London.

Only a few days after moving into their new residence, Saul and Lias decided to play at Easycome as Champagne Holocaust, a sardonic adaptation of Oasis's 'Champagne Supernova'. They were joined by Anna and Georgia, who provided backing vocals for them, and rehearsed a cover of 'I Hate You' by the Monks, which Saul intended to sing.

Outside, the band chain-smoked cigarettes before taking the stage, and walked up the stairs into the room with its cathedral-like atmosphere. Saul was adorned in redneck attire and launched into 'Wild American Prairie' and 'Borderline', two songs inspired by Ben Wallers' Country Teasers and *Psychedelic Glue Sniffin' Hillbillies*, a Super 8 film of trailer-park trash, two-headed cows, conjoined babies, meth and squalor that Saul watched on repeat. The sound that emanated was cracked country, dishevelled and ramshackle in places, and when Saul finally started playing the Monks the audience were impressed by its ferocity. Lias played guitar, dressed in a black polo neck, as Saul pushed his hand away from the strings, annoyed at the sound that emanated from them. His ability was no way perfect enough for Saul's exacting standards, a fact that he reiterated until one day Lias would give up and take hold of the microphone instead.

Many of Easycome's acts were earnest, political folksy types, with songs about the current Tory regime or leftist utopias. In contrast, as the earliest iteration of Fat White Family, Champagne Holocaust were noisy, messy and chaotic. The same fifteen people would come to every show they played, until the fifteen became sixteen, and the sixteen became seventeen. At which point they conceded it was time to host a proper gig and began promoting their own shows upstairs at the Tulse Hill Tavern.

When they played at a squalid basement bar in Dalston a necromantic and atonal transformation occurred. Lias metamorphosed by taking a pill an hour before the show. He walked out onto the tiny stage with all of the lights dimmed, removed all of his clothes, and as the ecstasy started to run hot through his veins and he tasted its sour tang in the back of his throat, started to primal scream at full volume, almost shedding a layer of his own skin under the red lights above him.

It was more akin to performance art than music, and Lias began to release himself, rolling and writhing on the stage as the audience alternated between horror and intrigue at the spectacle playing out in front of them. Honing in on the worst things that had ever happened to him, then exfoliating with an MDMA scrub, Lias threw his writhing body into the throbbing congregation. Like a maggot transforming into a bluebottle, for forty-five minutes that night the eruption of a reconfigured Lias began to take place.

☪

After their early shows the band held parties at Sturdy Road, which had taken on a decrepitude of its own; wasted aristocratic fashion girls on poverty safari lined the stairs, nodding out with cigarettes still burning between their fingers; ripped-up floorboards used for firewood left gaps in the floor. Upstairs in the bathroom, rings of black dirt lined the bathtub, each one a carbon date of the residents who had stewed in it without ever cleaning the residue of their vile brand of squat gumbo. The toilet contained welded-on skid marks and the scent of male urine reached into each crevice of the lino; an ammonitic stench rose through the floor. It was a familiar odour; one that nestled in the stained corners of bedroom walls when the inhabitants were too drunk, high or lazy to make it all the way to the bathroom, just along the hall.

In the front room, Dan's drum kit was set up. Saul shared with him, both of them sleeping on futon mattresses in between making an unholy racket. A curtain separated the two, and Saul would have to listen to the sticky slap of Dan having excruciatingly slow sex with his girlfriend six feet away as he tried to listen to the clock ticking instead.

There was an anything-goes policy on clothing in the house, amplified by Dan's uncle who worked at Spitalfields Market and ran a second-hand stall. He would regularly swing past and drop off clothes including designer suits, Ferragamo loafers and military coats.

'Get that shirt off your back! Change it NOW,' Saul would say to the flaxen-haired Dan, who was often restyled by his bandmate before a public outing.

Saul pilfered the Sturdy wardrobe and had a particular knack for putting together an outfit from a pile of cannibalised clothes. He often took shirts from Dan's cupboards and his own father's closet to create the perfect look. Dan would wander around Peckham with him for hours, waiting for Saul to try on countless pairs of orthopaedic shoes.

'I want the most revolting pair possible,' he would proclaim to Dan, before stumbling across a rancid pair of granddad shoes in the indoor market, which when combined with his junkshop aesthetic resembled exclusively designed footwear. He could squeeze chic out of any old rags and had a queer sense of style. A plain yellow tie would be transformed into a scarf, he would cut off sleeves with kitchen scissors, or pair bright socks with Italian loafers, high waisters and immaculate vintage braces. His fastidiousness with style extended to others in the band – any discrepancy in their overall 'look' would be brutally dealt with.

☪

When a gig the Saudis were booked to play was cancelled, the inhabitants of Sturdy chose to form a new band to play as a last-minute stand-in. It would be a development of Champagne Holocaust, named after James Endeacott's DJ moniker as the 'Fat White Duke' and a butcher's shop in Camberwell that sold the cheapest cuts to families off the local council estate. Their new name would be Meat Divine and the Fat White Family.

A friend of theirs, Aussie Jack, had a bottle of liquid LSD, which he sold to the band. Dan and Lias decided to take some at their first rehearsal at the Fortress Studios in Hackney. The pair kept it a secret from Saul, who turned up to play and was convinced at his own comic genius when he walked into the room like a crab and the two of them rolled about on the floor cackling at each movement he made. But there was a gaping absence that day: Nathan. His guitar playing was not deemed to be good enough by Saul's exacting standards, and when he eventually found out about the illicit rehearsal, he locked himself in his room for a month playing Metallica at full volume every day as a sonic retribution. Four weeks later, when Nathan emerged from his pit, he was carrying a new instrument, an organ, which he had taught himself to play during his exile, and from that moment on he was reinstated in the band.

As Lias, Nathan, Saul, Dan and their bass player Jak rehearsed in the house they frequently guffawed as their neighbour banged on the wall pleading with them to turn down the noise. She was elderly and aghast at the appalling sounds that emanated through the walls and ceiling. After many months, she ceased battering the living room wall with her sweeping brush. As the band started to load up a taxi with their equipment for a gig one night, an ambulance pulled up outside; a few minutes later, she was carried out on a stretcher zipped in a bodybag. Unbeknownst to Meat Divine and the Fat White Family, their neighbour had been suffering from cancer and her final few days were spent in torment. She had laid dead in her house as they hammered through their songs at full volume, but at least she finally had peace from the torturous drone that boomed through the wall.

Nathan shook his head as he watched the paramedics load her into the ambulance and the police take statements.

'Do you think we killed her with Krautrock?' he asked Saul, who threw his guitar case into the taxi boot.

'Probably, yeah,' Saul said, shrugging his shoulders as he spoke. 'Death by Damo Suzuki. It's quite a way to go out, don't you think?'

'Oh man, it's awful,' Lias said as he shook his head from side to side. 'What a rotten set of bastards we are.'

☪

The contents of my bedroom at Sturdy Road consisted of a large rectangular hunk of yellow foam I was using as a mattress and a small clock radio plugged into the wall beside it; draped across the window was a haggard sheet of green felt like the skin of an old pool table. Sophie, a friend with benefits, feigned admiration upon her first visit. She didn't have a problem with the poverty, quite the opposite. I'd met her friends and I'd visited her house. She was not of this earth, my earth, but the world up there: her ilk were all musicians or photographers or artists as well, yet none of them had the piteous, forgotten demeanour of my crew; the background hum of dynastic wealth and power from which they emerged kept them safe from our brand of self-loathing and doubt. They would almost certainly never achieve anything creatively but were full of adventure and gladness and – most importantly – they fetishised my unfamiliarity. I wore my bitterness like a badge of honour and told them tall tales from the kingdom beneath.

Sophie's body, golden and firm, was the ultimate refutation of my humble beginnings. Art school was too hard. Being in a successful band was too hard. Making a living was too hard. Making love to her released me from all of that failure. I'd finally found a valid exit strategy, one that would leave both friend and foe alike wallowing in a haze of bitter jealousy. Shortly after screwing for the first time on my lump of yellow foam, we heard loud screaming emanating from the kitchen below. I wrapped a towel around myself and rushed downstairs to find Dan, drunk and sobbing, having sliced a gash across his own wrist about a half an inch deep with a kitchen knife. I'm quite sure it was Sophie's wailing that set him off.

Her family lived in a mansion in West London. Save for the odd weekend visit to a National Trust holding with my mum on weekends back in Ulster, I'd never set foot in a gaff quite like it. What struck me most was the proliferation of lounges; I counted at least five different living rooms, each one a statement, each one a deeper shade of grandeur. Sophie's part of the house consisted of an entire annexe; a turret-laden side building just shy of what you would have had to call a wing had it been extended any further.

135

I was never introduced to her family. The reason for this being that her family and the family of her boyfriend were in cahoots, a tighter-than-tight-knit mutual masters of the universe, mergers and acquisitions sort of thing. He was away touring the States in a rock group with the spawn of Mick Jagger for three months, three months I considered to be my window of opportunity, within which I had to love my way from dirty little secret to romantic primacy. Should her parents be home when I came to call, I had to enter the premises through a side door in the garage. In the dark I had to fumble my way through the disused furniture of lounges in order to make my way into the main house, where Sophie would be waiting to lead me up her stairs to the secrecy and sanctuary of her chambers. She would disappear briefly at mealtimes, returning with a tray of pilfered foodstuffs for the 'Algerian in the attic'. I thought this pattern would eventually dissipate – that after a couple of months I might be treated as an equal – but how sadly mistaken I was. It didn't matter how deeply we stared into each other's eyes while making love, it didn't matter about our adventures in the steam room and nor did the laughter I worked so hard to inspire – through the dog flap still did I cometh.

This arrangement came to a disastrous head late one night towards the end of our dalliance. Sophie, as was frequently the case on a summer weekend, had been out of town at a music festival. She'd told me to wait up for her, that she'd be back early enough for us to work out a rendezvous. I waited and waited, watching the hours peel away on my clock radio, until eventually my phone started buzzing around 3 a.m. She would be back home in half an hour, could I make my way over? I told her that, as desperate as I was to lie beside her after the agony of so much anticipation, there was no way I could make it from Peckham at that time; on public transport it might take hours and as she well knew I couldn't afford the cab. Not to worry, she insisted, simply jump in an Addison Lee and I'll cover the fare at the other end. Within minutes I was in the back of a seven-seater hurtling westwards. The cab driver kept looking back at me as we made our way slowly past the assorted chateaux that constituted the rest of Sophie's neighbourhood, asking me if we'd maybe taken a wrong turn at some point? I proudly reassured him otherwise as we rolled up outside the gleaming white pile.

I called Sophie.

No answer.

I called again.

Same thing.

The cabbie had just driven across the whole of London through the arsehole of a Monday morning and he was quick to get militant about his fare. It swiftly dawned on me that, drunk, Sophie had simply passed out the minute she'd got home. By this point in time the driver had begun pouring forth a hot flow of profanities, peppered with the odd mention of the police. Ringing her phone was obviously a non-starter, there was nothing else for it, I was going to have to march up to the front door and ring the bell.

I stood atop that giant porch an eternity in my woolly jumper and jeans, clasping at the foolish hope Sophie might hear me ringing first, that I wouldn't have to meet her mother in circumstances as utterly damning as these. Not to be, sadly. The look on her mother's face when she came to the door in her nightgown was one of complete disdain, like she had just been awoken by an insect. I had expected a little fear perhaps – what with me being a strange man rapping on her door at 4 a.m. – but no, gazing into her eyes was like watching a dog maul an infant behind a film of Plexiglass. Her mother was confused – yes – but first and foremost she was enraged.

I began trying to explain the situation, or at least some version of it she might find tolerable. Me and Sophie were good friends . . . dear friends. My bank card had disappeared. That man over there in the taxi gesticulating at us, well, he needed forty quid. If he didn't get it, he was going to call the police. Managing to corroborate my identity through a series of queries and questions relating to her soundly slumbering daughter, I was eventually granted access. I'd only ever set foot in the main house several times – what with my persona non grata status it was largely out of bounds. Now I found myself having to make my way through a maze of lounges in the dark in order to find my way to Sophie's annexe. I had of course been sure not to ask her mother for directions before commencing my quest, as she might have thought I was bluffing out on the steps. God knows how long I stumbled up and down flights of stairs, through billiard rooms, conservatories, personal cinemas and drawing rooms. Just when I thought I'd sussed it out I would wind up at the same spot I'd started from. It was like a bad acid trip, the type where you find yourself stuck in a time lock, where reality starts folding in on itself and it takes all of your composure not to collapse into the foetal position and start screaming in terror like a helpless child on the floor.

There was nothing in the world more endearing to me at that point in time than the sight of Sophie sleeping. The struggle through the labyrinth and the humiliation on the doorstep melted into nothing the minute I caught a glimpse of her passed out on the bed. I gently brought her back to consciousness. She giggled a little, asked me to fetch her bag, passed me the fare then passed out again. I quickly retraced my steps back to the front door. By this time the cab driver had joined Sophie's mother on the doorstep. They were screaming at each other. Both of them threatening to call the police. That was the last I ever saw of Sophie's mother. And three weeks later I got the call: Sophie's boyfriend was back, she couldn't see me again, under any circumstances. I couldn't make head nor tail of it. She didn't sound bothered about it at all. The call only lasted around four minutes. I thought we were in love. I didn't hear from her again for years. Not until I started appearing in music magazines, by which point it was too late . . . because by then I was very much in love with myself, at long last.

☪

A job was advertised at the Agile Rabbit in Brixton, and within a few weeks Lias, despite a lack of any culinary ability, had signed up as pizza chef, where he rolled dough and chopped up basil behind a glass counter in the village market, tortured by the daytime soundtrack of BBC 6 Music playing numerous bands he loathed from south London. One performer booked to play at the café was the one-man band of Adam Harmer.

An affiliate of the Toilet Factory set on Old Kent Road, but originally from Bournemouth, Adam was rockabilly cool, could play slide guitar like a country blues pro, and sported a huge pair of sideburns. Lias was immediately intimidated by his looks and charisma when they first met over the pizza counter, a sign which he took to be positive. When he saw Adam play, he instantly invited him to join Fat White Family, providing he passed the crucial Saul test.

Opposite the kitchen, where Lias kneaded dough and pulled at the gloopy testicular mounds of buffalo mozzarella, was a butcher's counter. At the end of each Saturday, a broad-chested man with plump bloody fingers sold cuts of meat at a reduced price. Chicken feet, brains, oxtail and kidney, chunks of liver, knuckles and tongues. One item that sold for £2 before market closing were pigs' heads, with expressions of blissful bleeding sleepiness. Sensing an opportunity for the absurd, Lias bought three for a fiver one afternoon, and brought them back to Sturdy in blue carrier bags. When he walked into the kitchen, he peeled off the bags, and left them oozing on the table.

'What the fuck are they?' Dan asked, almost retching.

'For tomorrow night's show,' Lias laughed. 'Set dressing for Nathan's organ. We can put one on each end and maybe a photocopy of Charles Manson's face hanging from the side. Trust me, Dan. It'll be like Rammstein at Nuremberg.'

A promoter at a ropey north London venue called the Purple Turtle had booked the band to play as part of a line-up that included Black Daniel (featuring Clams Baker and the May Brothers). It was Nathan's birthday that night and Saul had designed Nathan a T-shirt as his birthday present with the lyrics to one of his solo songs, 'Let Me Fuck Your Face', printed on the front.

The audience was polarised, even more so at the satanic falsetto and unpalatable lyrics of 'Cream of the Young'. Alongside Adam, the recently acquired bassist Curly Joe paced about at the front of the audience; his performance was a vast improvement on his debut show with them at a New Year's Eve party in Brixton, where he'd fallen asleep mid-set and collapsed snoring onstage on a concoction of heroin, crack and downers.

As the crowd at the Purple Turtle began to move, Lias started to wail and scream, and at one point threw a tambourine into the audience which accidentally hit a girl on the head. The music soon ground to a halt when the plug was pulled.

Lias was gesticulating at the security guard who had pushed his way onto the stage and tried to pull the band off. He dropped his trousers to reveal a pair of long johns and flashed his pecker at the raging security guard. Then, as Saul was wrestled to the floor, Lias took matters into his own hands and started protest wanking at the crowd, spanking his insolent prang at the screaming front row who howled and cried with revulsion or glee at each motion. Within moments, the band were thrown out one by one from the backstage door, and a large brawl erupted outside. A team of muscle men in black bomber jackets dumped their instruments onto the pavement as Lias writhed in the wet gutter.

Liam May from Black Daniel had invited a few people from the music industry to the show to see this strange new band. One was a publicist for a prominent Mancunian musician from the Hacienda era, who took it upon himself to start throwing punches at Lias and Nathan outside as February rain bucketed down on their amplifiers and drum kit. Adam crept out of the venue quietly, carrying his guitar, wiping sweat from his brow. It was one of the most demented scenes he had ever witnessed and was his formal baptism of fire. He was now a fully fledged member of Fat White Family.

☪

Liam had his own small independent label, Trashmouth Records, based in New Malden. After the Purple Turtle gig, Liam was convinced Fat White Family were the most exciting band he had seen in years. He arranged to meet them in Trisha's basement bar, where they drank bottles of wine and Saul implored Lias to sign on the dotted line. He was anxious about it, and vaguely aware he should call a lawyer, although at this point in his life, Lias had never met a lawyer or had any clue as to how he would find one, even if he could afford it.

Within weeks, a recording session had been arranged, and Liam booked out a slot to record their album, which would be released as a digital-only download. They had been obsessively listening to Country Teasers, the Fall and the Make-Up at Sturdy Road, bands they hoped to regurgitate in some haphazard way when they reached the studio.

At 11 o'clock in the morning on the first day of recording, just as Liam was testing channels on the mixing desk and connecting leads, he received a phone call from Lias, who was sounding sheepish down the end of the line.

'Alright Liam, listen man. I have some bad news . . .'

Liam paused and took a deep breath.

'Go on,' he said.

'Slightly depressing, you see, me and Nathan are here, but the rest of the band, they've been up all night. Well, actually, they've been up for two nights and haven't slept at all. So they're saying they can't come.'

'You know what,' Liam replied, 'I'm not having that. I'm not rearranging to do this. Just get them down here. NOW. Otherwise you can forget it. Give them some speed or something.'

Five minutes later the phone rang again. It was Lias.

'Erm, I don't suppose you know where we can get any speed?'

'No, I fucking don't! Just give them some Red Bull. It's not brain surgery. You need to get them off their arses and out the door.'

Another five minutes passed and his phone rang again.

'Yeah, Liam. Alright. It's Saul. Umm. I'm at Sturdy and I've got my guitar, but I haven't got any strings on it.'

By this point Liam's face was burning with rage.

'Well get some strings and string the bloody thing up then!'

He hung up convinced that the session was a write-off but was pleasantly surprised to receive another call from them an hour later asking for a lift from the train station. They were all waiting outside the bus stop when Liam pulled up in his estate car to collect them. Saul was carrying an old, beaten-up Spanish guitar and Nathan had a synthesiser under his arm.

'At least you made it,' Liam laughed. 'Only another two weeks to go.'

Lias pulled his coat over his head and curled up on the back seat, attempting to stop his hands from shaking. 'It's like herding autistic wasps,' he groaned, as if he was the only one holding it all together, a fact that couldn't be further away from the truth. Equally culpable for the situation they had landed in was their frontman, who had dished out the drugs the previous evening when the rest of the band had voted for an early night. Maintaining the illusion of the stoic leader, Lias was not the one who had roused the troops that morning. It was Saul and Nathan who dragged *him* out of bed, despite the story he was now peddling in the studio.

As Liam predicted, the next day was more productive and within a week they had established a routine. They weren't particularly drunk or high but the main intoxication in the studio appeared to come from the band abusing each other. A peculiar negative energy was by far the strongest chemical in the room.

Frustrated, Saul kept repeating how it needed to be perfect, but perfectly *bad* – he wanted it *to sound shit*. Anything that made him cringe had to be removed immediately. Certain sounds, vocals or lyrics that revealed too much of who they had been previously in their musical lives had to be cut out. It was Saul's chance to obliterate the cross around his neck that was the Metros; it was a legacy that he was burdened with, more than he would ever admit to at the time.

A year later, in 2012, their debut album *Champagne Holocaust* was mastered, and the band organised a series of chaotic release parties, with the final one at their new favourite hangout in Brixton, the Queen's Head. Saul had met the Landlord on the tail-end of a bender, and believed he was the rudest man he had ever come across. He wore a T-shirt with 'London, My Arse' on the front, Alan Vega shades and a Baker Boy hat, which made him a complete tosser in Saul's eyes. Saul played drums at a gig in the function room with Curly Joe on guitar on the night of the London riots. The entire pub was locked up as petrol bombs and screaming erupted outside. Saul and the Landlord shouted encouragement at the rioters from the upstairs balcony, a sport that they quickly bonded over. By the time morning came, Saul and Nathan agreed he was possibly the only person in Brixton who could put up with their revolting behaviour and a firm friendship was formed. The Landlord convinced them to hold a party for their album in his venue, which he gave them for free, providing they could fill it.

It was decided by committee that the Fat Whites would play their last ever show as a band, considering how much of an ordeal they had already gone through trying to live with each other and record the album, which nobody would be remotely interested in hearing anyway. There was little interest beyond Brixton, and any chance of success or a pop career was rendered obsolete by their provocative and frequently offensive actions onstage and lyrical content. The band was only ever meant to be a way for them to earn money to buy more drugs and avoid getting a proper job. Lias, Nathan and Saul made the decision to break up the band and leave for Barcelona, which had taken on a utopian quality since their brief visit a few years prior.

After a final debauched party at Sturdy, Fat White Family uploaded their album online, packed up their belongings, and made their way to Victoria to catch the coach to Paris. The house was completely ruined, but with a small envelope of cash in their back pockets, they waved goodbye to Peckham to pursue a future in the clear Catalan sunshine.

Who's the Whitest Boy on the Beach?

We alternated for a while between being 'beach bums' and 'mountain bums'. The worst thing about beach bumming was that you could never get away with setting up camp down there; the coast was well policed during the day, so you ended up just sleeping out under the open sky once night fell. This was fine until the sun came up and started cooking you alive, or until the coppers clocked you, then you had to shift onwards to your next stretch of nothing in particular.

As we adapted to mountain life, we became more ambitious with our hiking, prone to deeper and deeper treks into the wilderness. Each morning we would pick out an arbitrary target on the map – somewhere you could buy wine, invariably – and boulder along across whatever country came our way. With temperatures soaring in the high Catalonian summer, we eventually settled on a small patch of blue as our destination, assuming it represented a mountain lake. The best of both worlds we figured. It took us two days just to reach base camp. Two days of slogging it up the sides of main roads, through haggard little mountain towns and across arid scrub before we were within reach of what we surely assumed to be our salvation.

Our mountaineering tackle was sub-par. Nathan carried a rucksack and tent, Saul an antiquated red canvas hold-all and a strapless, case-less Spanish guitar, myself a tent and an imitation LV shoulder bag I'd borrowed from the Landlord shortly before leaving London. Each of us wore an echo of what you might once have called a pair of trainers. Our only real concern was water. We purchased a six-litre bottle prior to the *ascent, the carrying of which would test our ability to function as a team to the utmost. Few words were said once we settled into a steady stride, we were 'as one', panting and gasping our way upwards, save for the nature of my luggage, which in my opinion was so ill-suited as to warrant me spending less time on the water-carrying detail.*

'I can't, this fucking bag is cutting my shoulders open, someone else take the water . . .' I pleaded.

Several hours into the trek it occurred to us we'd barely seen a soul the whole time we'd been marching.

'Weird no one else is heading up there, no? In this heat you'd think loads of folk would be headed up to the lake . . .'

Nathan was onto something, but we put it to one side.

'Nah, they all drive down to the beach,' I said. 'They're not a lake-faring people . . .'

When the path finally opened up and gave us a full panoramic view, our 'lake' turned out to be a reservoir, each side of which constituted a sheer cliff face that had been hewn from the rock by man and machine. It was basically a quarry with a giant puddle at the bottom of it. There was no question of even accessing the sinister waters below; to attempt to do so would have meant suicide.

'Wicked boyo!' Saul exclaimed, in the faux Irish reserved by each of us to describe moments of exquisite shittiness. Red-faced and sweat-drenched we collapsed in a heap along the path, staring out silently into the grey abyss as we refuelled on yet another tin of sardines in tomato sauce. We had taken a blow, to be sure, but spirits remained high.

'What next? Continue? Go back?' I asked.

'I reckon we scale the summit, it's the only way of reclaiming our honour,' Saul suggested, and what with the marvel of youth still resident in our blood and lungs, we all agreed. We would take the mountain. We would not bid retreat. Not having come this far. Somewhere upon the peak there was a vista worth struggling for. It felt good to march. Your head emptied out. It lent clarity to your thoughts. We looked at the map and figured it couldn't be more than another three hours to the top.

Another stretch of hard trek went by. The sun was at its highest point in the sky. We'd meandered from the path and began cutting through patches of beech forest and pine in lieu of a perceived shortcut. Atop a clearing on the side of the mountain in the distance we spotted a villa, vaguely resonant of the homestead denied Russell Crowe's character in Gladiator; a mirage of Iberian splendour.

'Maybe they'll feed us?' Nathan asked, taking a toke on his inhaler as he spoke.

'Maybe it's full of beautiful women?' I said, slightly delirious. 'Maybe this is where the chiquitas have been hiding from us all along? Welcome señores! Welcome! Stay with us, please stay with us! Play us song on your geetar señor! Is been so long since we heard geeetar on the mountain. We are so sick of listening to just the wind . . .'

We walked up to the large wooden door at the front of the house and knocked several times. Our clothes were clinging to our fetid, long-unwashed forms. As we were about to call it a day, a tall dark monument of a man made an appearance. Handsome in the Javier Bardem vernacular, just to look at him made you feel vulnerable in your masculinity. His voice was calm and gently enquiring.

'Hey amigos, puedo ayudarte?'

'Eh, speak English?' Saul replied, still gasping slightly from the long haul.

'Yeah, I mean, just a little. My name is Juan, pleased to meet you. What are you guys doing up here? You walk all the way up here with those bags?! You're crazy, you must be tired . . . come, come inside, rest a moment . . .'

He walked us through the cool marble miracle of the interior, out to a veranda peppered with lemon trees overlooking a sea of rolling hills. The island of tranquillity upon which we'd just stumbled was quickly disrupted by the appearance of the lady of the house. All olive skin and raven hair, the softness of her voice rendered each of us fourteen years old again in a heartbeat.

'Ola, my name is Celia . . . you must be hungry?'

'Si, si . . .' we responded in unison, clambering over each other to introduce ourselves.

147

Our hosts disappeared for a moment and returned with a tray of red vermouth on ice, a platter of ham, olives, fresh tortilla, anchovies and bread. He was a filmmaker and she a fashion designer. We explained that we were in a band called Fat White Family, but not to bother looking us up because nobody knew we existed. We told them that we'd given up on London because of the merciless gentrification of our neighbourhood, or some such spiel, and that we'd decided to take our chances busking on the streets of Barcelona, only to discover that playing music in the streets there for money was totally illegal, hence our becoming the wanderers of the hills they see before them today.

Having listened attentively to our tale of woe, they lined our stomachs, kindly rolled us a joint and then offered a way out of our current quest.

'You are going to return down the mountain? Perhaps I could drive you part of the way?' Juan asked.

We weren't for turning, however – we all felt renewed by this chance encounter. Moments like these were the reason you march off into the middle of nowhere in the first place. Collectively we felt energised.

'Thank you very much for the offer, but we need to make it over the top. Do you know which direction is the best to walk? To get up there . . .'

Saul pointed up towards what we believed to be the peak, a jagged claw of black rock scraping the afternoon sky off in the distance.

'Honestly guys, I myself have not been up that way, I think is pretty far you know.'

'That's fine, we've got tents, we might camp out on top. Obviously, we can't go "that" way, how do you reckon we get around it, go left or right?'

'I would take the left. But seriously guys, be careful, it is really quite far.'

By the time the afternoon waned it occurred to us that we were not the mountain men we believed ourselves to be, and perhaps never had been. Our faith suddenly transformed into desperation.

'Man, we're not setting our fucking tents up here, you're fucking crazy! You have no idea how far we are from ANYTHING . . . we barely even have any fucking water . . . we're lost . . . this is fucked . . .'

Saul was exactly right. We hadn't seen any other human life in over four hours. The people we had seen were travelling in the opposite direction, decked out head to toe in professional hiking gear. Beyond the peak we'd spied from the villa lay yet another peak, and yet another peak still.

The torn map that Saul carried in his top pocket had long since become irrelevant. There were no more mountain trails to speak of, and no landmarks whatsoever. There had been no spectacular vista awaiting us at the apex. There was no apex. You reached a certain altitude and the landscape flattened off into eternity. It was cold, barren and misty. All the vegetation became suddenly familiar. It looked more like Saddleworth Moor than the Pyrenees.

'Alright, alright . . .' Nathan shouted, in an exasperated and slightly desperate tone. 'I'm just fucking knackered. We've been going for ten hours. I'm burnt out. Why don't we just chill here until morning? There's gotta be water up here somewhere.'

'We're on top of a fucking mountain,' Saul said. 'What if we don't find any?! You want to hike across an entire mountain tomorrow in that heat without a drop to drink? We'll be found dead up here.'

Out of the three of us Saul was most in his element out in the country, he'd attended summer camp as a youth, and out of us all he was the only one with the slightest clue about this sort of tribulation.

'Why don't we just trace our steps back?' I suggested.

'This fog's coming down, we might just end up even more lost than we are already, we have to find the quickest way back. That's the smart thing to do, whichever way is down, that's what we should do . . .' Saul replied, as he fastened up the laces on his ancient Converse.

We'd come across a signpost several hours previous. It had demarked two options. We had placed our trust in the route that looked like it would lead us to a glorious summit. This had proven our moment of sublime folly. I pointed at an endless stretch of void to the right of us and suggested a new direction.

We settled on this compromise reluctantly and we marched solemnly, in complete silence, as the sun started to fade. Within two hours we found our way back onto a trail. When it became clear we were finally on the descent a whisper of relief crept through the party. Once again, the inclination to set up camp and rest took hold. Nathan's brow was coated in dust and sweat, he sat by a boulder, took off his trainers and let his feet breathe. His soles were burning bright from hot blisters.

We decided to make a camp beneath a cluster of pine trees. Evening was well on its way, the forest fast becoming a kingdom of shadows. We cast down our bags, unsheathed the pop tent and sat gawping silently at the floor a moment. There was no question of starting a fire, it would have burned the mountain to cinders.

Nathan pulled the dwindling water bottle from his bag and tossed it down in front of us. Reality then hit home with renewed vigour. We had about half a pint's worth of fluid to keep the three of us going.

Saul almost had tears in his eyes as he delivered his appraisal: 'We're fucked. We can't do this. We're not going to make it on that. It could be miles. Fuck knows. It must have been thirty-five degrees out there today.'

With barely a word exchanged we all took to our feet and began packing up the tent. The trek had to continue by twilight. We began pummelling our way down the scree-ridden hillsides fuelled by fear alone. Our eyes adjusted to the dark as we stared out at what must have been a village on the other side of the gorge. Eventually the mountain trail fed into a mountain road. And just as total darkness took hold, we heard the bass rumble of an engine in the distance.

'Quiet, quiet, what was that?' Nathan muttered. We stood there in silence a moment, each of us now no more than an outline of a human being amidst the inky gloom. Somewhere up the road behind us we spied a beam of light through the wilderness, a beam of light that slowly morphed into a four-wheel drive. A park ranger arrived as if by the grace of God.

The drive back from the mountain was a long one. It took around twenty minutes before we hit civilisation. In the back of the jeep it occurred to us just how badly we'd fucked up. My lips were caked white from dehydration. There was no way we would have made it off the mountain on foot. Perhaps a stretcher.

The park ranger dropped us off at a roadside service station, where we stormed through the doors guzzling a litre of beer each to slake our thirst on the neon forecourt. In a litter-strewn ditch around the rear of the store we set up one of the tents and packed our aching bodies inside, lulled into a deep, exhausted sleep by the sound of articulated lorries that groaned and clunked behind us, echoing into the humid Spanish night.

'What do you reckon Juan's up to right now?' said Nathan, before slowly sinking into slumber.

When all hospitality had been exhausted in Barcelona, and the three men had nowhere left to turn, they made a decision to go their separate ways. Lias, who had saved money from flipping pizzas, booked a flight to Berlin and paid for a flat for two months, where he would meet up with his old friend, Jordan the Australian. Nathan was heartbroken after having been unceremoniously dumped and decided he was going to head to Venice to win her back. He remembered her affection for Heinz Tomato Soup and had brought a tin all the way from Peckham, hiding it deep within his rucksack.

Nathan bunked the train to Italy with Saul, with the two friends dodging fares and hiding in toilet cubicles as they sped through the landscape towards Tuscany, where Saul's dad was on holiday. They stopped with him in Vernazza, ate all of his food, rinsed his wallet of cash and then caught the train on to Venice the following day.

When Nathan arrived at his ex-girlfriend's flat to surprise her, she was confused and shocked at the two grubby travellers who greeted her on the doorstep. She let them stay with her that night, but Nathan's romantic gesture was a failure: she had already met a tall, ravishing Italian. Before he even had a chance to wrap his arms around her, Saul passed out on her bed, seriously inebriated, and threw up on the pillow.

The next morning, she booted both out onto the street, which is where they remained as buskers, sleeping beneath archways and playing outside the railway station each day. As vagabonds, they earned enough money to buy a large litre bottle of Pastis, which Saul proceeded to drink all to himself, swilling down the warm liquor until nothing was left but the saliva dregs. In a deranged state, Saul lost all control and pulled a blunt bread knife on a pair of tourists. As he lurched between the alleyways, seeing with double vision, he laughed and yelped with aniseed steaming from his breath. Through his paralytic state, he truly believed it was a joke, and was astonished that the two women he accosted believed him to be serious in his intent.

Nathan was adept at bunking trains and had been capable of living on his wits since his teenage years; he always used the self-service checkout at Waitrose, where he paid for a quarter of the goods in his bag, and was an expert shoplifter, having never been caught in his many years of filling his inside pockets with ingredients. Squatting was a way of life, and despite his periods on the dole, he had learned it was easier to be a continual student than to sign on for jobseeker's allowance. He studied at Goldsmith's on a History foundation, just to claim the student loan, only attending the first few months of lectures.

The following year, he enrolled on an English Literature foundation just to claim the maintenance grant, with no particular interest in the subject. He decided that life in perpetual education was an excellent way to avoid ever getting a proper job. When he joined the degree programme, he calculated that he could receive an income that would keep him alive for a bare minimum of work. The small amount of money he had saved to travel Europe helped him survive with the pittance he and Saul could raise from begging and busking.

When they arrived in Berlin they made their way to Lias's flat, where the owner, who was a depressive with a deep suspicion of junkies, explained how he was happy to rent his apartment that contained a four-poster bed and two singles to Lias, but he drew the line at Saul staying there. 'Your friend with no teeth and the funny eyes can't stay here,' he grumbled. 'But your brother can. He looks okay to me.'

Saul's missing front tooth was a permanent reminder of the punch he was awarded in his teenage years by his bandmate in the Metros, Curly Joe, who had knocked it out when Saul pressed his face up against the tour bus windscreen, made a windowlicker gesture at him, and Curly Joe retaliated by smashing his fist into Saul's mouth from outside. It shattered the glass and, more importantly, gave Saul a new facial feature that would make him stand out from the crowd.

After wandering the streets of Berlin for a few hours, Saul contacted Jordan, who had lived at Sturdy for a few months, spending his days smoking hydroponically grown skunk and listening to death metal and esoteric Nordic folk. Jordan was handsome and sophisticated, but heroin had started to take its heavy toll. Their friend, who had once been into drone, noise and minimalist composers was now junked out of his head playing Kings of Leon's 'Sex on Fire' on the cajón all day, every day in Alexanderplatz to pay for the next twenty euro bag of brown. Even Saul was shocked to see a ravaged Jordan cooking and shooting up down alleyways, hustling for money, or trying to sell copies of the free *Vice* magazine on the underground. Sensing their desperation, he offered Saul and Nathan a place to stay, and they spent autumn sleeping on his kitchen floor, busking by day and smoking heroin when enough money could be made. Nathan, who was still heartbroken, quickly adapted to the drug. It was cheap and cushioned him from all of life's problems. Heroin was the ultimate form of avoiding responsibility, a perfect cocoon to carry him through the ride of early adult life. Together with Lias, the young men spent hours of each day playing ramshackle rock 'n' roll to passing tourists when the trains stopped at War-schauer Straße. Lias sang, Saul played guitar through a crackling amp, and Nathan played rhythm with a wooden spoon, a brick and a piece of fencing. They performed Bo Diddley's 'Mona' and

Chuck Berry's 'Maybelline' as swathes of oblivious commuters passed by. Occasionally, the music would stop as Saul interjected to chastise Lias for screaming too much. More often than not they played to an audience of Polish drunks or other wasted smackheads gouched on the pavement. For their pitch, they had to pay Jordan and their host an equal cut of the takings, which came in at fifty euros a day.

As his brother attempted to survive on the street while nursing the early stages of a drug habit that would eventually become a full-blown addiction, Lias lay in his four-poster bed and scrolled through his laptop feed. In the time they had been away, *Champagne Holocaust* had been uploaded to SoundCloud and had unexpectedly gained a whiff of online traction. It was the last thing he had considered when he left Peckham Rye, but Liam had messaged saying that it was getting played enough times online to warrant being pressed up.

Lias rolled back into his soft quilt and contemplated the vaguest possibility of public acclaim and how that might manifest, the beauties that would drip from each arm, the money and fame, the ensuing critical attention, and how the whole world was waiting for the masterpiece they had created. Yes, it felt good to be Lias Saoudi at that very moment, as he gazed longingly at the comments thread. At least three of his friends, and Michelle, had left rave reviews beneath the SoundCloud link.

Later on, when Nathan announced that his student loan had landed in his bank account, the three bandmates made the decision to return to London. There they would press up a thousand copies of their debut LP, funded by the Student Loan Company. Literary deviant and patheticist supremo Lewis Parker was promoting a show with Ben Wallers from the Country Teasers and asked if they would support him at the upcoming gig in Shoreditch. They were content being bums on the streets of Berlin, but after some discussion the offer forced their hands and carried them home.

It was agreed that they would move back to Brixton to live at the Queen's with the Landlord, who had spare rooms above the pub. The band would rehearse in the function room there; in return for the roof over their heads, they would play regular gigs and Lias would knead dough and become the in-house pizza chef. Anything had to be an improvement on the Sturdy Road abyss, and in the Landlord they had found a new 'team coach' who was ready to lead them further into the seven rings of hell.

☪

The bodies of the broken men climbing in and out of the Queen's every evening looked a lot like the war on disappointment they'd been attempting to drink their way through: overextended and overwrought. Each face was like an eternally slapped arse, like a molested patch of rhubarb. Suspended above their crummy little cocaine mandalas their eyes would lock and something resembling conversation would unfurl, but it was as two mirrors placed on opposing walls – immaculate vacuity. The loudest voices were the only ones that mattered. Those willing to show and tell.

The two-hundred-year-old brickwork hummed with impotent confessions. It also hummed with song. There was no such thing as humiliation. That belonged to a previous life. Some of the younger punters might be gone the next day, gone forever with a tale or two to tell, back to something tenable, something they might be able to endure. The regulars corralled here though were dedicated to the nightly onset of drought. What began with a green shoot always left them in the same desert of howling impossibilities. These men would make up our surrogate family, our assurances as to a future shorn of all responsibility. And we would be their champions, their brand ambassadors. We would export their defiant decrepitude to the world . . .

☪

The walls of the pub on Stockwell Road were built in 1786 as a staging house on the road into London; there was a historical resonance to the place, through which thousands of travelling men had passed for two hundred years, on their way to seek the city's fortunes.

The exterior of the Queen's was painted black, the boarded-up windows were painted black, and the walls inside were also painted black. A fading old Victorian boozer, the disreputable establishment was populated by barflies and desperados, many ravaged by alcoholism and drugs, often in their older years, still clinging to the myth of the men they once were before dementia eventually bedded in.

The suppurating attitude and gnarly character of the Queen's gave the band an extra layer of skin against the world; it created a sense of resilience in them. Its poison converted into playfulness; there was functionality in its chaos, and a sense of belonging. Music was the only thing that was taken seriously. In their dysfunctionality they created a new family within its walls, one that allowed for the trickiest behaviour and vilest aspects of each member's personality, and somehow in this heart of darkness they all found solace in that.

The week of their return, the Landlord had decided to host an exhibition of a local artist who specialised in creating photographs of rectal hand insertion, and on each large-screen TV images of hairy fists being shoved into black holes cascaded throughout the day in the same room where families ate Sunday roasts. In the main bar, the resident 'drunkle' – once a famous Ibiza DJ back in the day – salivated at the food being served and wandered between each table begging for money so he too could eat a £5 roast. He was so wrecked he had taken to living in the pub, reminiscing each hour on his previous life of mass adoration and repetitive beats.

The Queen's was Brixton's very own Last Chance Saloon, an establishment that welcomed those cast out by others, one that encouraged bad behaviour, lunacy and extreme states. One New Year's party was so packed that a punter stuck outside attacked the venue's door with a burning Christmas tree. Nevertheless, the Landlord was tolerant of the terrible mess his young tenants got into, even forgiving Curly Joe, who pissed all over his bed one night, blind drunk and higher than the sun, and was let back in the bar at opening time, no questions asked.

Recognising Saul's musical ear, the Landlord gave him a job booking acts for the pub in exchange for a room upstairs. Prior to Barcelona, Saul had lived in Hank Dog's cupboard in a council house in Clapham, which he paid £70 a month for. But even that was luxury compared to what he was offered at the Queen's. His new abode was the broom cupboard, which had a sloping floor, so that even with his mattress he slept on an angle, sliding off and downwards into the night. Like the other rooms at the Queen's, it was infested with bedbugs, and they quickly took hold of his bedding, crawling through each layer of fabric as he attempted to sleep. As the bedbugs had no interest in the Landlord's blood, he didn't bother to fumigate the place, but the fat cochineal insects were delighted with their new hosts, who clearly tasted far better than he did. Each evening, Saul tucked his long johns into his socks, tightened his hooded top against his face, and buried his hands inside his jumper, so all that remained were his large eyes peering out. But even that had little effect, and when he rose each morning the small area of exposed skin on his face would be covered in bites and blood and little scabs, forming a patterned mass of feasting on his eyelids, chin, nose and mouth.

Heroin was an easy way to escape the torment, but the noise that emanated from downstairs, sometimes until 4 a.m., frequently pounded his brain. The Landlord held Bashment nights in the bar, as lock-ins or wedding events for his friends, the *boom boom boom* of dancehall rhythms being enough to send Saul into a spiral of doom. His opiated sleep was frequently interrupted when his host kicked his door open at 3 a.m., pulled the sheets from his tenant, and shouted at him to 'Get the fuck out of bed, I need the glasses washing.' Saul would have to run downstairs, rub the bleeding mess from his face, and start washing the hundred glasses that had piled up on the bar.

Upstairs, in the function room, the band rehearsed new songs. In the kitchen downstairs Lias made Hang Cameron calzones, smoking spliffs and throwing rodent corpses into the bin before each shift began. The menu at 'Grande Finocchio's Stonebaked Pizza' was adorned with a photograph of Lias in his underpants, wearing a worker's cap and swinging a large salami suggestively by its string:

For Grande, pizza is more than something you put inside your body, it IS the body. For over nineteen years, the maverick Italian chef has been refining his highly esteemed dough, and in that period has served pizza to the leading lights of the global scene: from Berlusconi to Bono, Obama to Osama. In 2012, however, Grande was exiled from his beloved Italian homeland on account of what the Italian state deemed 'belligerent sexual deviancy', and was forced to take up residence here in London, home of the open-minded and liberal man. So it is with great excitement that we here at the Queen's Head Brixton can announce the arrival of Italy's culinary prodigal son, Grande Finocchio. Enjoy.

Culinary ambitions aside, the bar's true culture was far from gastro; it was a breeding ground of savage ridicule. The drinkers all had something to prove, although none were sure what that was exactly. On certain nights there were more drug dealers than customers but there was rarely any violence. At least they were contained, and local coppers turned a blind eye to the venue.

Exactly who was allowed to go upstairs after the Queen's gigs was regulated: only 'VIPs' were permitted into the drug den that was locked behind a numbered door code. Word of the number quickly spread, and before long members of the general public would wander in at all hours to gawp at the scene. After one particularly chaotic late-nighter Saul woke up supine, almost snowblind, on the bar's banquette, after passing out three hours earlier. He opened one eye to see his friend Lenin staggering around the bar – he took a half pint glass, filled it with Smirnoff and drank the whole lot in one go before brushing himself down and going off to catch the bus to work. It was 7 a.m.

As the windows had been smashed in twice by the same vendetta-fuelled ex-customer, they were permanently boarded. The Queen's was Tardis-like; those who entered became unaware of time or daylight hours. The upstairs window had been broken when Saul got into a fight with Nathan and Curly Joe, who were playing the Beatles' 'Let it Be' on repeat as the sun came up. Unable to tolerate yet another rendition of McCartney's eight-minute pseudo-religious ballad through the floorboards, Saul politely asked them to turn it off, then returned to the broom cupboard, slamming the door behind him. Five minutes later, Nathan put it on again even louder, singing noisily so that his bandmate would be certain to hear it.

The lights finally went out behind Saul's eyes. Nathan had pushed him too far this time. As he smashed the door open he snatched a cymbal from the drum kit and frisbeed it at Nathan's head, who only narrowly avoided a partial decapitation. Nathan and Curly Joe tried to take Saul to the ground. Nathan pulled Saul up, threw him against the wall and screamed at him, 'Don't fucking push me.' Saul pushed him, and Nathan rammed Saul's head straight through the window, scattering its glass onto the pavement below.

After a few flashes of ultra-violence, the argument was quickly forgotten and the soft warm glow of heroin abuse supplanted the fight. Saul and Nathan taped binbags up against the broken window frame, preventing daylight filtering into their eyes, and embarked on an epic four-day session, locked away together from the world and cocooning themselves in the festering comfort of tinfoil.

☪

I suppose everyone in the band brought a certain amount of disgrace to the table. It is therefore unwise to try to work out whose contribution most lowered the tone. That being said, were I forced to point a finger,

I would point it at Curly Joe. I've never come across a less professional human being. In a way this is what gave him his appeal. A Neanderthal on bass made perfect sense. It was a strong aesthetic. Rhythm isn't about thought after all, it's about sex. Joe was keen on sex.

It didn't take long for Joe to find himself sacked from the group. The minute we started getting paid for shows, the minute we had a schedule that stretched beyond forty-eight hours into the future, he struggled to keep it together. Even the most basic tasks could prove calamitous should you prescribe Curls to carry them out. In the early evening before one of our shows at the Queen's, during that period when our star was very much at the beginning of its meagre ascent, the Landlord realised the bar was out of limes. Joe piped up. He'd fetch the limes. The Landlord gave him twenty quid and sent him off to market. Discredit where it's due, he made this call despite the fact Joe had given up on wearing shoes by this point in time. He was in the middle of his 'barefoot phase', which to the best of my memory lasted some two or three months. Many a time you would catch him out and about around Brixton, in a liquor stupor, his clothes covered in filth, his feet almost black, having just inspired a brawl.

An hour went by. Then two. Then three. By this point in time the place was heaving. Still no limes. Still no Curls. 'What a fucking cunt,' said the Landlord, over and over again, to nobody, much to our mirth. As showtime approached at the tail-end of the evening, the funny side started to disappear. 'What a fucking cunt,' we said to one another, 'you couldn't pack another body into that room downstairs', so and so's here from such and such a magazine, band, label, etc . . . Not for the first time in his life, Adam had to start working out the bass parts. We began snaking our way through the audience towards the stage without him around midnight, when Curls finally made an appearance in the doorway. He was naked except for a hospital smock.

It turned out that he had managed the purchase after all. He'd picked up a crate in the village market as required, he just hadn't managed to make the four-minute walk back to the pub. He'd taken a detour on the way there to score a load of Xanax. Instead of waiting until after that night's coke binge to swallow these, he'd gotten a head start, and gobbled

161

a few the minute he got his grubby hands on them. After picking up the Landlord's order he'd bumped into his latest squeeze somewhere on Atlantic Road. Again, being a man of the moment if nothing else, a man of appetite, he decided on yet another detour, this time to the nearest park so he could have a fuck in the bushes. Then he passed out completely. When he came to, he was in hospital. The paramedics had found his unresponsive body in the foliage, surrounded by a hundred stray limes.

☪

'Touch the Leather' was the most notorious of the band's unholy trinity of films made at the Queen's and owed much to an obscure video, 'Chase the Dragon', by the Australian blues band, Beasts of Bourbon. As an homage, a wooden frame was built in the function room with a plastic sheet draped across it, behind which the band planned to dance and make vaguely menacing gestures, just like their idols. After building the set, the entire group embarked on a day-long binge and, consequently, nobody turned up for the actual video shoot on the following day, nobody except for Nathan.

When Lias emerged from his chamber, a small room situated on the second floor above the establishment, he discovered that his errant bandmates were absent without leave. Their plans were quickly rearranged to mimic another of Beast of Bourbon's videos, 'Psycho', instead. Lias decreed that Fat White Family's version would be far more lo-fi and that it should be injected with a degenerate pornographic element.

After knocking back two tequilas, the brothers were prepared for the filming that would be shot by director Roger Sargent in real time, over three minutes, in one take. In close-up, Lias smoked a cigarette and grimaced as he sang in front of a candlelit table. Behind him, Nathan rolled across the floor in slow motion, then, with his trousers pulled fully down, exposed his bare-naked arsehole straight at the lens as he balanced on top of a hardback flight case. Lias attempted to keep a straight face as he sang in the foreground. As he gyrated up and down, Nathan's ball sack swung between his legs like a Newton's Cradle. Behind them, their friend Lenin, who had been up drinking with the Landlord all night, sat by the piano, playing stabberscotch between gaps in his fingers.

Only days after being uploaded onto YouTube it was removed for indecency, but by then it had caused enough controversy to create the desired effect. When Saul first watched it, he immediately denounced the video as juvenile, and the song rudimentary. But despite Saul's protest, 'Touch the Leather' quickly caught fire online. When the producer Tony Visconti first heard it, he believed it to be the best thing he had heard since Iggy Pop's 'Lust for Life', and was keen to produce their second LP, *Songs for Our Mothers*, before working with David Bowie on his swan-song, *Blackstar*. Not that the offer appealed to Saul. The idea of working with Visconti was quickly dismissed as far too obvious. The same went for former Smiths producer Stephen Street, who was also interested in collaborating. Why would the band want mainstream acclaim? Fame held no allure for Saul, who preferred the idea of the band producing themselves. He was vehement in his vision to create one of the most doggedly unlistenable records of the coming year, an opinion at odds with that of the band's manager, Stuart Green, who as a hardcore Bowie fan could not see the reasoning in such a decision.

☪

Throughout their tenancy at the Queen's, Brixton was undergoing a period of significant change. Streets that were previously populated with market stalls, Jamaican record shops or fruit and vegetable shops were slowly shutting down over rent increases. What replaced them – chic coffee shops, expensive restaurants and organic food stores – were an indication of the wave of gentrification that would flood Brixton in the years to come.

At the village market's Granville Arcade, where Lias had worked at the Agile Rabbit, a new store opened called 'Champagne + Fromage'. Sensing the injustice towards its previous tenants, the band set up an anonymous gentrification hate page called 'Yuppies Out' on Facebook. It was puerile even by their standards, with Soviet imagery that bled into Islamic iconography plastered on its home page. Their aim was to ridicule the new wave of upwardly mobiles that were making their way onto Brixton's streets, those who were pushing property prices up and local people out. Anthony Gormley's bollards on Bellenden Road took a pounding, as did Saul's dad, whose photograph was doctored with crudely drawn red swastika eyes and posted on the page.

Yuppies Out was littered with explosive acts of MS Paint détournement; anyone or anything the Fat Whites didn't like was fair game. Because the band were social rejects with nothing to lose, they opted for an old school hard left/class war visual approach. Lias's most successful contribution was a scathing two-thousand-word viral essay on the Campari rooftop bar in

Peckham. It was a vicious full-frontal assault on everything he despised about himself, his non-existent future and the world around him that refused to cough it up, through the prism of a bar he wanted to drink at but couldn't afford to.

When a Foxton's estate agency opened in the Brixton area, they took it as a bad omen and immediately switched into riot mode, arranging a street demonstration attended by fifty people in army jackets waving banners outside. Behind the loudhailer was Lias, who wore a Palestinian keffiyeh scarf around his neck. He had previously posted a message online:

> A dark cloud is ominously looming above the once pure skys [sic] of Brixton, this cloud is called CHAMPAGNE AND FROMAGE and from the 15th of October it will rain on us until we drown in a sea of estate agents, champagne swilling yummy mummies and the so called 'fizz fiends' . . . cunts! WE WILL NOT STAND FOR THIS. DEATH TO CHAMPAGNE AND FROMAGE! YUPPIES OUT!

The bar's owner was perplexed by the commotion his new bar had caused – its previous Covent Garden location had been innocuous – but the protesters believed it was symbolic of something bigger: the middle-classes were moving in and ejecting the community who had always lived there. He stared up at the handmade cardboard signs emblazoned with 'TAKE YOUR GRILLED SALMON PANINI AND CHAMPAGNE WITH YOU!' and the small child who held a 'YUPPIES KILL CULTURE' banner and wondered how his empty little bar selling afternoon tea for £29.95 or bottles of Waris-Larmandier Cuvée Empreinte for £110 had caused such a provocation.

Nathan took it upon himself to feed the masses, distributing packets of processed cheese slices stolen from Iceland and a bottle of Frosty Jack's cider served in plastic cups as the rain bucketed down outside. When the *Evening Standard* caught on to the story they believed a serious militant group were behind the action, having no idea that the political agitators posting images of Stalin online were actually the drug-addled Fat White Family, uploading screenshots live from Saul's mouldering broom cupboard.

☪

Within a matter of months, the band's talent for provocation and relentless troublemaking online resulted in their very first front page, but perhaps not one they had predicted the night before their celebrations began. On 8 April, Saul was stirring on his mattress, attempting to shake off the previous day's crack comedown when he heard excitable voices rising from downstairs.

'She's gone! I can't fucking believe it,' the Landlord shouted.

'Yes!' yelled Lias. 'The greatest news I've heard all year.'

Outside, car horns started beeping. The television was turned on to the BBC at full volume. Nathan tapped on the door lightly and appeared cocooned in a duvet which covered his head and body.

'Saul? You up?' he said, as he poked his head into the darkened pit. 'Guess who's dead?'

'I don't fucking know and I don't care,' Saul replied. 'Told you not to wake me up . . .'

'Alright, misery. But you're going to love this. Thatcher. She's gone. Ding dong!'

Saul rubbed his eyes and broke out into a wide smile.

'A day for celebration.'

'Yeah, too right,' he said. 'Coach is going to love this.'

Up the road, at Windrush Square, revellers had started to gather. Nathan pulled on his trousers before running out of the door to see the commotion. By the time he returned, Saul, Lias and the Landlord were rubbing their hands with glee.

'There's a soundsystem there already,' Nathan said. 'And at least thirty people. They've all got banners.'

On the television screen above them the news rolled with

footage of the former prime minister, leaving Downing Street in tears, missiles exploding in the Falklands War, children drinking miniature bottles of milk, striking miners being chased by marauding police on horseback at Orgreave, newspaper headlines screaming THIS LADY'S NOT FOR TURNING, stockbrokers waving filthy rolls of cash at the camera, and the smoking shell of a cremated Brighton hotel.

'Wait,' Saul muttered. 'I have an idea.'

He scratched at a spotty scab on his face, struck by a bolt of inspiration. He vanished, and a minute later reappeared with his stained bedsheet, grabbed a roll of tape from behind the bar, and gaffered it to the floorboards.

'You got any of that black paint left?' he asked. 'And a brush . . .'

'I'll have a look in the cellar,' the Landlord replied. 'But no spelling mistakes. Make it good.'

By the time they arrived in the centre of Brixton, Thatcher's Death Party was in full throttle. Hundreds gathered outside the Ritzy Cinema, where the joyous crowd had scaled the front of the building and rearranged the billboard letters to spell 'MARGARET THATCHER'S DEAD. LOL. OH, AYE.' A shop window was smashed, and paint was thrown across the fascia of the local Foxton's estate agents. Anti-Thatcher graffiti was scrawled on the walls in red paint howling: 'You snatched my milk! & our hope.' Music boomed out across the square, as revellers sang 'Maggie! Maggie! Maggie! Dead! Dead! Dead!' and politicos congregated from the Anti-Bedroom Tax Federation, the Communist Party and the Socialist Party with members of the Brixton public to mark the occasion.

Dressed in a combat jacket, with a freshly shaved head, Saul's eyes were larger than usual that day. It was noted by Alabama 3's Larry Love that he had started to resemble a crack gopher in his emaciated state; Larry found it hilarious when Saul had recently been admitted to hospital with a constipation-related hernia.

Saul lit up a Marlboro Red and carried the banner along to the crowd with Nathan, who wore a leather flying jacket and a broad grin. Brixton junkies, crackheads, desolate outpatients of the Maudsley and anarchist gutter-dwellers joined their celebration; one had served time for setting fire to an empty scab bus used by miners in the 1980s and was particularly overjoyed at the passing of the dreaded Milk Snatcher. The rapidly accumulating rabble would not be outdone by the 'Rejoice Thatcher is Dead' flag that was attracting attention from a pack of swarming photographers.

'It's our chance to shine!' Saul shouted, as he unfurled the first of two banners he had handmade for the special moment.

His gut feeling was correct. When he held it up towards the sky all cameras fell on him and Nathan. A journalist gravitated towards Saul, sticking a microphone beneath his mouth, to which he gladly gave a quote.

'We are here for a celebration,' he said. 'I have never seen such a joyous atmosphere for someone's death. She was so particularly evil and hated by everyone; there are twelve-year-olds here . . . I wasn't even alive to witness most of her reign, but people are here because of the effects of it. It is the celebration of the end of a tyrant. And Brixton is the right place to do it.'

By midnight riot squad officers had been deployed as missiles exploded and crashed in the same location as the 1981 riots that Thatcher had provoked. Lias and Saul smoked crack to mark the occasion. As Lias pulled the pipe away, reeling from the intense rush rising through his lungs and into his face, he puckered his mouth and exhaled the smoke. Within a heartbeat Saul, who had already finished his portion, snatched it from his hands and ran off into the corner of the room, hunched over like an evil maniac in a miracle posture as Lias tried to wrestle the pipe from him.

'You little prick! So much for socialism,' he said.

'Socialism . . .' Saul replied, blowing the last of the gear from his mouth as he booted Lias away. 'Fuck your socialism!'

Despite the wave of protests across the country, it was not their brand of public outrage that generated the most headlines the following morning. It was the defining image of three emaciated reprobates standing on the balcony of the Queen's, in front of a handmade banner taped to the wall reading: 'THE WITCH IS DEAD'.

It was the first and possibly only time the Fat White Family would ever make the front cover of a national newspaper, but it was a moment they would treasure for the rest of their lives.

'We've finally made it, brothers!' Saul proclaimed when he saw the photograph plastered across the *Independent* the following day. He tore the image out and sellotaped it behind the counter at the Queen's.

'This is *my* greatest moment,' he said.

A Type One Situation

The band had been formed out of sheer spite. Spite unto the world that rejected me and my companions on account of our obvious defects. Our being drug-addled, socially crippled, mentally ill reprobates wasn't posturing. It was like a club for useless, angry young men driven to breaking point by the job office. We pooled our collective sense of embittered enfeeblement, our childhood traumas, our flaccid rage, turning them into a kind of public exorcism, one that eventually became too vulgar for people to ignore. 'Success!' we thought, not realising the implications of having to actually live in that moment, every night, seemingly forever. We were going to see the world, or at least its backstage rooms. We'd never have to pay for a drink again, and large crowds of strangers would applaud us each night on account of the very things for which we were once shunned.

☪

Stuart, the manager of Fat Whites, assumed control of the band's peripatetic existence by creating a plan that would see them acquire a record deal, a chain of gigs in the UK, a sold-out show at the 100 Club and, later, Brixton Academy. It was not beyond the realm of possibility to make this a reality, but it required a launchpad. They were booked to play at South by Southwest music festival in Austin, Texas.

The first indication of their American journey was made public at that year's NME Awards at Brixton Academy. The once-legendary (but now flailing) music publication had bestowed a Philip Hall Radar Award on the Fat Whites as the best emerging band in the country, and they were duly invited to receive their trophy at a live event. Lias was packed off to the ceremony dressed in a wool overcoat and suit. Saul refused to attend as he believed award ceremonies to be cringeworthy, and gave strict instructions to Lias not to let Dan onto the stage under any circumstance.

It had been decided that Pat Lyons, the Godfather of South London's music scene and errant MC, would make the acceptance speech. He delivered a free-form rendition in his slow American drawl, much to the bemusement of the audience.

'Where would we be without the Fat White Family?' he bellowed as he rolled out the lines dressed in his tweed hat and crumpled suit jacket. 'Don't let's get ready, NME. Let's get down and dirty, we're in the River City. And Fat White Family are going to be like . . . the wild American prairie . . . be like that, wildfire . . . all the way from Texas, Fat White Family might just SAVE AMERICA with the MUSIC . . . and it's so good . . . Hey Lias, step up to the microphone . . . get the people in your vocal zone . . . another tourist struggle . . . dig in . . . don't forget about the afters . . . and that's why they nearly collapsed tonight . . . I'm so happy to say . . . I AM A BIG FAN . . . of the Fat White Family . . . see 'em live . . . 'cos that's reality . . . hahaha . . . get ready, America . . . Austin, Texas . . . let that wildfire burn hot and long . . . thank you, I'll gladly accept this for Fat White Family, you know how they say it . . . hey! I LOVE YOU . . . they're going to entertain you and me . . . and for all the critics . . . *you gotta see them live* . . . this is Patrick Lyons telling it like it is . . .'

The previous week, a press release written by the band had appeared online as an open letter to the general public. Funds were required to pay for visas, flights, accommodation and vehicle hire to take them to South by Southwest (SXSW), followed by a tour of the eastern seaboard finishing up in New York.

Lias crafted the words at a sticky table in the inner sanctum of the Queen's. It was his last chance to escape the dismal English winter and the relentless poverty his band was trapped in. He leaned over the foolscap pad and wrote a heartfelt letter in green biro, slopping pasta and tomato sauce from his chin as he forked Sainsbury's Taste the Difference microwaved bolognese into his mouth and smeared the splatter from the page as he honed the lines until they clicked.

> *In return for your pledge we are offering ourselves up body and soul, for the next six weeks we are on sale . . . there is no low to which we shall not comfortably stoop; the future of bad taste is in your hands, don't let it slide through your fingers and mucky your shoes.*

For their investment the public could bid on a list of wonders from the band, including a 'special massage' from any member, a primal scream workshop with Lias, drum lessons with Dan, dinner for two cooked by Nathan, the opportunity to dance and sing backing vocals onstage with Fat White Family, a personalised answerphone message, a night out with the band, a tattoo by Dan, an anthology CD of rare tracks with handmade artwork, a customised Yuppies Out crack pipe and a one-man-band show with Adam Harmer.

Much to their surprise, within a few weeks the band had raised the £15,000 required from their fanbase. Even though the fan experience could sometimes be intense, it was their audience who supported the band early on, by donating to their fundraising appeal and enabling them to fly to America, to eat, hire a van and fill up with gas.

Live dates they had played in the previous two years attracted similar faces at each show, and fans often brought new friends along to see what all the fuss was about. The attention was heart-warming if a little peculiar at times: frantic starstruck fans started to appear in backstage areas, or in their bedrooms at the Queen's. Perhaps the most ghoulish fan encounter was at Nambucca in Archway, when the band found themselves covered in white powder thrown from the audience. Even the record label staff were covered in it. Afterwards, when Lias stumbled outside to smoke a cigarette in the humid London air, a funeral service programme was thrust into his hands, featuring the photograph of a middle-aged man who had recently passed. He was cremated to the sound of 'Bomb Disneyland', and that night his partner had chosen to spread his ashes in the place he loved the most: in the moshpit of a Fat White Family gig.

Despite his genuine excitement at touring America, Saul was openly terrified at the prospect of boarding an aircraft for such a long journey. He hadn't flown since the Metros, and he tossed and turned each night in the broom cupboard, scared of bailing out and letting the rest of the band down. A toy plane with flames painted up the side hung from his bedroom light, and each night before he closed his eyes, he fixated on it as it moved from side to side. He was convinced that he was going to die that way, with fire burning him alive as a plummeting plane soared down towards the earth, its engine exploding in the clouds.

☪

Bands were given stages to play around the festival site, and were required to play up to three times a day. Performers covered their own travel and lodgings and were given wristbands in return for playing live. For a band like Fat White Family, with six members plus a manager, the money required to play there had to justify the expense. It was a place where bands were broken into the industry, where every booker, mogul and producer visited; a good performance could make a band, a fact they were all well aware of.

As part of their shoestring budget, band members were each allocated an inflatable bed between shows, where they nursed hangovers and quietly masturbated their way through the small hours. At one Burger Records event, Sean Lennon appeared in the crowd and watched them with his friends, the Black Lips. Much to Saul's irritation, Dan made a beeline for Sean and immediately started talking to him, as Sean had worked with Dan's girlfriend on a video shoot. Dan needed somewhere to stay in New York and thought Sean would be able to help. Saul sat on a beer crate in the backstage area glowering at him as Lias smeared his torso with a carton of I Can't Believe It's Not Butter before heading out to play another show, one in which he would writhe and scream on the dusty ground, coating himself in the Texan dirt like one half of a melting Twix.

Later Dan took a call from Sean, who had lost his girlfriend and was searching for her. He jumped in a rickshaw with Saul and Lias and they travelled up to Sean's hotel, stumbling into the penthouse suite where he was sprawled on a large velvet sofa, playing music and talking with his friends. For the Fat Whites, unbeknownst to them, their fortunes were about to change.

As the heir to the Lennon estate, Sean took it upon himself to support emerging bands. Adorned in cherry-picked boutique fashions, he poured a glass of whisky for Saul, who immediately started jostling with Jared from the Black Lips. As a fellow antagonist, Jared took an instant shining to Saul that first manifested in a verbal sparring. Little had changed, but in America Saul had inadvertently joined the in-crowd.

☪

Upon their return to the digs Dan was awake and restless, and when Curly Joe rolled in stinking from daytime drinking they opted for a nightcap at a place that sold two-for-one shots along the road. Within a few hours, they had started talking to a gang of redneck Jesus-freak teenagers who hung round the bar outside; they shared their OxyContin homebrew with them, a sweet fizzy purple mixture named Texas Tea, and when they were invited back to their house for a party, it seemed like the perfect conclusion to the day.

They jumped in a hillbilly wagon with two Japanese girls and an hour later arrived in a desolate apartment block by the freeway. The party was non-existent, until a group of men in hooded tops turned up with a bottle of Fireball whiskey and a bag of crystal meth. The instigator of the party had gold grills on his teeth and played loud trap mixtapes from his speakers before offering Curly Joe a pipe. He declined, but Dan, who had recently been watching *Breaking Bad*, hit the pipe immediately. It was his first time taking the drug and for six hours he was high. As the sun came up, Curly Joe, who had been slumped on the sofa, started stirring. The sound of Gucci Mane's 'Lemonade' pumped out from the speakers, and as he staggered into the kitchen, a shoeless girl with giant hoop earrings who had been rapping to herself asked if he wanted a smoke.

'Sure,' Curly Joe replied. 'Why not? Breakfast . . .'

He held the lightbulb to his mouth, lit the ice and inhaled deeply on the meth that flowed deep into his lungs and fizzed through his morning fog until the world became sharp, bright and alive. He was exhilarated, alert, awake, agitated, a touch paranoid, and aroused.

As he started peaking on the meth, Curly Joe looked up through the doorway into the living room and saw some of the party boys had balaclavas. They unpacked shoe boxes from closed cupboards and started putting handguns together, waving them around. Then they bellowed, 'This is how we do it in Austin, man . . .' and ran out into the street shooting their guns up into the morning sky.

Curly Joe clutched the lightbulb and started spinning out; a wave of intense fear raced through him as his heart started to palpitate. Then, he felt a hand on his shoulder. Dan was rocking from side to side, the sugary smell of alcohol oozing through his pores. His peroxide hair glowed neon in the dawn light.

'They're just having a laugh,' Dan cackled. 'I swear they've done that three times already. You were blacked out . . .'

The meth whirlwind continued into the day. When they arrived back at the venue to play another show, Nathan and Adam had necked a bag between them; it was the cheapest and most easily available drug they could find. Nathan's face was deranged and had transformed into a Cubist ruin.

'You alright, man?' Curly Joe asked. 'Why did you swallow it?'

'Thought we might as well neck it. But it's okay because now I feel like superman, an insane amount of confidence. Fuck!'

Curly Joe shook his head and wiped beads of sweat from his brow. When he caught sight of his reflection in the mirror behind the bar, a fifty-year-old man stared back at him. It had been a long day.

As he ordered a drink to calm the comedown waves, Nathan started talking to a girl standing next to them and Curly Joe overheard the tone of her voice change.

'Excuse me?' she spat. 'What did you just say?'

Taking a deep breath, Curly Joe tuned into the conversation playing out behind him as the bartender pushed a pint over the bar, and he handed over the dollars, at which point Nathan proceeded to drop his trousers in full view of everyone in the packed bar, pulling his hairy buttocks apart and shouting, 'FINGER ME!'

A swarm of jocks surrounded him and pushed Nathan away, then launched at him with a pile of kicks and punches. Nathan squirmed around on the floor, taking a severe beating with his trousers down. Curly Joe rolled up his sleeves and quickly intervened, landing his fists into the maelstrom.

'We've gotta get out of here!' he shouted. 'Fuck's sake, we've got to play in an hour.'

The day's derangement continued, and the fallout of sleeplessness kicked in. Tyler, the Creator incited a riot. By the witching hour, Lady Gaga had been vomited on by a performance artist called Millie. Outside, on the pavement, a drunk driver crashed into the queue waiting outside their venue.

Four people died and twenty were injured. An aspiring rapper on his way to a gig drove up the road the wrong way and ploughed straight through the barricade. Chaos had erupted inside and out.

☪

When the turmoil had cleared, Nathan wandered with a parched, meth-comedown mouth towards a Fata Morgana of a garage along a dusty road, searching for fruit. He was alone and felt ill from the lack of food and vitamins. The rest of the band were disinterested in joining him on his mission but he knew his body would not survive without it.

When he finally arrived, he imagined he had been walking for hours. Each step towards the garage made it move half a mile away. The heat rose through gluey tarmac beneath his feet, but all he could visualise was the counter of fruit he would find when he got there: bananas, oranges, kiwis and mango, papaya and pineapple, apples and pears. What he found when he opened the door was a shabby, dingy shop with long lines of Reese's Peanut bars and bags of salted buttery popcorn.

A large woman behind the counter was chewing gum with her mouth wide open. Above her, an irate TV evangelist was waging a war of fire and brimstone on the screen overhead.

'Excuse me,' Nathan said, after looking around the aisles. 'Do you have any fruit in here?'

'Frood? Come again,' she replied. 'What d'ya mean?'

Nathan looked down and along the counter. There was one dehydrated lemon amongst the candy and crisps.

He held it up and said, 'Look, that's fruit, you've got fruit.'

'Aaaah fruit . . .' the woman replied. 'We don't have any fruit here.'

For Nathan, this was the summary of his American experience. A long walk on a dusty road to a place always out of reach.

A woman numbed by religious TV who didn't know the meaning of the word 'fruit'.

'She had it,' Nathan muttered on his way out. 'She said she didn't have it. Fuck me, that's not real is it. Nothing is real here . . .'

He trudged back along the freeway drinking a carton of sweetened pineapple fizz, his feet beginning to blister. When he pissed behind a streetlamp the smell of his urine grabbed at the back of his throat. He sat down by the speeding traffic and put his head in his hands, wishing the arid ground would swallow him up.

☪

There weren't a great many people at our first show in Chicago. There weren't a great many at our second either, for that matter, or our third. Stateside, we were forever painting the Forth Bridge. It's the calibre of one's audience that counts, however, not its size, and in Chicago Cynthia Albritton AKA 'Cynthia Plaster Caster' chose to honour us with her presence. Giddiness and enthrallment swept through the Fat White camp: to be cast by Cynthia meant canonisation.

We ended up sat in a blues bar together after the show, nervously guzzling margaritas. We'd been skirting around the prospect of my getting cast for several hours. Cynthia was nothing if not gentle. She had a tremendous knack for making you feel at home in your own skin. The rest of the band had disappeared aside from an exhaustingly drunk Dan, whose attention-seeking tendencies at that point in time were reaching fever pitch. He desperately wanted in, but she was having none of it. She'd have been more than happy to include Saul, and possibly Nathan I suspect, but the drummer was clearly out of the question.

Once he'd finally taken the hint and scarpered, me and Cynthia were left free to unpick the finer details.

'So, my fluffer's out of town . . .'

I necked the dregs of my cocktail and cleared my throat.

'Eh, what do you mean by that?'

'Fluffer, you know, to get you "ready" for the cast . . .'

She explained that she'd be busy preparing the pot of plaster in her kitchen, and that I needed to be 'solid' for the big dip. In normal circumstances, she said, she would have someone take care of that side of the operation, to 'lend a hand', as it were. Cynthia had been perfecting her art since the 1960s, a beatification ritual that takes around fifteen minutes. Soon I would find myself nestled amongst the likes of Jimi Hendrix, Wayne Kramer and Jello Biafra; part of a sacred lineage for all eternity. All the same, I was slightly disappointed about the fluffer thing. If there was no fluffer, why mention it?

'Shall we head back to mine?' she said as she tucked her long silver hair behind her ears and smiled at me, her latest muse. 'I think it's time . . .'

We disembarked from our taxi and walked up the black metal steps to her front door. The living room contained her complete collection proudly displayed on a variety of cake stands and plinths. I stared at the smallest example, in its erect state no bigger than a weathered cocktail sausage . . .

'Whose is that?' I asked her.

Cynthia rolled back on her sofa cushions and a smile broke out.

'Ariel Pink,' she replied. 'I couldn't get him going . . .'

'All shapes and sizes then?'

'Well, yes. The male member never fails to amaze me. Although I have started doing women recently. Yours will be number seventy-seven, perhaps one of my final great casts.'

She began pulling the necessary utensils down from the shelves. I started pacing around, then walked into the kitchen, where I was struck by the ubiquity of penis-themed memorabilia decorating the place. No surface was safe: penis tea towels, a penis pepper grinder, penis oven gloves. The interior was a shrine to male genitalia.

Cynthia followed me into the kitchen and started to mix up a bowl.

'So, depending on what lies beneath, we'll pick out one of these . . . then you hold it down here like this . . .'

She put one hand on her hip, arched forward slightly then hovered an empty cup between her upper thighs.

'It's not gonna feel pleasant, kinda like cold porridge or something . . . that's the tricky part, it takes a few minutes for it to set. It's like a dental mould, it's called alginate, and once it has set, I'll pour the plaster in. I developed the method myself in my groupie days . . . Jimi was my first, although many of the rock stars who "volunteered" their services wanted to keep them for their own personal use. So they still have them in their wardrobes, I suppose. The rest I kept.'

I began feeling quite fearful. Performance anxiety, despite the tequila. She ushered me into her office and patted the chair in front of a large computer screen, then made her way back into the kitchen. I was instructed to find some pornographic material of interest, and then, having achieved sufficient rigidity, the casting could commence. I was left alone for several minutes before Cynthia poked her head through the door to ask whether I was 'doing okay'.

'I'm doing great,' I said, with an ounce of humiliation in my voice. 'I'm doing just fine . . .'

The first attempt was aborted, much to my disappointment. Cynthia consoled me, offering up a diplomatic excuse about the pot not being deep enough. If it weren't for raw fear I might simply have passed out. My head was spinning from the liquor. I fixated on the penis tea cosy in a bid to steady myself. Adrift in a tabernacle of the testicular: perhaps I was unworthy of initiation after all?

'I'm not sure if I can do this,' I whispered.

'You'll be fine sweetie, it didn't work the first time with Jimi either . . .'

I returned to the pornographic den for attempt two. Cynthia re-entered the room. On this occasion, she bent down on her knees and began slowly coating my nether region in Vaseline herself. This was a crucial part of the process. Without the Vaseline you were in danger of lodging your glans in plaster permanently. Having someone other than yourself apply it turned out to make a world of difference; who'd have thought? Staring straight up at me, gently insisting 'that's it, that's it . . .' under her breath, everything became simple, became pure . . . became gratitude. In that moment, guessing at the many worlds hidden behind those eyes, I became quite sure that Cynthia and I were in some way meant for one another. There had been a fumble up on high, some rupture in the space-time continuum; the gods had gotten it wrong. Why do people start bands? Why continue with the drudgery and pain and derangement? Nobody even buys records anymore, why risk ruining your life over it? It's because you're sick of being fed your culture from up on high. You want a chance to pour yourself into the human dilemma despite the bitterness and loathing and terror that inevitably blooms up inside you while you're a teenager. How much would you sacrifice for half a hand job from the great Cynthia Albritton? All in, I say.

The result itself wasn't too bad. Comparing it to the others on display it seemed a mid-table affair, might qualify for the odd European tournament, but certainly not a contender; Aston Villa sort of level, not quite Huddersfield Town . . .

☪

As the van reached the perimeter of New York the traffic began to slow, and the band slowly edged along Brooklyn Bridge towards Chinatown. Their manager, Stuart, pushed a CD he'd saved for the occasion into the stereo. It was the only time they had ever listened to Alabama 3, but collectively they agreed that driving over the bridge to Manhattan was the only justification to play 'Woke Up This Morning' and re-enact the opening credits of *The Sopranos*.

'Can you let us out now?' Saul asked when they reached the other side. 'I need to put my feet on the ground.'

He wound down the window and hung his head out the side. The city was laid out in front of them. It was no longer the New York of their imagination.

'It's not like *Taxi Driver* anymore you know,' Stuart replied. 'It's cleaned up since then. Don't be thinking the Lower East Side is full of punks. Even the Meatpacking District has gone corporate. There's no grime or dirt. No CBGBs. But feel free to walk to the hostel if you want. The bad air might do you all good . . . Besides, I could do with a bit of silence.'

Saul unfastened his seatbelt and pulled on his jacket. Dan and Curly Joe piled out of the vehicle that had been driven thousands of miles from Texas with a steaming bonnet, and together they stared up at the vast concrete valleys reaching up to the clouds.

Nathan tuned in to the sirens that echoed overhead. Elderly women with grotesque facelifts and lacquered hair walked designer dogs on jewel-encrusted leads beside him. Yellow cab drivers reached out of their windows to hurl abuse at jaywalkers. Subway steam rose from beneath their feet. The smell of pizza hung in the air. Every cliché from the big screen played out in front of them.

'I'm not sure if I want to replace the Lou Reed version with this,' Lias said.

'I've heard the Velvet Underground,' said Nathan. 'But I don't give a shit about them, unlike everyone else here who chases the old myth.'

'Oh come on, man. What do you mean by that?'

'Well, you lot are always harping on about what went on thirty years ago, rather than what it is now.'

'Judge Nathan laying it down. You've only been here for five minutes for fuck's sake,' Curly Joe said.

'It's like London. A bunch of middle-class kids who control everything: culture and the arts. A nostalgia trip. Looking down on the gas station attendant in the sticks with no education. Or teeth.'

'But you haven't met anybody yet . . .' Saul laughed. 'I'm middle-class, so what does that make me? Would you like to purge me?'

'You're in the twilight zone of class,' Nathan replied. 'Neither here, there or anywhere. A shit-sifter extraordinaire.'

'Yeah, maybe you're right,' said Saul. 'I can dine at almost any table, whereas you're condemned to a life beneath . . .'

As they crossed East Broadway Saul made the most of a pickled herring and gherkin bagel, shoving the last fishy morsel into his mouth.

'Mmmm. Better than Brick Lane,' he said. 'How long before we reach Piano's? I can't feel my knees.'

'Ten minutes,' Nathan said, before launching into his latest riddle. 'Being here now, it all makes sense to me. There are two types of people in the world. There's people that walk up escalators, and there's people who just stand on them.'

Curly Joe scrunched his face in exasperation.

'What's that even supposed to mean?'

'It's just the movement of things. Static people, climbing people. My people. I feel like we are walking up the escalator right now,' said Nathan. 'And it's about to come off its tracks.'

☪

At their first show in New York, at a small venue called Piano's on the Lower East Side, the guest list was oversubscribed. Word had reached the city that one of the best new bands in Britain were playing three small dates that week. Saul was secretly delighted when he saw Jon Spencer, Legs McNeil and Danny Fields written down on the list. He knew how significant those people were in punk history, and he made a point of performing well. In the audience that night Matthew Johnson, owner of the label Fat Possum, watched from the wings with a keen ear and beady eye. He promised to return the following night at Union Pool, knowing full well that he was going to sign them before anyone else caught wind.

The morning of the Union Pool show was idyllic for Lias. He had woken up wrapped in the arms of a blonde of a calibre native only to the streets of Manhattan. As an Englishman, his value within the sexual marketplace had risen exponentially on arrival through his accent and attire alone. He had exploited his newfound exoticism, and as he gazed out across the rooftops of Brooklyn, bathing in the spring light, he let out a long, grateful sigh. He drank a cup of black coffee and stretched his arms above his head and smiled. It was his twenty-eighth birthday.

He messaged Saul, who had spent the morning eating breakfast with Canadian relatives. They agreed to travel across town to the Empire State Building and take the lift to the top floor in tourist style to celebrate the occasion.

After a long lunch they journeyed to the venue for the sound-check, where they caught sight of Nathan walking down the street dressed in drag, wearing a pair of sequinned high heels and sashaying his hips from side to side. Curly Joe had his head rolled back with mirth, and cars were slowing down to watch his performance.

'Happy birthday, my old brother!' he said. 'I've bought you some chocolate orange matchsticks.'

They walked in together, and Lias pushed his cream cowboy hat up as he waved at the sound engineer and signalled five minutes to her. He ordered a margarita as Curly Joe started to unpack his bass on the stage. Dan walked through the door behind them, drunk already, and screamed happy birthday at Lias before pulling his hat from his head, throwing it down on the floor, stamping up and down on it and destroying it. In his inebriated state, he thought it was a joke, and that Lias would find it funny. The bar staff watched it happen, and then refused to serve Dan.

Lias was annoyed and irritated by the puny act of attention seeking. He picked the crushed hat from the floor and pushed it back into shape. It looked like a cowpat, having lost all of its Texan dynamism. The situation escalated when Dan stumbled towards his kit and kicked over the support band's amp. In his confused state, he didn't apologise or attempt to pick it up.

Saul watched it happen as he tuned up his guitar.

'Why are you such an idiot?' he seethed. 'Drop the rock star schtick.'

'Am I always going to be beneath you, Saul?' Dan replied.

'I should have stayed at Sean's. It's lovely, you know. It's so *kind* of him to let me stay there. I've been drinking his brandy all afternoon.'

'Yeah, don't we know about that.'

As Dan thumped on his bass drum, Matthew from Fat Possum arrived and shouted over to Saul, 'Man, we're just gonna watch the soundcheck. You don't mind us being here, right? We have other shit to do later on . . .'

The rest of the band weren't expecting to be watched by the music industry's answer to Lucifer, but Saul was keen to make the right impression. Dan sensed this and, becoming increasingly antagonistic, informed Saul, 'I'm gonna play shit on purpose.'

'You need to chill out,' Saul said. 'Have some water or something. You're rat-arsed. Don't embarrass us. Half of the label are here.'

They launched into 'Cream of the Young' and it sounded abominable, Dan playing in a style true to his word. He then spat at Saul from behind the drum kit, an act Saul returned in kind. Then Saul put his guitar down, steamed over to Dan and slapped him in the face. It suddenly dawned on Saul that he hadn't hit him hard enough, so he walked back and smacked his drummer even harder. Dan fell to floor from his stool, then skulked out of the venue with tears welling in his eyes.

After the storm had passed, Saul found Matthew outside, smoking.

'I'm sorry,' he said. 'That's not the way we normally behave.'

Matthew looked up at him through a cloud of smoke and hissed, 'If you've got a bad dog that goes crazy, you put it down.'

Saul put his hand out and shook the cold, sweaty palm in front of him, and realised that this was a man he could do business with. Matthew put his arm around Saul's shoulders.

'Let me take you out for dinner,' he said. 'I think we have more than a few things in common.'

☪

Saul believed the Big Apple and all of its trimmings had seduced Dan, giving him licence to behave badly. His drinking and drug-taking escalated, and the more he unravelled in public, the worse Saul treated him in private. There was little regard for the underlying issues behind his behaviour. Dan viewed Lias and Saul as a blackbird and boa constrictor. He failed to see the irony of the band's flirtation with communist imagery. In his eyes, some pigs were clearly more equal than others.

When Dan was intoxicated or became insulting, Saul would return the behaviour twice as hard, and set off a chain reaction – Dan would attempt to transfer the behaviour meted out on him onto Nathan, Lias and Curly Joe. The vicious cycle continued. When Dan started on Nathan after the soundcheck at Union Pool on the second night in New York, Nathan replied in the only way he knew to be effective, by hitting him in return.

As the unofficial diplomat of the group, Lias refused to get embroiled, but as Dan railed and ranted in Lias's face, Nathan intervened.

'Why don't you just slap him and sort it out?' he would say repeatedly. 'It's the only way to deal with him.'

Contrary to his stage presence, Lias wasn't naturally the argumentative type and would only intervene if pushed hard enough. He had a pathological fear of confrontation that often veered into spinelessness; his frequently lily-livered responses infuriated Saul. But Lias had enough self-awareness to recognise that when small events gather into a snowball of repression they take on their own momentum, and that's when they become a real problem. At the other end of the spectrum, Saul thrived on antagonism, for better and – of course – for worse. If and when it finally did come to a physical altercation it was always so puny and utterly non-lethal that the two warring bandmates invariably resembled two emaciated gerbils trapped in a cage, attempting to fornicate in the middle of an earthquake.

In his Metros days, Curly Joe had been the butt of all jokes, so he felt some sympathy towards Dan's situation, which only elicited venom from Saul in response. Lias believed that like his forebears Caligula and Richard III, Saul could be a tyrant who only wielded power thanks to his vastly superior musical talent. This was a typically melodramatic view of his bandmate. A born catastrophiser, Lias always viewed the situation as a worst-case scenario. The glass was always half empty. Nathan existed on Planet Nathan, and was so consumed by whatever his bizarre view of the world was he barely noticed what existed beyond it. In the absence of any real leader, it often fell to Saul to deliver the discipline. As Lias spent his days and nights chasing women, and Nathan spent it chasing the dragon or the latest conspiracy theory, it took the frequently erratic Saul to intervene and drive the music forward. Adam observed from the edges as Curly Joe and Dan soaked up the public attention, which was the most they had ever received in their lifetimes. Collectively, they were all so consumed by the nearest gratification that they barely noticed what was slowly poisoning them from within.

☪

Within a month of returning to Brixton, Nathan and Saul were flown back out to New York to sign a record deal. Numbed by the residue of Valium, Saul flicked through the pages of *The Fateful Adventures of the Good Soldier Švejk During the World War* by Jaroslav Hašek on the flight, incapable of reading a word. Nathan watched *Robocop* under a chemical cosh, and they discussed the virtues of Gary Glitter on their way into Manhattan. They agreed the new record should sound like 'Rock and Roll Part 1', with looped drums and layered vocals.

For ten days in Greenwich Village, Nathan and Saul embarked on a speedball marathon and imbibed an almost lethal concoction of heroin and cocaine. On the seventh night Nathan overdosed and stopped breathing properly; his lips turned grey and his lungs tightened in the first signs of respiratory failure.

'Please help me,' he said to Saul. 'I need an inhaler. Think I'm gonna die.'

Saul, sprawled on a leather sofa, let out a whimpering sound.

'You won't die. You just need to relax. Here, have some more. I've left you a line.'

'I don't need any more,' Nathan replied. 'I swear, this is enough. The heroin's slowing my heart down and the coke's speeding it up. I haven't slept for days. Hardly any food. I'm scared. Something's gone wrong in my body, Saul.'

'Go and get some fresh air then. You're having a panic attack.'

'Aren't you going to come with me?' asked Nathan.

'Too tired. Sorry, pal . . . I've had a hard day at the coalface . . . Come on, you'll be alright.'

Nathan ran down onto the sidewalk and towards a small green square. *If I can just put my feet on the grass I'll be alright*, he said to himself. But even when he reached the grass, took off his socks and shoes and splayed himself out on the turf, his breathing didn't recover. The tightening sensation in his lungs felt as though he was breathing through a straw. None of the passers-by he asked had an inhaler, and the fear grabbed him from within.

A few streets along, he saw a medical sign above a doorway, entered it, and walked through automatic doors into a dialysis centre.

'Please help me,' he said to the receptionist. 'I think I'm going to die. Please. Get me to hospital. My heart is stopping, I can feel it.'

Within seconds, a duty doctor dressed in a white coat and wearing a pungent aftershave started screaming at him, 'GET OUT OF THIS BUILDING NOW!' and pushed him along the long corridor from behind onto the pavement outside as all of the patients waiting for treatment gawped at him.

Nathan curled his knees up to his chest and started to count, holding his breath in and slowly releasing it until his breathing eventually calmed down and his heart stopped thrashing inside his ribcage like an angry woodpecker.

When he returned to Saul many hours later, he was shaken up.

'What's the matter with you? Where have you been?' Saul asked, as he bobbed his head up and down to an R. L. Burnside album pumping from the speakers.

'It's alright for you,' Nathan replied. 'You have a strong constitution. I can't keep up. I nearly died today. On my own. Out there on the street.'

'You didn't look as bad as the guy at the party the other night. He was properly ODing. I had to give him mouth-to-mouth.'

'Yeah, I fucking know that, I was there. This stuff is so strong. It knocked me sideways.'

Saul started to laugh.

'Great, isn't it?'

'No, it's not great at all. Drugs just bounce off you. Doing speedballs for this long is just madness. Where does it all end? I mean . . . on a pavement in New York?'

'It's alright out here though,' Saul said. 'If you know what you're doing . . .'

'Yeah, fucking trustafarians. Endless cash to pay for it. Well we don't have that.'

'I know. But thank God they're so generous with it.'

Saul opened a brown wooden box on the table, engraved with an ouroboros on the lid.

'Look, I've got works now. Makes the drugs kingsized. Anyway, you can't smoke the gear out here. My nostrils are burning from the lines . . .'

He tapped on the inside of his arm, just above his Thursday Night tattoo, and started to smile.

Nathan unpeeled his jacket, turned off the stereo and sat down in front of the television. The face of Louis C. K. filled the screen; it was the last thing Nathan saw before finally nodding out into a sleep that felt like it lasted for a thousand years.

Roll Over Abdullah

After travelling from Paris on the first Eurostar back to England, Lias was collected from the train in Cambridge by a fraught Bashir. Hours previously, the band had taken to the stage at Nouveau Casino, halfway through their first European tour supporting the Black Lips. Lias was by that point exhausted from touring and was running a temperature from a deep chest infection that he had failed to seek treatment for. He forced himself onto the stage, not wanting to perform.

Towards the end of the set, as he started to sing 'Bomb Disneyland', a metallic taste began filling his mouth – when he spat on the stage, it was bright red. A silvery film coated his skin, and he was finding it hard to sing. After the final chorus he floundered towards the dressing room where he filled the sink with splashes of blood from each hacking cough.

'Do you think I might be dying?' Lias asked as Saul burst into the room with a barely concealed expression of fear on his face.

'No, man,' he replied. 'Don't panic. You'll be fine. It's no big deal. People cough up blood all the time . . .'

Luckily for him, a doctor was in the audience and quickly made his way backstage, taking Lias's temperature and pulse.

'You have to go the hospital, immediately,' he advised.

Their tour manager, Pete, called a taxi and accompanied Lias to the nearest accident and emergency department. Nathan and Saul quickly evacuated the scene to spend time with the Parisian glitterati who had been at the show. Only Pete remained with him.

Speaking to the doctors in pidgin Algerian-French, Lias described what had happened that night and was given an X-ray. He was diagnosed with pneumonia and told he'd be kept in hospital for at least a week. A decision was made to return him to British soil as quickly as possible.

When he finally arrived in Cambridge, Lias had never been so relieved to see his father. He was taken straight to the hospital and put on a drip in the TB ward for the next seven nights. Upon his discharge, Lias was taken back to Bashir's under strict instruction to stay in bed and eat his way back to health. He was anaemic from the blood loss.

The mollycoddling of his stepmother and her homecooked food worked miraculously, combined with ferrous iron tablets that bunged up his insides and had the silvery tang of liver. He slowly started recovering from his illness. The relative calm was interrupted when one morning, as he rolled out of bed, Bashir stormed into the room.

'What's bloody going on here!' he shouted. 'The family have seen pictures of you on Facebook. Out in Algeria. You know it's haram! Why do you bring such shame on us?'

'What are you talking about?'

'What do you mean what am I talking about? This! Look. You stood on a bar naked with some woman hanging onto you!'

Lias coiled back onto his bed.

'It's *performance*,' he said. 'This is what I do. This is ART.'

'Why can't you just have a proper job!' his father screamed. 'You are wasting your life. And your intellect! You could have been successful by now, but look at you. No money. Nowhere to live. You almost died in Paris and now you have disgraced yourself!'

'Please don't shout.'

'Don't tell me what I can do in my own house.'

Bashir's face filled with fury as he stomped around the bedroom.

'I'm only shouting because I care! I hate to think one day I get a call saying one of my sons is dead . . . you don't have children . . . you will never know how that feels . . .'

'We are adults, you know.'

'Well why don't you look after yourself better?'

'I do, it's just I don't have money. We live off a pittance. You know how hard it is trying to scrape a living in London. We barely have enough money to eat.'

'Always enough money for the bloody drugs though, eh? I guess you have different priorities to the rest of us!'

Bashir shook his head and turned off the light switch. He slammed the door so hard it shook the frame and barked at his son as he walked down the stairs.

'When are you ever going to be a man? Get a woman. Pay for a roof over your head. You can't stay eighteen forever. You were gifted at school. You could have been engineer . . . like me! Now look at you. Living like a tramp. Kaci would not accept this! I will send you both to bloody Kabylia and arrange a marriage if you don't sort yourself out.'

☪

When he first started working as tour manager for Fat White Family, Pete Hambly had an inkling that his new job might be somewhat eventful, but had not anticipated the chaotic load that was about to descend. An old face from around the Brixton squat scene, Pete was a familiar presence on Electric Avenue, and worked intermittently for Alabama 3. Originally from Calgary, and at one time a professional ice hockey player, Pete had studied sports psychology before following the path of punk rock, and had a particular understanding when it came to motivating groups of hopeless junkies incapable of getting on a tour bus or even a stage without a certain level of prodding.

When Pete first started working with the Fat Whites, he devised a plan that would transform them. He'd spent a year touring with a heavy metal band, and he was exhausted and bored by that world; he wanted to work with a band he could develop.

As tour manager, production manager, driver, front of house, backline and tour co-ordinator, Pete fulfilled numerous roles officially. Unofficially, he became the band's de facto manager. By the time they had worked together for four years, they had burned through a multitude of 'official' managers that were either sacked or walked away from the unruly mess. He was the only constant. By default, he became the seventh member of the band.

When they needed money, he gave it to them. When they needed drugs, he bought them. If they got arrested, he bailed them out. He was there for hospital admissions, brothel trips, mental health breakdowns and police enquiries. Submitting to their demands frequently pushed him into a corner, but he held this philosophy tight to his chest: 'Fat White Family are the real deal. So let's do this right and turn them loose.' Turning them loose often meant overspending the tour budget to make the shows happen. It manifested in Pete bribing Saul to get him to play, as otherwise he would refuse and simply not turn up for the tour bus, the flight, or at the venue, leaving all the other band members in the lurch.

'If I get you £100 of crack right now, then you're getting on that flight tomorrow and you are playing that gig,' he would tell him.

'Alright then,' Saul would reply. 'Fine.'

He often wondered if he would be the one who became the band's sacrificial lamb, getting shanked down a dark alleyway one night before a show attempting to buy several bags to dole out between them.

Still, this was the only approach that worked; if they needed to get out of London to tour Europe, America or even around the UK, Saul was frequently the sticking point. And then in turn, other band members would kick up a stink and refuse to leave Brixton.

When Pete joined them permanently in 2014, they had a reputation for unreliability, erratic gigs and appalling behaviour. This didn't put him off; far from it. He knew he was possibly the only man around who could handle them.

☪

A bidding war erupted in 2014 to sign the band, and after a series of ecstatic live shows that were filled to the rafters with industry insiders, various offers were put on the table. The amounts from major labels were eyewatering, but Saul was immediately suspicious of them. Having had his fingers burnt in the Metros, he was belligerent and refused to concede to the same system again, no matter how much cash they pushed under his nose. Any whiff of mainstream was rooted out by him. He knew that money meant compromise, something that he was not prepared to do. Integrity and authenticity in music meant independence, not becoming corporate shills. Their lifestyles and personalities would never wash with the demands of the middle-aged men in suits who ran most of the industry. Saul knew this and rejected it without blinking.

A deal was negotiated with [PIAS] that would fund their second album and give them their own label, which was named after one of their more *challenging* tonal works, 'Without Consent'. With hindsight, it was an absurd idea to let Saul and Nathan run a label in their current state. Although Lias knew the project was doomed to fail, he went along with their ambitions. The first and only act signed to the new label was Sheffield's Eccentronic Research Council and their side project with Lias and Saul, the Moonlandingz. Other acts were mooted, but in the whirlwind of band life, most fell by the wayside. One thing they were certain of was that their new album, *Songs for Our Mothers*, would be released on Without Consent, and dedicated to the tireless efforts of the women that raised them.

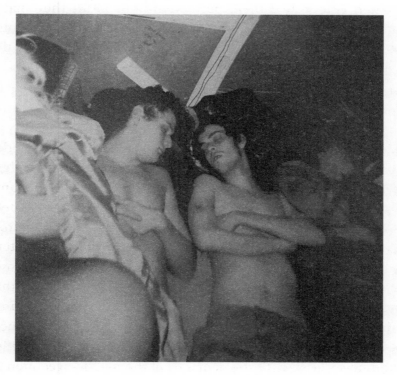

It was the Landlord's birthday, and the pub was heaving with punters. Palestine flags hung from the walls and pamphlets were scattered on each table. During the gig, Nathan took his shirt off and whipped it across Dan's back. Its button caught him in the face, in the same eye on which Dan had had a serious operation as a teenager for a detached retina.

'You fucking arsehole!' Dan screamed from behind the drum kit, before standing up, kicking over his drum stool, then grabbing hold of Nathan's keyboard and throwing it onto the floor, mid-set. The gig continued at pace.

Nathan stood back grinning at him, before picking it up, plugging it back in, and making a throat-cutting gesture across his neck.

Afterwards, Dan attempted to apologise but Nathan was irate and had to be pulled away backstage. He felt belittled by Dan's act. It wasn't just Nathan who was angry; the entire band wanted to throttle him. Sensing this, Dan ran out of the pub and went out drinking and drugging: he sank into such a state that he conveniently forgot they were playing the next day at a festival in Cambridgeshire. He'd also chosen not to turn up to the band's album launch, opting to play in Misty Miller's band instead. He was on a retainer with them so had left the Fat Whites in the lurch.

For years he had been living the myth of the rock drummer – attempting to be the next Keith Moon, John Bonham or Ginger Baker. But Dan had serious mental health issues and didn't seek any treatment until after he left the band. He experienced manic episodes and extreme mood swings, and he self-harmed. Other band members provoked his behaviour and his internal disintegration accelerated. He found himself sucked deeper into the band's malevolent realm, which initially had a whiff of glamour but revealed itself to be a damaging and emotionally toxic environment.

When the band played in Liverpool, Dan tried to take his own life and was hospitalised. His cold hands still rattling with medication, Dan had been driven in silence to the Liverpool show with bandages around his arms covering the lacerated wounds. He needed urgent psychiatric treatment but opted to do the gig instead. What he didn't foresee at the time was that he would be sacked before the summer was out.

Dan was officially given his marching orders because he didn't show up to play their first major festival booking after spending the previous night on the lash with a trending film director. He joined a new band, Phobophobes, fronted by Jamie, Lias's sexual nemesis from his art-school days, whose drummer, Jack Everett, was immediately poached by Fat White Family. After an initial honeymoon period, Jack would go on to prove himself an even more cataclysmic personality behind the drums. When their 'Tour of Tenderness' finally ended at the Electric Ballroom, Saul announced on the microphone to the sold-out audience: 'Dan is dead to us.' He may have been the first official casualty of the band, but he certainly wasn't the last.

G☪

It's difficult not to find yourself drowning in cliché when what you do for a living is travel around the world with a bunch of guys smoking crack and wearing ski glasses. Despite having known her for less than six months, and most of my friends expressing their opinion that it was a terrible idea I would bitterly regret, I had made up my mind. Within twenty-four hours of touching down at JFK I would marry AB. And a day later, I would perform on the Late Show *with David Letterman. One unreality fed straight into the other.*

The reasons behind my marrying AB were manifold. There was the usual, of course: she was the kind of girl that wouldn't have looked at me twice in my previous life. She was all glamour and hype, bangs and buxom; one of the 'in' crowd. I recall flicking through a copy of Rolling Stone *on one of my earliest visits to Brooklyn, searching for a tiny article about my own band, and wondering how many times I'd have to appear in this rag for a woman like her to go to bed with me.*

You might add to that the allure of Manhattan where she lived, an allure impossible to differentiate from the fear being there brought on – that you might in fact be peaking in life, and that the smart money rests on finding a way to stay put, come what may. The band were on the brink of implosion, after all; more of them were on the gear than off. When the bottom finally falls out, maybe US citizenship will come in handy?

In New York there was the sense that anything might happen. Its scale quickly became your own; if you were down, you'd never been so down in your life – if you were up, you were basically divine. I'm not saying that me and AB didn't have some kind of connection, but in the same way a holiday romance depends on its exotic locale, the minute that backdrop was removed, out went the illusion with it.

The wedding was scheduled for 1 April at the Soviet-themed KGB bar, our favourite haunt in the city. When I arrived in town the previous morning, we visited a Native American fashion emporium and bought two silver rings with embedded criss-crossing patterns of turquoise gemstone. She'd borrowed for the occasion a coat with tails, a wide-brimmed hat and some other items from Sean on my behalf. I was to be dressed in the same clothes donned by his father John Lennon in the video for 'Mind Games'.

I think some small part of what attracted me to fashionable girls like AB was my willingness to play the unquestioning mannequin. Sean himself would be absent from the humanist ceremony. He and AB were old flames; I think the prospect repulsed him in some way. Neither would Saul be making an appearance. Sometime in the week leading up to this momentous double barrel – my marriage and our appearance on Letterman – he'd once again misplaced his passport. For a previous video shoot we'd bought six matching military shirts, all of which ended up in a pile at his place afterwards. Weeks after our only ever appearance on American television he located it again in one of the six identical breast pockets.

The rest of the band would be at the wedding ceremony though, with Pete, our new American label boss Matthew, and a smattering of AB's friends and her parents, which made me feel like a bastard for leaving my own mum out in the cold. I'd called Tam from the Queen's a few days earlier to hassle him about the music selection. I didn't normally run to him for music requests, but I felt he would have an intrinsic understanding of the surreal gravity of my situation, the preposterousness of it and how best to highlight that. The recommendation of 'Koyaanisqatsi' by Philip Glass sprang from his lips almost instantly.

The Ed Sullivan Theatre on Broadway had the same kind of backstage rooms you get at the BBC: underwhelmingly utilitarian. They perfectly analogised the impotence of spirit one feels the day after knocking yourself dead with Xanax at the end of a coke binge.

One of the guitarists from Mystery Lights stood in for Saul onstage. Later that evening Matthew expressed a desire to strangle him. He pulled a windmill. On air. Fuck that guy, man. We all agreed we should have played 'Touch the Leather' instead of the more generic 'Is It Raining in Your Mouth?' – which Matthew had insisted on – and woke up the next day disappointed that we'd failed to achieve a viral Future Islands-esque moment while we had the chance. The States would remain decidedly uncracked. For a brief flash we were beamed into millions of American homes, the Ed Sullivan filled up with one rapturous round of applause and then it was over. I remember thinking David Letterman had the softest hands. It was more airtime than we had ever received in Britain. For a brief period, Saul had been peddling a 'Jools Holland is a Cunt' meme from the Facebook page, ruling us out of that one for good.

I was in no position to make the move Stateside at that point in my life. I had touring obligations and a summer of festivals back in Europe. AB and I decided she would move over to London to try to make things work on that side of the Atlantic. She would give up her SoHo loft, her DJ residency at the Roxy, all of her New York privileges and together we'd see what happened when we spent more than ten days in each other's company.

Upon returning to London after that New York visit I submerged myself in the same old sleaze, plagued with doubt and regret from the start. I would wander from punter to punter at the Queen's ravaged on cocaine and dithering about having done something terrible I now had no idea how to get out of. The exact same people that had told me unequivocally not to get married in such circumstances now told me in equally certain terms that I had to come clean – before she emigrates at your behest at least – but I ignored them all a second time.

I knew in my heart and soul there was no way it would work, but laziness, cowardice and vanity – the great trinity of personal failure – had been left breeding too long in my person; a few years of flattery on top of a decade of drug abuse had reduced my once nimble mind to a self-infatuated rubble, my sensitivities now inclined towards immediate gratification and nothing else. Instead, I rented us an apartment, a temporary place. A lowlife I may well be, but not so low as to expect her to move in above the Queen's upon arriving in the UK.

It took just eleven days for a warm embrace at the airport to morph into bitter resentment. Wilful detachment isn't an easy thing to hide from people, and from the person you've just married it amounts to pretty much the most offensive course of action one can take. The more AB demonstrated her desire to make things work the more indifferent I became, and so began a vicious cycle that reached its apogee in the flat one late spring evening. We'd been out with two of her friends at the Barbican, and I had worn the revelation of my spineless ways like a millstone around my weary neck the entire day. In the cab home from central London the bickering began heating up. I remember ordering us a pizza from Domino's, the little dialogue with them on the phone feeling like a brief reprieve from the disaster I'd set in motion. Eventually we settled on silence, both of us staring out of the windows as the morbidity of evening began swallowing up the city. I made up my mind then that once we were inside, I'd come clean. I held her gaze for a moment and told her that I no longer wanted to be with her. There was a sudden flash of comprehension, then came the blows.

A more deserved hiding you'll never find.

In the middle of this ugly altercation the doorbell rang; the pizza delivery boy was outside. As I opened the front door and made my way down the single flight of stairs to the ground floor entrance of the council block, AB appeared out on the porch to continue with her recriminations. An unceasing cascade of abuse at my back, I opened the door and told the delivery guy I was happy to pay for the pizza but had lost my appetite. He could eat it himself if he liked.

☪

The band returned to America as the leaves started to fall, ready to record their album with Sean as producer initially, before moving on to an analogue studio in the wilderness, a place where no heroin or crack could be found. After Curly Joe had been turfed out of Sean's New York apartment for putting his fungal brogues in the fridge one night 'to get rid of the smell' and ruining all of the food, only Saul was permitted to stay in Manhattan.

Gazing out across the crooked skyline, Saul plotted his next move for the second record: Lias would write the lyrics, and he would create new songs as an antidote to the bedwetting lifestyle-muzak and festival-moment themes that permeated the independent music scene in London and New York. The tepid beige tremblings of daytime radio gave him sleepless nights. The blandness needed banishing.

By the time they reached the Lennon Ranch in the Catskill Mountains, Nathan, Saul and Lias had tucked into a sheet of acid to celebrate the occasion. They were exiled to their own luxury quarters in the estate grounds and began ransacking the guest house CD collection under the influence, with Nathan eagerly trying to hunt down a copy of *Magical Mystery Tour*. 'I don't understand it. Why wouldn't they have "I Am the Walrus"? It's the only thing I want to listen to . . .'

Daylight was breaking. Stumbling across the piles of crumpled beer cans that had started to accumulate, Nathan walked out into the grounds, traced his hands around tree trunks and squeezed at the pale lichen that hung from branches above him. The lake was partly frozen, and as the fading moonlight bounced off the ice he was overwhelmed by a desire to cross it, heading towards the full moon's gaze, wrapping his arms around its reflection in the rapidly freezing water.

'Where's Nath?' Lias asked back at the house, as he pulled a packet of Rizla into a hundred paper pieces.

'In the middle of the lake, out there . . .' Saul replied. 'Do you think he'll drown?'

Lias staggered out of the front room and ran towards Nathan waving his arms. The ice was thin, and Nathan was skating on top of it in his woolly socks, crouching low as an aircraft passed in the sky above him, adding to the lattice of contrails that he had become fixated by.

'Come on!' Lias shouted, as his voice echoed over the ice. 'Get off the fucking ice . . . what am I gonna tell Mum if you drown?'

'I'm the lakewalker!' he replied, his voice reverberating into the trees.

Pirouetting towards his brother, Nathan felt the ice beneath him starting to crack. His cheeks turned carmine from the deep hoarfrost.

'Come on,' Lias said. 'Almost there.'

He held out his hand and pulled them both onto the brittle ground as his brother started to laugh manically, taking the occasional stab at his cloudy dragon breath. They walked back into the flat and collapsed in a heap on the goatskin rug.

Saul, who had watched the whole scene from the window, took a swig of Collis Brown cough medicine from a bottle and tutted at the pair in front of him. The two of them rolled about on the sofa, Lias with his goofy 'Uk-uk-uk' laugh, and said: 'Let's go wake Sean up? I swear. Yeah. He'll have more of the good stuff.'

Lias, Nathan and Saul marched up to the main house, listening to the Pogues' 'Streams of Whiskey' on a Bluetooth speaker.

'You know what would be really funny . . .' Nathan said.

'What?' Lias replied.

'If we murdered Sean.'

A wave of devilish joy broke out across Nathan's face, before he let out a howl and bent over double with tears of joy rolling down his flushed cheeks.

'Yeah, man! Our place in the history books,' said Lias. 'Immortality guaranteed. It's not the worst idea I've heard today.'

When they arrived at the house the front door was locked, but they knew where Sean's bedroom was located. Saul gave Nathan a leg-up to the nearest window, which led into his mother Yoko's empty bedroom. Lias watched Nathan's feet vanish over the balcony ledge and then bent over, giving Saul a leg-up, until both had broken into the Lennon residence.

For a few minutes, all was quiet. Lias watched his bandmates creepy-crawl around the house until he heard Sean shouting, before appearing waving his arms behind twenty-foot-high French windows, dressed in a silk kimono.

'You can't do that!' he heard Sean say. 'It's not right to break into my house. That's my mum's bedroom! You can't just come over here at six in the morning begging for more of this and that. This is not cool. AT. ALL.'

☪

The analogue studio at New Paltz was built thirty years previously on an old veal farm, eighty miles from downtown New York on the Shawangunk mountain ridge. It housed an echo chamber inside a disused grain silo that was once the old slaughterhouse's bloodletting tank. It was recommended to their producer Liam as the perfect location in terms of living accommodation, the right kit and, more importantly, being miles away from any opportunity to purchase drugs. The band would all be held captive until the record was completed.

Liam was flown out of London to produce *Songs for Our Mothers*. He'd been informed that Marcata Recording Studios was renowned for making confrontational sounds, and would therefore fit the vision Saul had expressed for the record: a distressed, remote, obtuse, abrasive and enveloping noise. Nathan had spent the previous months obsessing over the drum sounds on Gary Glitter's records, how he'd slow down the drums, play over them, then speed it up again. With this in mind, Liam was instructed to slow down the original take on 'Duce' until it sounded weird and nasty. When it made Saul and Nathan feel 'bad' inside, they knew it was right. It was designed to act as a sonic weapon.

Throughout the *Mothers* sessions, Curly Joe was miserable. Saul had been using heroin heavily in the weeks beforehand and became completely nocturnal. He was withdrawing when he arrived. Adam had also gone cold turkey, as there were no drugs left onsite for either to take. When the shakes and vomiting and nightmares had subsided, Saul emerged from his pit only to dismiss Adam's ideas in the studio, which were often agreed to be excellent by the rest of the group. No matter what happened, he refused to be outshone.

Outside the studio, three feet of snow had fallen. Curly Joe would drink all day with Nathan and try to make music. The new drummer Jack Everett joined in, and Lias would work with Adam on the bones of song ideas. Saul isolated himself from the group, waiting for the right moment to reassert his authority.

For six weeks, Nathan shuffled around the farm wearing a turquoise Puffa jacket the size of a double quilt that looked like it was stolen from a street sleeper, and spent his quiet hours watching LiveLeak videos of people being beheaded. He had borrowed John Lennon's mellotron and used it on one of their emerging tracks, a dirty Krautrock number called 'Whitest Boy on the Beach', inspired by their disastrous Barcelona trip. The instrument used in the session was the same one used by the Beatles on 'Strawberry Fields Forever'. Other tracks emerging in the initial weeks never saw the light of day: 'Come to Me Villa', 'Our Drummer Met Sting and Then He Went Insane' and 'Iain Duncan Smith's Eggs'.

'Whatever we make must be an antidote to all of that awful music being made in London right now,' Nathan would say.

Liam shook his head from behind the desk.

'You've come a long way from when we last did this though,' he added. 'You were all living in a squat back then. Now you're swanning around with New York glitterati. I don't know if you're quite prepared for the different realm . . . Where's Saul anyway? Because we've been here since ten, recording. And it's now almost five. The studio gets shut down in half an hour.'

Slurping on a mug of stewed tea, Lias scribbled a few lines down in his notepad, before chewing on the end of his pen.

'The eternal question,' he said. 'Do you want me to wake him up? He was still on Facebook when the sun came up. I could hear him tapping away.'

'You can try,' Nathan quipped. 'But approach with care. He bites.'

Lias wandered out of the studio and into the snow to wake up Saul. Inside the digs there were only two tiny electric radiators, and it was -6°C outside. An error had been made when the rooms were booked. There were only four futon beds available and six in the band, which meant they had to book shifts to sleep. It was miles from the nearest shop and nobody onsite had a car, and there was only one hob to cook on, which was a BBQ outdoors in the snow. Nathan made a stew each night beneath the stars, stirring the steaming pot in the crisp winter air. For weeks the band lived off cereal and Pop Tarts. In New Paltz, it was so cold they fought like starving dogs over the plug-in radiator.

'Come on, Saul,' Lias shouted as he walked through the door. 'Only thirty minutes left before we have to finish.'

'Fuck off, I'm staying in bed.'

'We're doing "Tinfoil Deathstar". It'll sound like dogshit if you don't get out of bed.'

Saul fell silent and pulled the duvet over his head.

'Don't feel well.'

At 5.23 p.m. Saul charged into the studio, immaculately dressed, and picked up his guitar just as Liam was packing up for the day.

'I'm ready to go now,' he said, before nailing the track in a single take.

'Tinfoil Deathstar' was based on the veteran David Clapson, who had his benefits cut after missing one appointment at the dole office. Police found his body in his flat. He had diabetes and couldn't afford to keep his fridge on to cool his insulin. He was found next to a stack of CVs with £3.44 to his name. The autopsy revealed he had no food in his stomach when he died. Clapson had worked his whole life and only started claiming dole so he could look after his mother.

Set at a south London party, with hipsters sitting around smoking heroin and thinking they have problems, they are then visited by David Clapson's ghost knocking at the window, holding CVs in his hand. The song was a morality tale of sorts, reminiscent of the Ghost of Christmas Yet to Come. When Lias read about the story in London he had been enraged, but the cynical part of his nature had sensed an opportune moment for a decent lyric.

After recording the vocal, over the next few days Lias was gripped by a blazing fever and spent forty-eight hours sweating out flu on an old mattress at the back of the former slaughterhouse. The air drank his body dry, and pools of salty sweat trickled from his forehead. He rocked back and forth relentlessly as he was tormented by rumination, hallucinations and purgatorial scenes from the past. When he finally regained some sense of clarity, he opened his eyes, only to see Saul looming over him, his face awash with frustration. He leaned over Lias and prodded his ribcage through the sheets. Through the crack in the door a malformed bass rhythm drifted into the air. It sounded like the muted death pangs of a drowning elephant.

'Are you going to be joining us today or are you just going to sit on your fucking arse?' Saul shouted. 'This thing's not going to write itself . . .'

☪

The album was unfinished when they returned from America. Strung out on heroin, the prospect of completing the record was too much pressure for Saul. For weeks, he kept absconding in London and only joined Liam and Luke at Trashmouth for 10 per cent of the *Mothers* sessions. Liam drove around Peckham trying to find Saul, hoping to persuade him to lay down the absent guitar lines. He refused to answer any messages on Facebook. Even his father didn't know where he had vanished to. The grip of addiction was tightening, and Saul became incapable of recording his own music, being anywhere on time, feeding himself, even changing his clothes.

Liam finally caught wind of where he was hiding, managed to find the flat and knocked on the door out of desperation.

'What are you doing?' Saul asked, wiping sleep from his eyes at the door. 'What, now? We need to do it now?'

'Yes,' Liam shouted. 'Get in the car.'

Upon its release, *Songs for Our Mothers* was panned.

One review described it as akin to 'snorkelling in a septic tank', another believed it to be 'a quagmire of seasick shanties and zombified country dirges'. *The Times* praised it for its transgressive wit but commented that 'this disappointing album has the feel of an in-joke'. The *Evening Standard* thought it sounded 'like a bad dream'. And those were the favourable ones.

Record Collector said it was 'a mostly meretricious, self-important record with delusions of grandeur', and *DIY* that it was 'an incomprehensible mess barely worth acknowledging'. The reviewer at *Crack Magazine* was nonplussed: 'The whole shtick leaves a foul taste, and *Songs for Our Mothers* is a grim reminder that while Fat White Family might like to think they represent our supposedly doomed generation, their brand of vain nihilism is probably the one thing that's holding the rest of us back.'

Saul joked about fashioning a 'Nazi disco' album in the Laibach vernacular. He genuinely believed that the record had to contain a real sense of nastiness and took pride in the sense of menace it had captured. Throughout its creation the band had treated each other with contempt, and therefore the music sounded utterly contemptuous.

Although practically unsaleable, the record stood as a testament to their lack of morality, or sense of hope. It cemented their position as perennial outsiders and was hard proof they existed in a realm beyond acceptability.

☪

For years Curly Joe's drinking problems had escalated, and so in turn had his mental health issues. He relished being in a rock 'n' roll band, getting drunk and getting laid. But there was alcohol at every venue they visited, and no place to escape it or the drugs. The constant flux became part of everyday life and eventually erupted in his own erratic behaviour. Each day there was needless aggravation, and he was unable to cope. Curly Joe never owned anything, not even his own shoes. The only money he ever had was the per diem Pete doled out to him. He didn't even own a plectrum. When he returned from a US tour, he experienced a mental breakdown; there was scant support for musicians in those circumstances.

He was already on thin ice after a previous no-show supporting the Pogues, a gig which was a dream come true for the band. Spider Stacey had personally invited them, and even though he was wasted on heroin, Saul flew in from New York to play and arrived for the show early. Curly Joe, on the other hand, didn't turn up at all. Consequently there was no bass, so Adam was forced to stand in an hour before stage time. Lias and Nathan were furious. It felt like the ultimate humiliation.

Their bass player was always causing trouble: in his worst moments he was entitled, pig-headed and chauvinistic. The night before he was sacked, the band had been out drinking in Paris, stopping over on a European tour. Manhandled onto the street by bouncers, Curly Joe showed up at the soundcheck in Brussels the next day covered in bruises.

Before the show at the Botanique, he was steaming drunk and stumbled onto the tour bus with two young women, where Lias was sitting reading on the backseat.

'This drinking has to stop,' Lias said. 'If you start at 2 p.m. every day it's only going to end one way.'

Curly Joe let out a large yawn, leaned over to the fridge and pulled out another beer.

'If you crack that beer open now, you're out. Tonight. Mark my words. And it won't be me who does the sacking.'

The two young women looked embarrassed and slowly edged their way out of the door. Curly Joe looked at his bandmate, pulled a lighter from his top pocket and used it to flick off the bottle lid, before downing it all in one go.

'Go fuck yourself, Liazzzz,' he replied.

At that night's show, he played the entire set a semitone out. He was completely kale-eyed throughout, and Saul glowered at him from across the stage. After the show, Saul cornered him, unleashing his full dictatorial ire at Curly Joe after he flicked the end of his cigarette in Saul's face.

'You're a fucking disgrace! A pig of a man. You've got no respect for any of us or the audience. All you give a fuck about is yourself. Yeah, don't fucking look at the floor. We work hard at these songs, then you show up and piss all over them. This isn't just some holiday for Curls!'

Behind Saul, the rest of the band nodded in agreement. In moments such as these they were glad of Saul's taste for confrontation.

Following his dressing down, Curly Joe was so loaded on drink and drugs that he climbed into the driver's cab on the tour bus and attempted to drive it, before crashing it into a fence. The driver had gaffer-taped up the tour bus toilet at 6 a.m. that morning, which had become his custom since the first night of tour when Curly Joe had taken a large shit in it despite being explicitly forbidden from doing so.

After stealing the driver's Ray-Bans, Curly Joe smashed up Saul's laptop and was subsequently fired on the spot by Pete. He then made his way to Germany on foot. It was the last time the band would see or hear from him in years.

As a last-minute replacement, a new bass player was found for the remainder of their tour. Taishi Nagasaka was the Fat Whites' tour support and occasional theremin player. Saul asked him to fill Curly Joe's boots at their next date at a festival in Dijon. With only nine hours to practise, Taishi rehearsed watching their live YouTube videos, and from then on assumed the position on bass.

A Brand-New Kind of Pain

Before their next US tour commenced, Lias and Saul started bickering at Heathrow, another petty argument that erupted in front of staff and early morning drinkers attempting to settle their nerves. Annoyed by his bandmate, Saul had followed Lias around the terminal persistently goading him until he finally snapped. It was another act of self-sabotage: Saul had no desire to get on the flight and it was far easier to cause an event that would scupper their collective chances.

By the time they reached the boarding gate security had been called, and Nathan, who was dressed in drag from their send-off party at the Queen's the night before, had a bruise on the side of his face, smudged mascara and leftover lipstick.

'How much alcohol have you drunk today?' the flight staff asked.

Nathan cracked a smile as he waved his Irish passport and said, 'Two Guinness.'

'Just the one glass of wine,' said Pete.

'A pint and a half of lager,' Adam added.

Taishi shrugged his shoulders and lifted his paper cup, saying, 'Green tea only, officer.'

'I haven't drunk anything at all,' replied Jack the drummer.

Lias nodded along with his bandmates and said, 'One glass of whiskey to settle my nerves.'

There was a pregnant pause as Saul's turn came up.

'Eight Guinness, a couple of tequila shots and a Valium,'

he replied as he unleashed a chain of hiccups. 'I'm totally fine . . .'

The staff took one look at Nathan, who was swaying from side to side, and the errant lead singer and guitarist, who had already been reported to security, and called for the captain. They were then informed the entire party was refused boarding. £4,000 worth of tickets were lost, and Pete had to cancel a gig, rescheduling two others.

Over the next few hours, the band slowly made their way back into the city via public transport with their tails between their legs. All of the band aside from Saul and Nathan, that is, who opted instead to hail a taxi. They were in such a paralytic state that no driver would collect the fare. By the time the rest of the band were back in their beds, they were still marooned at the airport, desperately trying to flag a hackney cab.

In a frantic state, Pete could only find seven seats the next morning within budget, on Air Kuwait, the only dry airline in the world. The band were dressed for court as they boarded the flight the following morning on best behaviour. When they were safely airborne, Nathan opened his bag and pulled out a bottle of gin which had been smuggled onto the flight adorned in gift wrap. The boys discreetly passed it between the seats, taking a warm juniper hit each time the stewardess was out of sight.

It was the band's first full-length American tour, and for the next few weeks they squabbled and scrapped across fifteen states, playing dives and basement venues, leaving a new trail of recrimination and remorse behind them.

☪

'Listen, when the album comes out, everything will be settled,'
Lias said, as he fielded yet another call about the album costs that
had overrun. On top of that, the band asked for additional tour
support for the coming year, a request the band's accountant was
not willing to concede to.

'I know,' he winced from the van's passenger seat as they
drove through San Francisco. 'That cash was important because
we needed to get Saul straight, otherwise he wouldn't play. Yes.
That too. What more do you want me to say?'

Pete tried to grab the phone off him, which he resisted.

'The album will sell. And then we can pay all of this back. It's
just a bridge loan. Until we clear Europe. Tickets are going well
already, that's what the booking agent said . . .'

A wave of trepidation flooded over Lias's face as the account-ant read out the escalating debt that Without Consent Ltd had accrued, and how every show they played for the next year would be used to pay off the deficit. Collectively, the only money they would receive would be from radio play, via their publishing deal. All ticket sales would be used to attack the deepening well of monies owed.

Pete was just relieved they had survived the road trip relatively unscathed. He met up with a crew of his Canadian friends, and after he had cleared the venue and loaded out, Lias came into his hotel room and asked for the van key.

'I need clean clothes. And my toothbrush.'

'Sure,' Pete said. 'Make sure you lock it.'

'Do I look like that kind of tool?'

Pete slurped down a beer and let out a large belch.

'Uh-huh,' he replied.

On the third floor, Adam sprawled out on the bed in his room. Taishi and Lias shared a room together, the corridor outside dec-orated with peeling wallpaper and a freshly laid human turd. Lias was in a catatonic state, a malaise. Depression and quivering anxiety had set in. Emotional breakdowns were a regular occur-rence for him. The road lifestyle was unsustainable, especially for a frontman who performed in such an extremely physical way. The rest of the band had washed their hands of his histrionics and, aside from Adam, were all partying downstairs. Only Taishi attempted to calm him down.

For two hours he collapsed on his bed, sweating and sobbing under the sheets, wailing and spasming in his own personal abyss. Suddenly there was a knock at the door. Taishi opened it, and a young Latino man pushed his face into the room and stared at Lias.

'Hey, you guys,' he said, with a twinkle in his eye. 'How are you doing? Can I come in and party?'

'Sure,' Taishi replied, naively unaware he was a meth head.

The man strutted across to Lias's bed, pulled back the sheets and got into bed with him.

'What the fuck are you doing?' Lias screamed.

'Can I suck your cock if I give you $20?' he replied.

Downstairs, the band partied in the rotten digs until the early hours, content in the knowledge that they would have one extra day to decompress before catching their flights back to London the following night.

The next morning, Pete kicked the covers from his body, scratched at the bleeding bites that mapped his back, and trudged into the shower to revive himself. Mildew fixed the tiles together and a sewage stench radiated from the plughole. He brushed his teeth, took a long shit that made his head pound, and forced himself back into his room, where he ate a few dry crackers and a handful of Nurofen. The rest of the band were still snoring, so he prodded them out of their somnolent state, picked up his keys and suitcase, and put on his baseball cap before heading down to the van.

The spring sunshine was already burning bright on the tarmac when he walked across to the vehicle, which contained the gear for Fat Whites and the support band, LA Drugz. Plus all their clothing and belongings. He reached over to open the van door and found it was unlocked. Pete pressed the handle down, opened it, looked into the back of the van, then closed the door in front of him and let out a small, deflated squeal of pain.

'Yeah, it's all gone,' he whimpered.

'What's all gone?' Adam asked from behind him.

'All the stuff, the gear. Everything.'

'What do you mean?' Saul said. 'Who's taken it?'

'Some fucking tweakers. I don't know. You tell me!'

Not only had the band had all of their equipment stolen, but within that kit was a rare guitar loaned to Saul for the tour by Sean; John Lennon's original 1964 Danelectro Hawk that had recently been valued at $120,000.

'THE HAWK,' Saul cried. 'I fucking *promised* I'd take care of it.'

The three band members sat on the pavement with their heads in their hands.

'Shiiiiiiit, man,' Adam coughed.

Nathan reached his hands up to the sun and started to wail.

'And Sharif Dumani's organ as well! He's gonna go nuts!'

'I gave Lias the keys last night, and I told him . . .' said Pete. 'Now, to me, that van was not broken into. Look at the lock. It's not damaged. He was drunk and didn't lock it properly.'

Lias bounced over to the van waving his arms, with his travelling bag in his hand.

'What? No. I locked it. I SWEAR I DID.'

'Everything is gone,' Saul said, as his face turned pallid.

'Let's not panic,' Pete replied. 'No point in trying to blame someone now. It's happened. It's done. All of you, you need to go and leave me to try to fix this. I don't need to be dealing with your shit. Lias, I'm calling the police now. Then the accountants. You need to message them and tell them to pick up the phone this time. We'll need more cash for the next few days. We need to find somewhere to stay . . .'

'I locked the fucking van,' Lias said.

'We'll have to wear those LA Drugz band T-shirts in the foot-well, at least they left those for us,' Adam laughed. 'Walking advertisements to just say no.'

Saul pulled the T-shirt over his head and wiped the salt from his brow that had accumulated from the Pacific air.

'Ground down to nothing again,' he said. 'Square one.'

For the next few hours the band wandered through the city's streets, soaking up the carnival of acid casualties and parade of Haight-Ashbury dropouts. Everywhere they walked, gangs of people would laugh demonically at the band, until they turned a corner and saw a man sitting on the sidewalk, balling up a piece of his own excrement in his hand and throwing it onto the floor. He then picked it back up again, stood up, started walking, put it down, shouted at the shit, leaned over, scooped it up, and squashed it around in his palm like a satsuma, before screaming at it and throwing it violently onto the floor all over again. The gruesome scatalogical scene playing out in front of them was the perfect metaphor for their current situation. For the first time in months they were desperate to return home, wherever that may be.

☾⋆

The Landlord had been assuring me for some weeks that the solution to my Glastonbury 2015 dilemma – we had two slots on the Sunday, one at 4 a.m. on the Hell Stage, another at 4 p.m. – lay at the other end of a meth pipe. The second show meant a great deal to me; we were on an hour before the Fall. The Landlord had sent a festival stash down to the site with an old friend two weeks prior to its opening to the general public; his mate was building sets down there, so was given the parcel to avoid any run-in with security. When we arrived on the Saturday afternoon, neither of us having slept for two days, we made our way straight up to his tent round the back of the Park Stage.

The Landlord's pal, a reassuringly well-spoken deviant, was more than happy to show me the ropes.

'You trace the flame gently back and forth across the bulb. No, no, like this, let me show you . . .' he gently exhaled, his sallow yet thoughtful eyes pinned to the procedure. 'That's it, that's it, now just suck it all down, that's it.'

A seam of laughter buried deep within the Landlord came unstuck. A miraculous clarity washed through my being. I found myself in possession of a clean slate, a new beginning. I'd been reborn.

'How long will this last?' I instantly demanded, eager to work out the math.

'You'll be good until tonight,' beamed the Landlord, the corners of his mouth pulled back in pseudo-parental glee.

'Look, whatever happens over the remainder of this weekend, we might get separated, our phones will die . . . I need you to be here, on this spot right here, between these tents, the red one and the blue one, the one with tassels and the flagpole . . . with that pipe, every eight hours, on the dot, come hell or high water. Will you promise me that? I need you to promise me . . . my career depends on it . . .'

'Is that Vivienne Westwood?' queried my mother in astonishment at the Park Stage bar. She and her husband were both sporting bright red Fat Whites T-shirts, sipping mojitos. They'd never been to the festival before

and they were on a high, despite finding out that our set the next day clashed with Lionel Richie's.

'I think so, yeah,' I replied, achingly proud that my mum was getting a chance to rub shoulders with the rich and famous.

'Bloody Nora . . .' she cooed under her breath, steadying herself with another sip of her drink.

You could see the little girl in her eyes, the sweetly bewildered child. She was glowing. 'The innocence of this moment will haunt me soon,' I thought to myself. 'I will gaze back upon this moment of maternal tenderness through a glaze of tears from the wreck of my sinister over-indulgences. Mother will have drifted away from me by then. I will have betrayed her and this body she bore and raised. Those eyes will become two thunderbolts of guilt. The love in them will soon lacerate.'

I was glad I invited her. She looked like she was having a ball. But I was also wishing that I hadn't. The rest of the afternoon was an absolute blur.

This was a period in my life when people that I'd previously only ever seen on the telly were suddenly swaggering into my reality on a semi-regular basis. Amidst the multitude marching through Shangri-La on their way down to the Hell Stage that night, my brother and I were accosted by 'uber-producer' Mark Ronson. Mark's aura and his fame didn't correlate. His voice sounded unfinished, like it was stumbling over its shoelaces on the way out of his mouth. I couldn't work out whether he was American or British. His partner, a demure and painfully involved French aristocrat, seemed to be hanging off the wrong arm. Or at least that's what I thought.

I began formulating designs on her instantly. This man may be hugely wealthy and successful, but just wait until she catches a glimpse of my kebab-wheel torso turning in the fresh morning light! Mark and his partner invited me back to their nearby hotel after the gig. They were residing at Babington House for the duration of the festival, an offshore fantasy of effortless comfort and gourmet everything. I told them I was in. My next meth appointment wasn't until sometime just after lunch; I had time to burn.

221

Mark was exactly the kind of music industry insider I'd gone out of my way to ridicule up until quite recently at that point. The problem is, with that kind of carry-on, it's very difficult to stick to your guns once they show you the slightest bit of attention; it goes too well with the cocaine you're forever sniffing. It's even harder when they turn out to be quite pleasant human beings, on the surface at least. Suddenly you find yourself with two sets of friends, one half of which renders you a turncoat with the other, less fortunate half. The part of you that started the antagonistic punk outfit is tired. He deserves a break, you think. You've done your bit. You might as well indulge, be indulged in turn. Nobody's watching, after all. Why shouldn't you and Mark become bosom buddies for a bit? It's not as if you're in Sleaford Mods . . .

We spent what was left of the wee hours quaffing Grey Goose and champagne, elaborating on our superiority over all things living. I kept playing tracks from our forthcoming LP on the stereo, every now and then demanding silence in order to draw the pair's full attention to the lyrical dexterity occurring before their very ears; with a heart full of furious self-love I would mouth out each syllable, lost in a reverie of gormless early morning joy.

I'd re-piped before making my way to the show the next day. I felt fresh as a newly hatched dove. A picture of confidence. Then began the inevitable search for Saul. A search that, through the years, took on the form of a permanent and fairly stable panic attack. He'd been at the festival since Wednesday, squeezing every penny out of his new-found fame. When all was said and done the Guardian would go on to proclaim him the festival's 'best-dressed man'. Disgusting. We were ambling onto the stage a man down as he made his heroic late appearance, a manoeuvre that always left you self-loathingly grateful.

I had the distinct feeling that my life was hurtling towards some kind of crescendo. Ten years had gone past since getting involved with music. For the most part those years had fallen on top of each other like layers of snow, in silence. Nobody paid any notice. But suddenly there we were, sat at a table with the Hip Priest himself.

We ambled backstage post-performance, and the Fall's frontman was casually sat at the end of a bench wearing a white shirt and black leather jacket, hunched over a bottle. This was a moment akin to seeing a famous landmark or monument for the first time at the end of a lengthy expedition. Bathed in the same weary afternoon light as everything else, it seemed almost indecent in its unreality; he was like a weathered clipping from a magazine, like a barely animated postcard.

Then he took a sip of his drink.

Then a drag of his fag.

It actually was Mark E. Smith.

How much time had I spent with that man's voice rattling through my skull? I had to abandon his music at the start of my recording career because I couldn't help but imitate the guy whenever I finally got behind a microphone. Now he was near enough to spit on.

I took a seat with the rest of the crew from south London and my mum. I tried to explain to her the stature of the haggard little guy with the grey skin and the eyes like sunken battleships on the table opposite. She hadn't a clue. We were all muttering under our breath like schoolchildren at the back of class.

'For fuck's sake, at least one of you lot has to get off your arse and say something . . .' the Landlord insisted, excited at the prospect of a little north-south cross-pollination.

'What are you supposed to say to Mark E. Smith? "Uh, uh, hey man, love your band, especially that tune about 'bringing out the obligatory niggers'",' I scoffed back.

The last thing I was going to do was introduce myself. Starstruck doesn't seem the right expression somehow. 'Goblin-struck' would be more appropriate. He looked terrible. His band were all wearing the same pub-rock 101 black leather jackets: they looked heavy, despite sipping champagne out of ridiculous little cardboard cups.

Nathan, a Marvin Gaye man through and through who didn't really give a shit about the Fall, back then at least, saw an opening. Puffed up after playing the biggest show of his life he bounced across to their table and nodded at Mark.

*'Alright Mark, how's it going? My name's Nathan, from Fat Whites,
mind if I have a little cup of your champagne? Sharing is caring, bro . . .'*

Mark invited him to sit down.

'Sure thing, kid,' he drawled, pouring out a measure.

*I felt a mild pang of jealousy. Nathan was bonding with him. 'It's
alright,' I told myself. 'I'll just wait until he's broken the ice and then
ingratiate myself.' God bless Nathan, fearless as he was. A true trailblazer.*

*Mark then proceeded to hurl the contents of the cup he'd just poured
straight into his face.*

*The cowardice at the core of my being burned more fiercely than ever.
He'd needlessly humiliated my little brother in front of everybody, and I
just stood there dazed, wrapped in silence. Nathan stood up, began pacing,
wiping the wine out of his eyes. He kept saying: 'That wasn't right, Mark.
You shouldn't have done that, Mark,' as he marched up and down in a
barely contained rage.*

*'You rotten bastard, what have you done that for?' I heard my mum
exclaim through a fog of astonishment.*

*The rest of the Fall were having a good chuckle about it. Mark could
see that he'd been out of order. He re-engaged Nathan. 'Sit down, I'm
sorry pal, sit down. Here, d'you want a glass of cider? We've got plenty
of cider.'*

*With some trepidation Nathan entered into peace talks with the
garrulous Salfordian.*

*'If I sit back down there, are you just gonna toss that in my face again?
I'm not fucking having it, man, we're all just trying to get on here,' he
warned him.*

*'No, no, sit down, sit down kid, you're alright, I'm sorry, here you go,
have a drink, come on, just messing, just messing like . . .'*

Mark's lips were still wearing a wry little smirk.

*Nathan got hold of the freshly poured vintage and without a second
thought dashed its contents straight into Mark's face and down his trousers. Mark doubled over melodramatically and let out a scrawny yelp as
the whole of his group took to their feet in violent protest. Nathan was
the one wearing the smirk now, and suddenly it was Brixton that was*

pissing itself while Salford spat venom. A slanging match ensued between the two parties. Threats and abuse of all kinds were fired back and forth. My mum was really letting Mark have it by this point. He began looking quietly pleased with the mess he'd inspired. A few of the guys from the Fall looked like they were going to strangle Nathan.

We were on the cusp of a full-blown brawl when the Landlord's voice broke out above the din. 'Oi! Calm down you miserable fuckers, the lot of you just calm fucking down! He threw that first and he got what was coming to him, fair enough, but these boys fucking worship you lot so shut the fuck up and have a drink for fuck's sake!'

His extensive experience dealing with exactly this kind of scenario proved fruitful. Apologies began seeping out, animosity began thawing into a kind of camaraderie, Mark obviously found it all quite amusing. Before too long my stepdad was sat with him enquiring about maybe doing his accounting. Mum maintained a little frostiness, she kept lecturing him on his crappy manners, but we all sat down together for a drink.

'You're not very nice, you, are you Mark?' she kept saying.

'Have any of you lot got any speed?' he asked.

'No, but we've got crystal meth, you'll have to trek up the hill for a hit though, it's frowned upon down here,' replied the Landlord.

Mark passed on that one.

I was perfectly, supremely wired at this point. I was perched atop one of those moments in life that calls into question the validity of everything. At moments such as these it becomes hard not to collapse into total faithlessness. All is just a computer-generated solipsism. These things don't actually happen. The sun was beating down hard.

Mark, who was sat right next to me, began quizzing me about the group. 'Was that you up there just now? All that screaming like, that was top that, sounded like the Seeds or something . . .'

He made no mention of the fact that we'd just performed a song called 'I Am Mark E. Smith', although I later found out from the Landlord that he'd stood and watched the whole thing, arms folded, the beginnings of a grin on his face.

'*Just one thing man, just one reservation . . .*'

He was staring into my eyes, munching his own speed-ravaged features, making an awful gummy sound as he did so.

'*What's that then?*' I said, expecting some pearl of ethereal wisdom from on high, some nugget of total truth only available to those that reach the source.

'*Lose the Jap on bass,*' he replied.

We shuffled from the communal area into our respective backstage wigwams. Saul, who had disappeared briefly straight after our show and had missed the drama, appeared back on the scene. We were excitedly filling him in when some kind of heinous commotion could be heard unfolding in the adjacent tent, Mark E. Smith's tent. He was being told in no uncertain terms by his girlfriend, who also played synth for the group at the time, that he didn't have another pair of trousers to change into. That he'd have to march up on stage with what looked distinctly like a streak of piss running down his thigh brought him much chagrin. You could hear him growling profanities in a semi-drunken stupor: a dribbling, hectoring totem, a cabaret washout gone to seed and taking it all out on this poor woman.

By this point my hopes weren't particularly high for their set. I'd seen them murder an audience before, and I'd also seen them when they were awful enough to walk out on after three tunes. We marched out to the arena and were proven dismally wrong on this count the second they started playing. The Fall were in charge.

Worlds were reimagined where restraint and chaos merge, where the literary and idiotic are force-fed one another. The weird and frightening realm of the Fall at its best: something elusive and beyond categorisation; you are granted only temporary access. You glimpse something beyond the pale, a kingdom of strange, self-multiplying, libidinally outraged doubt. There is nothing total. Nothing you can break down into convenient pieces and carry off elsewhere. A glorious indictment of the banality you swallow everywhere else, it is arguably the least patronising guitar music ever made.

A loathsome autocrat he may be, but a genius also.

Of course, this didn't stop someone from the BBC reporting that he'd taken to the stage after having pissed himself.

As the sun bade its retreat over the horizon, I said my goodbyes and began my wearisome trek back towards where I thought I might find my comrades. My peripheral vision was beginning to cloud, ominousness was setting in. For an hour I rambled amongst the depleted, ravenous, hollow faces. For an hour I found nothing but further exhaustion. I then chanced upon Larry Love, aging singer from fellow Brixton narco-country syndicate Alabama 3. He was also adrift, sat at a bench alone under an

227

awning, chopping up a small mound of white powder. He invited me to join him briefly, to partake.

'I can't hack it,' I said. 'I keep thinking I can hear the Landlord's voice, calling out to me from the crowd, but when I turn around he's nowhere to be seen. I shouldn't have done all that meth man, it's proper fucked my head. I keep hearing voices, they're calling my name, voices coming out of nowhere . . .'

'That's exactly the reason I take it . . .' he responded, in that bottom-of-a-disused-Welsh-mineshaft baritone of his. 'It reminds me of when I used to be famous.'

His drugs had no effect. My nostrils were almost totally defunct by this point. What did manage to find its way up there amounted to nothing. I was doomed. I felt like a condemned man. I had to escape. I told Larry I was going to make it back to my tent, at least try and close my eyes for a while. I hadn't slept in days. I had to get some rest.

'Bad idea,' he warned. 'I'd ride it out here if I were you, without downers you're just going to writhe alone, it'll be horrible.'

It had been a little over twenty-four hours since I had erected my tent on top of the hill behind the Park Stage in a meth blitz and this was the first time I'd seen it since. I unzipped the entrance and looked inside. There was nothing in there save a bottle of Corsodyl. No sleeping bag. No pillow. No drink. No food. No other clothes. Nothing. I lay there for a moment in that glorified plastic bag, listening to the hideous carnival rage on without me. I started writhing. Then I unzipped the entrance flap, sat there and stared out at it all: a light drizzle descended across the scene. I was seizing up with disgust.

At first this feeling was directed outwards, towards the sound of the rabble at play, the giant metal spider coughing fire into the once-innocent night sky, and whatever outfit happened to be having its big moment over at the Park Stage that day. I then felt some weight from within drinking it all down, pulling my conscience away from it all, like it had been snagged on fishing wire cast out from someplace beneath my soul.

My chest filled up with lead, then all the lights began fusing together in my eyes.

228

I was weeping.

The wretched, hollow glory of it all marched through my mind, and at the end of the parade stood my mother in her red T-shirt, eyes beaming with proud joy. I gave into it. I shuddered and sobbed, letting the tears burn across my face. The sadness felt like home.

When the cold eventually got the better of me later that night, I marched over to Strummerville, where at least there was a fire to sit around. Saul had a DJ set there in a couple of hours; I sat desolately staring into the flames waiting for him to show up, being accosted by the odd stranger. When he did finally arrive, he was in great spirits, which I found frankly insulting.

'The miracle of heroin,' he explained.

Don Letts was on the decks, playing a reggae version of Coldplay's 'Yellow'. Me and Saul both agreed that he must in fact hate reggae. There was no other explanation.

I was routinely offered lines of gak and halves of pills, but it was no use. I just kept asking random people if they'd seen the Landlord, a loud guy wearing a pinstripe suit and a flat cap.

Negative on all counts.

By this time Saul had started his set and could be seen coolly shimmying about behind the decks wearing a pair of sunglasses and military fatigues, dropping one unborn hipster anthem after another. My loathing for him in that moment was the only thing keeping me going, the only solid ground left.

When the sun came up, I decided to split for the stone circle. It might well have killed me, but I had to try and find the Landlord. If he was anywhere on the Monday morning, he'd be there. You could hear cranes in the distance dismantling the party infrastructure, the BBC were on their way out, the glamour was going, Lauren Laverne was no longer there. It brought to mind the film Event Horizon *– all those mutilated jawlines strewn out across the hillside in the early morning light. This crew had attempted to reach the stars and wound up in an alternative dimension of pure pain, each one reborn to their own private vision of hell.*

The gusto with which the revellers throw themselves into this Hogar-thian disarray year-in year-out brings a flutter of pride to my heart; only here in the United Kingdom have I seen public life sling itself so low as a matter of course.

I wandered around the human wreckage for an hour, spotted the Landlord a hundred times, heard his voice call to me a hundred more. The true measure of my crisis began asserting itself. I had no means of travel home, my van having left the previous night. I had no money and no phone. I was wandering around a stone circle in Somerset sometime just after dawn on a Monday, asking groups of people I'd never met if they happened to have any crystal meth.

It was then that fortune struck.

Nestled between two of the most obliterated old ketamine casualties I've ever seen, wearing a pair of black Wayfarers and spinning his own demo tapes through his phone on a Bluetooth speaker, sat the uber-producer himself, Mark Ronson.

'You fancy heading back to the Babington after all this?' he asked.

'Yeah, yeah, I reckon so,' I replied. 'Good shout . . .'

Dr Johnson's Got the Feeling

Yards before the sorting office on Wynne Road, on a side street near the centre of Brixton, a series of windowless basement flats had been converted with flimsy partitions under the guise of 'affordable live/work units'. A stable of students lived there, ambitious middle-class creatives, and a handful of drug addicts, including Saul and his girlfriend. The walls were constructed from polystyrene and the sole toilet would occasionally pump out excrement, flooding the place with the entire block's waste. It was a grim contrast to the life Saul had been living in New York, but at least it was a roof over his head.

Down in the bunker the lack of light made all sense of time disappear, and waves of paranoia washed through the unfortunate souls who lived there – even the ones who weren't smoking crack.

One former resident of the basement in its previous long-forgotten history was Austin Osman Spare, the occult artist who created a series of automatic drawings in 1944 in the same room where Saul now lived, recalling the trauma and injury of being 'bombed out' during the Blitz. Spare slept on two chairs under a flea-ridden blanket, surrounded by easels and stray cats. Some described him as having a 'touched look' due to malnutrition, toothlessness and the intensity of his eyes – a description that could easily fit Saul seventy-five years later.

After returning from Glastonbury, Saul experienced a two-day blackout during which rage burned through his blood like powdered glass. He kicked and punched his way through the bunker's walls, and then tried to stab Alex White, a new friend and saxophone player he had spent the previous few days hanging out with. When he eventually regained consciousness in the back of his friend's van days later, he had no recollection of what had happened at all. According to Alex, Saul had been speaking in tongues and baying at imaginary enemies for days and the residents had locked themselves in their rooms to hide from him. He had experienced what he later believed to be a psychotic episode characterised by possession by the spirit of Spare, whose obsessive interest in spiritualism and psychic realms had caused some level of resonance that remained in Wynne Road.

That was Saul's excuse, in any case.

Dark days and nights blended into one. By this point there was no stronger force in his life than heroin and crack. Devoid of possessions, even a guitar, his life on a damp mattress, without daylight, was only manageable as long as the drugs continued to arrive. He was accustomed to *high-quality product* in New York. Arriving back in Brixton deposited him into an ugly reality. Drugs had fundamentally changed who he was as a person – the charming, funny and sensitive part of his nature had dissolved. Whenever he resolved to clean up, he was wary of who that shell of a person was; his reflection filled him with disgust and resentment. Being high was the only way to return to any sense of equilibrium.

Eventually, he was evicted from Wynne Road with his girlfriend. From there, the addicted pair moved into the only place that would tolerate them: a crackhouse in Peckham, in a flat not too far from his father's house.

Before moving into the crackhouse Saul would visit it occasionally to smoke drugs and play chess with a friend who was a Maudsley outpatient. Situated just around the corner in Camberwell, many of the psychiatric hospital's patients lived in the local area; some on the streets, some in sheltered accommodation and others in squats and crackhouses like the one that Saul now made his home. Long afternoons were spent wrapped in a blanket playing chess. His friend knew all of the openings by heart: the Sicilian Defence, the Caro–Kann, the Queen's Gambit and the King's Indian. The household smoked rocks bought from the side streets of Rye Lane, then returned to the flat to resume their narcotic-fuelled games of draughts and backgammon and poker.

After Saul set up camp in the corner of the living room, with its woodchip walls and the shell of a seventies gas fire, a Jamaican prostitute joined the household, and then moved her friends in. Various Yardies and ex-prisoners passed through; it was a place where all sense of morality was left at the door. Underage prostitutes frequented the flat, turning tricks for £5 to pay for their next rock. Saul and his girlfriend would spend most of each day attempting to scrabble £15 together to buy enough crack and heroin to keep the fear at bay. When she returned with the drugs, Saul would snatch them from her, keeping them all for himself and leaving her with nothing. There was an extreme selfishness in his addiction which gave birth to vicious arguments. Both were strung-out, capable only of focusing on one thing: where the next hit was coming from.

It was here that the mental health issues of his youth returned with bloodthirsty vengeance. His diagnosis still stood; it manifested in the form of serious long-term addiction and violent interactions in his day-to-day life.

Beyond the crackhouse, Saul had started to believe that Fat White Family were just side characters in his own story; his thinking became megalomaniacal. He discussed his own genius, of which he was convinced, frequently. In a fresh form of psychosis, for months he believed he could control Lias's mind.

In the weeks following a trip to the notorious suicide spot of Beachy Head, where the band filmed a video for their single, 'Whitest Boy on the Beach', a series of interviews were arranged to promote the record. Saul, as ever, was unreliable. It fell to Lias to speak to journalists. One who did manage to get both in the room at the same time was Miranda Sawyer, who sat down with them for a particularly awkward conversation that would appear in the *Observer*'s music pages.

At the time of the interview, Lias had moved into his aunt's house in Tooting, where he slept in his niece's room on a single bed. The Queen's had closed down, he was homeless and couldn't claim housing benefit. He caught the bus through Balham and arrived at the gastropub with a head full of intelligent lines that he intended to pronounce to the journalist over a glass of Châteauneuf-du-Pape.

Suffering in an advanced stage of starvation, Saul made an unexpected appearance that afternoon in Brixton's Trinity Arms, where he ordered a bowl of pasta that he held to his face and sucked up like water, slurping its contents into his mouth and slopping it over his chin. When their publicist left a £20 note on the table to buy a round of drinks, Saul put one finger on the note then moved it across the table towards himself, staring at Lias as he did so. Infuriated by the micro-aggression, Lias put his own finger on the note and slid it back to himself, away from Saul, then folded it up and put it in his own top pocket. They bristled at each other. When Lias talked, Saul contradicted him. They started to talk over each other. Miranda, sitting between the two, was caught in the crossfire, and recorded the conversation between them.

'Do you like playing live?' she asked.

'I love playing live,' Lias replied into the recorder. 'I think you find things in songs as you perform them, the songs reveal different things as you go along. You experience them in a different way.'

Saul interjected.

'What? It's boring playing live. You play the same songs every night, and I hate it. It's boring.'

They both talked about how being in the band was like a marriage that had reached the point of divorce. Miranda started to feel uncomfortable and asked them what it was they fought about.

Saul: 'Drug . . . habits.'

Lias: 'Saul's drug habits.'

Saul: 'That's about it.'

Lias: 'Saul's belligerence, Saul's aggressiveness. He's not going to argue with the fact that he can be a bit of a bully.'

Saul, starting to laugh: 'Well . . . your sexism.'

Lias, affronted: '*My* sexism? Excuse me!'

Saul: 'I'm serious.'

Lias: 'Let's not go down that road.'

Saul muttered a cutting remark about one of his collaborators, and Lias interrupted to call him out, saying that chance mutations are important.

Saul: 'Bollocks. That's just bollocks.'

Lias: 'Why is it bollocks?'

Saul: 'Because what you're saying is, it's nice when you have someone who can write songs for you, and you can write the words. Which is fine, but call a spade a spade. That's what it is.'

Lias: 'Well, who wrote "Hits Hits Hits"?'

Saul: 'Me.'

Lias: 'Who wrote the melody?'

Saul: 'I don't know.'

Lias: 'I wrote the melody.'

Saul: 'Well, I'm not sure about that.'

Lias: 'On banjo.'

Saul: 'Sorry? Oh yeah, a collaboration. It's a collaboration, yeah, fine.'

Lias: 'You turned it into something that I never could, but I had a skeleton of a song, and then you turned it into something much more interesting.'

Saul: 'Oh whatever, I can't be bothered. I'm going, sorry.'

Saul shrugged his shoulders, grabbed his jacket and slammed the door behind him, walking out into a stream of traffic that lined the streets outside.

'You see what I have to put up with?' Lias said, turning to Miranda. 'I wouldn't wish fronting this band on my sworn enemy.'

☾

It was Friday 13th of November 2015 in Paris, and the band had been booked to play a festival set at La Cigale, with other bands including Bo Ningen and Wolf Alice. Backstage, middlemen from record labels swanned around quaffing wine, and a nervous Lias observed the scene with a furrowed brow, pretending to enjoy the conversations.

Before the show that night, as usual, Saul had refused to sleep or keep the same hours as everyone else. When the bus was waiting outside, Pete would usually knock him up and spend an hour dragging him out of bed. In the run up to Paris, Saul's attitude had become more inflammatory, and by the time he checked into the hotel he had reached a tipping point.

Over the course of the European tour, Saul had started treating everyone around him with contempt, soaking up all available funds with his drug habit, helping himself to every morsel of credit and pulling those around him to pieces as a matter of course. Every now and then he would violently attack people, including band members; a pattern of behaviour that started early

237

on and blossomed into full-blown sociopathy, at which point he started to believe he was the heir to Phil Spector's throne. The encouragement from various friends he surrounded himself with gave him a shield; he was quick to get others to laugh along with him and made Lias feel stupid for pulling him up on his behaviour.

Paris was nothing more than the straw that broke the proverbial camel's back. Saul's banishment had been a long time coming.

By 10.15 p.m. the band were mid-set, playing to a crowd of 1,800 people who danced, moshed and nodded their heads in time. As Taishi started playing the bassline to 'Whitest Boy on the Beach', just down the road, in the 10th Arrondissement, a suicide bomber was about to detonate himself in Seine-Saint-Denis as others fired bullets at passers-by with automatic rifles.

The audience were oblivious to the chaos that was erupting only a few blocks away.

In the audience that night, watching his sons, was a very proud Bashir, who attended the gig with his wife and brother. Bashir supped on a bottle of Coke and shook his head, muttering something about how they'd be better if they sounded more like Cat Stevens.

'The notes are all wrong,' he said. 'Why don't they do something more tuneful that we can all sing along to?'

He beamed at Nathan and Lias for a moment, before noticing that all around him, the audience were checking their phones and shouting into each other's ears. They looked scared. Bashir and his brother shrugged their shoulders, wondering what had changed the atmosphere. Onstage, the band played on, oblivious. After 'Garden of the Numb', Nathan was pulled to one side by venue staff, who spoke urgently to him. He leaned over to Saul, who made an announcement on the microphone, stopping the song halfway through.

'Stop! This guy said we have to stop the concert. There's a terrorist shooting up Paris. I'm not even joking. I suggest you run for your lives . . .'

The house lights went up, and the venue manager announced a call for calm in French. The band put down their instruments and headed to the dressing room, confused about what was happening. They began to hear police sirens. Until they reached the dressing room and checked their phones they weren't aware of what had happened at the Bataclan, that 137 audience members watching another western band, Eagles of Death Metal, had been massacred that evening.

As the Cigale venue evacuated, Bashir was overwhelmed with panic. In his own country of Algeria in the 1990s, 200,000 people were murdered, raped and kidnapped during the Black Decade of the civil war with Islamic fundamentalists. He had a very strong sense of who was behind the incident at the Bataclan. He rushed up to the dressing room to protect his sons and take them out of the venue.

Saul had commanded the rest of the band to stay in the dressing room, informing them, 'It's the safest place we can be. We shouldn't go outside.'

But it turned out he didn't say it because he genuinely cared for the safety of the band, he said it because he had arranged to meet his dealer. He was waiting for the man.

'Just another ten minutes,' Saul kept saying, before a quiet, cautious man wearing sunglasses turned up, and he vanished into the night with him as the rest of the band shook their heads in disbelief.

When Nathan was finally released from the venue he walked through streets awash with police to an apartment where a party was happening, a place where he knew Saul would be. In the corner of the room his bandmate was crouched over, snorting lines from an album cover, surrounded by willowy-limbed models and Parisian bourgeoisie who hung off his every word. He beckoned to Nathan and made a space for him on the sofa, before leaning into his ear and beginning to speak. It was a conversation Saul would have no recollection of at all, even five years later.

For a moment Nathan was convinced he was joking about purging the lead singer, that it was the drugs talking, before he realised that what Saul mumbled was said in all seriousness. It was normally Lias and Nathan who plotted to remove other band members, almost on a daily basis.

'I can't believe you would even say that,' he replied, devastated by Saul's inebriated proclamation. 'It was me and Lias before you came along. We've always been together . . . but this is a problem now. What is wrong with you?'

'Why are you upset?'

'You aren't the centre of the universe. Telling people you write everything and we are nothing without you . . .'

This time, Saul had pushed it too far. In that moment, Nathan knew it was over for him, whoever 'that Saul' was.

'I know I'm being sentimental. But when I see you now, it's the end of someone I have loved, and I don't know if you are ever going to return.'

Nathan stood up, brushed tobacco off his trousers, zipped up his tracksuit top and pulled his beret to one side.

'Goodnight, Saul,' he said. 'I guess this is it for a while.'

Confused by Nathan's reaction, Saul made a gesture for him to come back, but he had already fled down the stairwell, out of the building and onto the street outside.

After hours of wandering, Nathan had eventually returned at sunrise to find his bandmate. Saul was restless after spending the small hours doing speedballs, and rang Pete first thing in the morning to ask where the van was and when he was getting collected. Pete spent half an hour attempting to get permission from the police to enter Paris and parked the van outside Saul's girlfriend's address to collect him. Nathan waited with Saul until Pete showed up at 7 a.m.

Pete wound the window down and leant out.

'Let's go, Saul. Get in the van.'

Saul shook his head and folded his arms.

'I can't go without her.'

'No,' Pete said. 'You *won't* go without her.'

'Fine, I won't go without her then.'

'Fine, then we're going without you,' Pete said, and checked the time on his watch. 'I've got your best interests at heart.'

'What are my "best interests", Pete?'

'To take your band as far as it can possibly go.'

'How are those my best interests?' Saul replied, in the most insolent fashion he could muster, one that Malcom McDowell's sneering Mick Travis would have been proud of.

An hour later, when Lias woke up on the backseat of the van as it hurtled through the outskirts of Paris, he let out a sea lion yawn and made a confused expression.

'Where's Saul?' he said.

'He didn't make it,' Pete replied.

A heavy silence filled the van, before Lias made an executive decision.

'Well that's it then, that's a sackable offence, isn't it?'

'I guess so, yes. He's calling now on the phone, ten times already. Nathan, can you answer that and put it on speaker phone?'

Nathan picked up the phone and held it towards Pete as he waited at a red traffic light.

'I'm not coming back for you, Saul. No. Not for the next gig, or any other gig. It's over.'

In that moment, it was easier to ask Pete to fire Saul, rather than Lias tell him in person. He was given a particularly weak, politician-style termination of employment, through the adjacent channel of the tour manager, rather than face-to-face. A fact that left Saul distraught. His bandmates' refusal to even discuss the previous night's events was devastating. Saul felt as though he at least deserved to be told in person. They'd passed the buck to Pete, and

Saul's view of his bandmates, who he had considered his brothers, was now in tatters. At the very lowest point of his addiction, they had abandoned him when he needed them the most.

Nathan leaned through the van seats towards Lias, Taishi, Adam and Jack.

'It's for his own fucking good. He's trying to destroy us. Look at Lias, he's scared to death. Saul refuses to play, keeps walking offstage, is being a total cunt to all of us and I've had enough. The biggest problem is that he goes round telling everyone that he wrote all the songs and never gives us any credit. I feel squashed out of existence . . .'

'You and Adam do just as much gear as him,' Lias said. 'But you always turn up and play. How much longer do we put up with him behaving like such a prick?'

The pine air freshener swung from side to side, batting Adam's face as he stared out of the window, with his shoulders scrunched up from the stress.

'What a fucked-up night,' he said.

'Yeah, too right,' Nathan muttered. 'It wasn't just the madness outside . . . two acts of violence at once. Maybe the universe was trying to tell us something.'

☪

The following morning, comments appeared online saying the suicide bombers hit upon the wrong gig and should have done the Fat Whites instead. This wasn't likely to be the worst feedback they would have that day, as the band waited for Saul's retaliation, which they knew would be forthcoming when he sobered up.

Two days later, sensing the upset his departure had created with his bandmates, the gravity of the situation began to dawn on Saul, who apologised publicly for his behaviour on Facebook.

Pete always believed that the difference between Saul being in the band or not was them being the real deal or not the real deal. Saul could conduct them flawlessly. Nobody could lead them onstage like he could. The pressure and trepidation he imposed put Lias in a clinical mindset, spurred him to do it right. Saul ruled through his presence, bringing cohesion and suspense. He knew this, and that's how he held the band to ransom. It was his ultimate bargaining tool. The bottom line was that they all needed each other, more than they would ever admit. Lias was the performer and lyricist that Saul could never be, and Nathan's innate outsider status curbed the other two whenever they chased fame or took the rock 'n' roll myth too seriously. Nathan was the core emotional force that held the whole project together.

After the night at the Bataclan, Nathan was the only person to call Saul in Paris. He was desperately sad about the situation.

'Man, you need to sort your shit out,' he said.

Saul was emotional and confessed to feeling extreme guilt about the tour and the night at the Bataclan.

'No one else has called me . . . I'm hurt,' he said.

'Guess why?' Nathan replied. 'Because they are scared. You've got to sort this out. I've tried to get you some cash to live on. I don't want you to starve. I know you're in a bad way. But they didn't want to do that. I just want you to know that I tried . . .'

'I appreciate that, Nathan. But it goes to show how little they really care about me.'

'It's not that, though . . .'

'What else is it?'

'You've been calling Pete off the hook and then you sent him that email saying you were going to kill his cat.'

'Come on, man. I didn't mean it. I was taking the piss. You know that.'

'Don't think you can go round saying that shit and get away with it.'

243

'I was joking.'

'No, you fucking weren't Saul. It's just not on. You've gotta get a grip of this, bro.'

'I don't know what I'm going to do,' he said as the line started to crackle. 'Feels like I'm drifting further and further into the sea.'

When he finally arrived back in London, Saul moved into the only place that would have him – his friend Leo's house. Leo lived there with his mother, who agreed to let Saul stay in the same bedroom as his friend for a while, sleeping on his floor. The windows were plastered with sellotaped copies of the *Sun* to block out all daylight, and the two young men spent each waking hour smoking heroin, until Leo developed a full-blown psychosis and was sectioned. Then, Saul was truly alone.

Hearing of his distress, Pete had contacted Sean across the Atlantic to tell him about Saul's predicament and asked him to intervene. The help came in the form of drug treatment. Sean arranged for Saul to be flown to San Francisco, where he attended a detox clinic and spent the next few weeks working his way through a jar of Fentanyl, staring at himself in the mirror, trying on different outfits and eating three doughnuts at a time. It was a drug so powerful it superseded that of the purest heroin. In comparison, Fentanyl felt like bathing in God's tears.

For days the clinic's staff were flummoxed at their recent arrival, believing Saul to be an unusual case; he was deemed untreatable. 'This guy needs completely reprogramming,' they said.

☪

Back in London, the band looked for a replacement for Saul on their upcoming *Mothers* tour. They were booked to play at the Bussey Building in Peckham, and approached Dale Barclay to come down from Glasgow to play with them. The former frontman of the Amazing Snakeheads was already part of the family after travelling with them on the NME Tour. He had stonemason's hands, a rockabilly sensibility, and violent, extreme vocals that Alex Harvey would be proud of. Lias adored him.

The Amazing Snakeheads had recently disbanded after a ridiculous argument on a clifftop, and Dale had walked away from the precipice of fame with his integrity intact. He was perhaps the only person in the country who could fill Saul's boots. Armed with a Telecaster and Fender amp, he turned up for rehearsals at Dropout Studios just a day after Lias made the call.

Initially, Dale believed Pete was from management or from the label, and when Pete suggested *exactly* how he play 'Special Ape', he shot him a thousand-yard stare and spat, 'Alright, mate. I know how to play.'

Dale had a serious problem with being told what to do, or how to play his guitar, particularly by the brusque Pete, whose machismo rubbed him up the wrong way. After rehearsal, they sauntered down Rye Lane towards the Bussey's courtyard gates, and it became clear that Dale had a problem. There had been crossed wires. As they passed through the alleyway, Dale grabbed Pete by the throat and pushed him up against the wall.

'Listen,' he seethed, in his guttural Glaswegian accent. 'See, you pay me the fucking money and you pay me for this RIGHT NOW. I don't give a fuck who you think you are, but I am doing this for Lias, and Lias alone. Not for you. And not for any fucking label.'

Pete held his hands up, then started laughing as he coughed.

'You laugh again, and I'll fucking kill you in this alleyway,' Dale said. 'Don't think that I won't.'

'Dale, you've got me all wrong. I don't think you understand this . . .'

Pete brushed himself down and bent over to catch his breath.

'I'll pay you after the gig. Whatever this is, whatever you think I am, I am with the band. Not with anyone else.'

Silence is Easy

Sometimes a butterfly flaps its wings in a Travelodge in Nottingham and a tree falls in Los Angeles, then several years later, in Sheffield, a whole forest is set ablaze. Such was the nature of my doom-laden dalliance with Hollywood.

I met Eva through a former publisher who used to work at Domino, whose job consisted of working out where the next trend in pop culture was going to emerge. A by-product of that was he knew who was who, all the scene kids, all the hangers-on, all the people with linked-in families and all the people who exerted any kind of influence over the ever-expanding universe of social media. After a show one night we were up in my 'suite', probably hacking away at a baking soda/Pro Plus melange and guzzling Guinness as per usual, when he mentioned a girl he had become infatuated with online. He showed me a message he'd written to a petite, ivory-limbed sybarite, a lengthy and pathetically adoring plea for attention to which she coolly responded 'No'. Intriguing. I decided, more in a bid at winding this industry goon up than anything else, to message her myself. I wrote on her public wall: 'So when is this going to happen then?' We agreed to meet in Berlin after striking up a rapport online.

She was only nineteen years old, eight years my junior. She had a butter-wouldn't-melt innocence about her that juxtaposed with the erotic ferocity of her online persona. An impossibly exacting stratagem. Her thing was fashion. My thing was hitting every kind of drug imaginable at that point in time, including heroin, although I smoked that in secret. She ended up joining us on the road. We had a splitter van with a double bed at the back situated over the compartment that held all the *gear. I remember hurtling down the Autobahn high on whatever was to hand, getting head on the sly while the rest of the junkies nodded out to whatever dirge they were obsessed with at the time in the passenger compartment. The quagmire of tedium and hopelessness of the bad old days was behind me; it seemed only natural to me that I should be dating this LA girl from a famous Hollywood family. Everything, for once in my life, was as it should be.*

Growing up in Cookstown, I used to collect video tapes. More precisely I used to buy blank ones, then when the TV guide came out each Monday I'd circle the five films I wanted to harvest from the week, eventually amassing a collection of around two hundred titles. Each night in bed I watched a movie on my own. Two of my favourites were written by Tarantino; these pictures were far more than entertainment. They constituted a cultural map invaluable to the small-town loner stranded way beyond the outer rim of any kind of cultivated, metropolitan existence. They were a lifeline to another realm in a way that music on its own never quite could be: wrought black humour, spectacular acts of erotically charged violence and luridly unconventional protagonists. For my generation they were absolutely crucial. Going out with Eva was a way of reaching through to the other side of that screen.

Given my ballooning addiction to downers of every kind, however, my libido was shrivelling up, much to her chagrin. Save for our respective inclinations towards tourism, albeit up and down opposing ends of the social ladder, there wasn't a great deal of common ground between us, although symbolically we complemented each other perfectly.

This limp pantomime dribbled on and on. I would take enough drugs to render Eva interesting to me and she would receive just enough attention to warrant the occasional manic outburst. With her in LA or New York or Paris or wherever, as is custom for people of her ilk – members of the dreaded jet set – there was ample remove to keep the game up, to sustain the illusion of a 'deep and meaningful' connection.

The band were scheduled to start our third US tour on the west coast, in San Diego. I had a month off before the first show and decided it was finally time. Hollywood was probably ready to embrace me by now;

the foundations had been laid, not with any particular vigour, but laid nonetheless. I made my way out there to stay with her, with my little brother in tow, freshly heartbroken having been dumped by his long-term girlfriend. I think eventually she tired of coming home from work to find Nathan half passed out on smack in her lounge, eight or nine days gone by without even bothering to wash. Fair enough. Eva very kindly agreed to put him up as well, which meant he had a place to try and kick his habit.

I had visited LA once before with the group, but without the necessary 'ins', just on the fly for one show and then a couple of days off. It's not the kind of place you bend your head around in a hurry. Its insidiousness, set to slow release. In a way there is no LA, it's just a micro-verse of utterly atomised sociopaths co-existing within the same one hundred square mile radius.

I'd never encountered hypocrisy on this scale; to be walked around one of five mansions attributable to the family, shown a babbling brook that runs through the middle of one of their Turbine Hall-sized lounges and then hear people bemoan the rise of Trump and the neglect of our natural environment by the powers that be left me giddy with the kind of excitement you can only feel when life truly exceeds your expectations. A rare phenomenon to be sure. Perhaps the only thing comparable to the feeling of spiritual desolation I encountered there would be the sensation brought on by strolling through one of our deserted peak-pandemic city-scapes, that profound and luxuriant emptiness. They were way ahead out there in Hollywood.

The month or so I spent living up in the Canyon burned every bit of fat off the illusion of our relationship. I couldn't feign interest in such proximity, and I ended up getting completely hooked on downers. The drug dealers in LA, the one my manager had hooked me up with anyway, provided you with a menu. You could get anything except smack or crack off this guy, and I mean anything. I'm pretty sure mescaline was on the list. I didn't get stuck into anything like that though, I kept it pedestrian: some Vicodin, some Xanax, some Valium, some cocaine and plenty of kush. Those pills really creep up on you. Before I knew it, I was popping a *mixture of the stuff from breakfast onwards, steeped in luxury. Eva wasn't into that stuff. Yet. She was in a constant state of disappointment at my libido or lack thereof. I was unconcerned and growing more indifferent by the day. The problem was that if you couldn't drive you were basically held hostage up in those hills. When our tour finally came around and it was time for me to get in the people carrier that was going to drive me the whole of the way across the US and then up to Canada, I'd seen enough. I'd made up my mind to let this affair peter out into nothing from a distance, the usual method of choice for disengagement then . . .*

☪

For four days Saul writhed on a hospital bed on the Baja Peninsula in Mexico. After taking a sample dose to check his reaction, he was given eight capsules of ibogaine over a thirty-six-hour period in a last-ditch attempt to cure him of his addiction. Taken from the bark of the iboga shrub, the extract was dried and powdered before being administered to the centre's opiate addicts, but its original use was in rituals: it formed part of coming-of-age ceremonies in Cameroonian tribal communities, opening communication with spirits and ancestors. For Saul, who had already spent weeks in a detox clinic, it was an attempt to rid himself of an addiction that had driven all of those closest to him away. He was standing at the precipice, and at that point ibogaine was the only solution. Desperate times demanded desperate measures.

After retching for three hours Saul was paralysed by the drug, yet, unlike most who take it and experience vivid hallucinations and dream sequences, all Saul could see was a bright blue square in front of his eyes. It pulsated for the next three days, but as Saul was unable to speak, he could not express the irritating banality of his vision. When he finally came round, he spent a day sitting outside in a bamboo chair. He was unable to walk or even hold a drink. Staff spoon-fed him bowls of ground beef molé and rice as teardrops rolled down his face. He could no longer remember who he was, how he got there, or what he was doing in this strange place. It was a complete cerebral annihilation that would, in theory, completely rewire the brain and dodge the inevitable bullet of a ninety-day withdrawal.

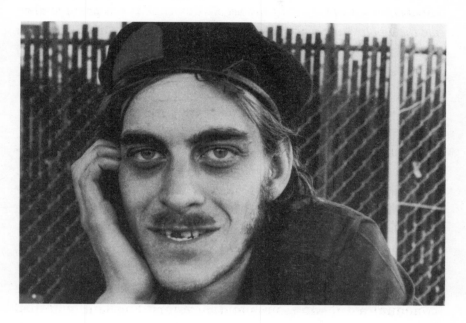

Throughout the initial days at the clinic, he had experienced a withdrawal that felt like maggots were feasting on his bones. By the time the ibogaine treatment was over, it was the lack of sleep that tormented him the most. In the garden of cacti and desert flowers that surrounded him, Saul stared across at the other patients with childlike curiosity. Having paid considerable amounts of money to be there, they were drooling in foetal positions on picnic blankets in the grass.

Some in the clinic had experienced seizures, others soiled the bed and rolled in their faeces, blissfully unaware. They were mostly American patients having travelled through the border at Tijuana to undergo this therapy.

Before Mexico, Saul was a shell. When he first arrived at the clinic and was sent into the reception waiting room, the same men that were now slavering in the desert garden immediately started laughing at Saul, who was wearing a raincoat and German military hat. 'Hey! It's Inspector Gadget!' they said. Later on, he learned they were all ex-marines, GIs or Gulf War veterans who had returned home and then became addicts. With no money, phone or laptop, Saul was helpless, but after they had detoxed and re-entered relative normality, they offered to drive him back to California.

Still unsure of his own name, and reeling from the industrial-level psychedelics in his system, Saul climbed into their van. Within seconds of him closing the door, one of the meatheads who resembled Fred Durst poked his head through the passenger seat and shouted, 'Right, guys. Let's go and score!' They were all still hallucinating.

The arid Californian landscape rushed past the window as they travelled through San Diego. After they had scored drugs, which they didn't share with him, the van hurtled towards the desert at sunset, where they pulled over in a layby, cooked up a fix and started shooting up into their armpits. Getting high was the last thing on Saul's shattered brain, and he physically recoiled at the sight of the drug. He found a piece of paper in his pocket that contained a series of instructions telling him where to go afterwards and a telephone number to call, and rolled it between his fingers. He was dumped in a motel car park on Santa Monica Boulevard three hours later, where he walked into the room and collapsed in a confused heap.

The following day, he opened the curtains to see a giant inflatable Santa Claus bouncing from the roof opposite. He could not work out if he was hallucinating or if it was really Christmas in Los Angeles. He sat static for an hour, trying to pluck up the courage to walk to the nearest phone box. His brain felt as though it had imploded. He was frightened, scared and hungry. After another few hours of rocking backwards and forwards on the edge of his bed, he finally hobbled out across the road and picked up the phone box receiver. He called the number and attempted to talk down the line. 'I am in trouble. Please can you help me? I don't know who I am anymore.'

The person who he called was the latest Fat Whites manager, who replied to him through a mobile line that crackled and popped.

'Stay there for four hours. I will send someone to pick you up.'

It was Christmas Day, and all Saul had eaten was a small packet of oat biscuits that were left by the coffee-making machine in his room. He waited. And just like his manager said, someone turned up; a bald man burning branches of sage in the doorway.

'I have come to purify you,' he said. 'This room is full of bad spirits. That's why you have been suffering.'

Saul rolled his clothes up into his bag and held out his arms to the man.

'Stand still,' the man said. 'You are now with the Spirit World People.'

The man started chanting as beads of sweat poured from his scalp.

'We are going to Las Vegas, get in the car outside. I'll buy you a McDonald's on the way.'

For the next month, Saul lived in a rehabilitation centre where he attempted to reconfigure himself. Each day, he was purified by gong baths, reiki, drum circles, Qigong and floatation tanks. He was even given toad poison to revive his brain. Occasionally he wandered out onto Tropicana Avenue, past the sign towards a place called Paradise, walking on towards casinos and miles of slot machines that flashed and exploded with light. In his emails to Ruth, he told her how much he loathed the place, that it was 'like the apocalypse with fake tits'.

The facility he was staying at was owned by DJs who were popular in the nineties and now played vocoder EDM at Vegas nightclubs. Saul was forced to go to the gym every day, where they pummelled him with appalling house music over the soundsystem. He had left one kind of nightmare for another. After weekly psychotherapy sessions, he tried to cry but could never quite manage it. Sin City was a long way in the wilderness from any of his friends. Loneliness was the price of sobriety.

☪

For the first time since the age of twelve, Saul was clean and sober. He was driven from the rehab centre and dropped off in Palm Springs at the holiday home of the Fat Whites' latest manager. The driver, a dedicated Aquarian who worked at the clinic, swallowed a microdot on the way as they headed south towards Joshua Tree in the warm afternoon sun.

Lias and his girlfriend travelled down from Laurel Canyon with the manager, in a car with the top down. As they passed a road sign to Bonnie Bell, their manager, a white man, leaned back with his dreadlocks blowing in the wind and said, 'So I brought a couple of grams of coke. Is that cool?'

The Saul that greeted them was vastly different to the one they had left behind in Paris. His skin was a deep golden brown, the spots and scabs had vanished. For once he was the picture of health, with a calm, contented glow that had all been burned out of him in the previous years.

'I'm really pleased to see you,' he said. 'If that doesn't sound too mortifying. How's Hollywood?'

'Yeah man, not too bad,' Lias replied. 'I can't walk anywhere, we're marooned without public transport. We went to see Ray Robinson though. Apparently, he'd destroyed every place that had been rented for him. But he's still loaded from his grunge glory days. So now he's living in this bland little bungalow in a forgotten corner of town to keep him out of trouble.'

'Is he still on the gear?' Saul asked.

'Without a doubt,' Lias replied. 'He was off his face. He had this table, right. In his kitchen. And in the middle was a broken chocolate cake with a dozen used syringes stuck into it.'

'Nice.'

Lias started to laugh. 'He kept showing me these weird videos on his phone, just random shots of the street and the sky spinning around too quickly to set your eyes down on anything. He's going through two phones a week, he keeps hurling them into the air, set to record. Fucking mental. Nathan says he's obsessed by the kaleidoscopic streetscapes they capture but oblivious to the fact that he's smashing up thousands of dollars' worth of phones on a regular basis . . .'

'I got a message asking if I'd write with him in London. He's coming over later this year. He's like a baby though, isn't he? That's what everyone says. A child trapped in a man's body.'

'Hope you're asking good money for that, Saul.'

'They said I'll get paid to turn up and jam in the studio, £300 a day, as long I can hook him up with a dealer.'

Lias started to smile and shook his head.

'You're fucking joking?' he said. 'Why should you bother doing that? He's a total wreck. Far worse than any of us by a long stretch.'

'Really?'

Lias nodded before slurping the dregs of a beer can into his mouth.

'He's a thousand miles further down the road than you are. Ray's far more extreme and that's saying something.'

The two bandmates took a walk together and wandered up a steep bank behind the manager's house, towards a hillside overlooking the town to watch the sunset.

'Seriously though, man. I'm glad you're feeling better. It's not been the same without you.'

'Look,' Saul replied. 'I'm sorry about all of it. I've had a lot of time to think. And I'm not proud. It got out of control. I was out of my fucking head.'

For a few minutes they stood in silence, looking out across the volcanic landscape, before Saul suggested they meditate. Lias was a little perturbed at the idea from his previously cynical bandmate.

'Sure, man. Let's give it a go,' he replied.

For ten seconds they sat in the lotus position in silence, the sound broken only by the distant hum of a freeway, until both exploded in laughter at the absurdity of the situation. Their cackles echoed in waves along the cliff face.

'I'm glad to have you back,' Lias said. 'You look healthier than I've ever seen. Putting us all to shame.'

They wandered back to the manager's residence, with an interior straight out of a 1950s mob movie, then ate a Caesar salad in the cactus garden. A crate of cold beer was left on the side, which they all tucked into. After cracking open the cans, their manager lined up four lines of cocaine as they sat on padded recliners by the poolside.

Saul paused for a moment as he leaned over, then picked up the rolled $20 note and snorted a line from the mirror.

'I never said I was giving up everything,' he said.

☪

With the band reunited they embarked on another UK tour, to culminate in a performance at the Coronet Theatre at Elephant and Castle. In Southampton, the night before the final date, a friend came down from London with a small bag of heroin in her pocket. By the time the tour bus reached the outer edges of London the next day, heading towards the venue, Saul was smoking crack. No matter how hard he tried to free himself of addiction, whenever he neared London, the Pavlovian response kicked in. The city equalled drugs. There was no escaping it, unless he fled to another country.

As Pete drove towards the South Circular that morning, Adam was struggling to breathe. He was experiencing the residual symptoms of a pneumonia that had hospitalised him before the tour. His absence left the band one guitarist down for that night's show at the Coronet. On the way there, Pete called Dale, who flew down from Glasgow as a favour to replace Adam. It would turn out to be Dale's last performance with the band.

The faded, formerly decadent interior of the Coronet was colder than a mortuary when they arrived for soundcheck. It was about to be demolished, like the rest of Elephant and Castle. The once-thriving community and their council homes had been displaced, the proud blocks of social housing flattened for international investors and empty deposit-box flats gaining interest each year.

Lias took to the stage wearing a Lee Brilleaux-inspired white suit bought by his girlfriend in Paris. He had recently been photographed in the city wearing a single Maison Margiela earring, posing with a group of fashionistas leaning up against a solid silver Jaguar in a white turtleneck. His 'modelling' sparked a tirade of mirth from his bandmates who thought he looked abominable. By the time he reached the Coronet, the suit had been transformed by shady stains of cigarette ash, red wine, cum, piss and skidmarks.

That night his vocals were fraught; he appeared distant as he balanced on the barrier and held his hands to the ceiling. Beforehand, the band had been smoking rocks in the dressing room, knocked back with shots of tequila. Against doctor's orders, even Adam had returned from the dead, like Lazarus loaded with antibiotics and black tar heroin. He made a last-minute appearance onstage, as ever the personification of dedication.

☪

When they reached Europe, two months later, the situation had deteriorated further. It was clear that Saul's extreme drug treatment had not had the desired long-term effect. Although he remained relatively clean for the first few months, it was

257

impossible to live in London or be in the Fat Whites and not be exposed to temptation. Drugs were far too easy to score, and even if he lacked the money to buy them there would always be someone willing to dole them out for free.

On their journey to play in Copenhagen as part of a European mini-tour, the atmosphere in the van was thick with dread. Lias spent the entire journey with his headphones on, as he often did, blocking out the voices around him. The band had played a few lacklustre shows, and perhaps unwisely chose to stop in Hamburg for a night on their way to Denmark. An argument over a Facebook comment had escalated between him and Saul, a fight that came raging from nowhere. Tensions rose in the van as Lias deflected Saul's interrogations and stared out the window in silence.

Outside, the rush hour traffic of Hamburg crept slowly along the motorway as Pete watched the bickering bandmates in the rear-view mirror. It had already been a stressful day. He had received news that his houseboat had sunk at Camden Lock, and all of his belongings were now under three feet of stagnant water. As Lias's temper frayed and Saul, tuning his guitar, continued to goad him, Pete held his breath and counted to ten. Like clockwork, as predicted, when Lias retaliated the lights behind Saul's eyes went out and his temper ignited. Saul leapt up and started battering the guitar against the driver's seat, before attacking Lias with its broken neck. The van rocked as Lias recoiled and Nathan, once again, was forced to intervene and put Saul back in his place. Pete was shouting from the front seat to no avail. Taishi pulled his hat over his face and vanished into his shell.

As the van crossed two motorway lanes towards the junction, Saul almost took the driver's head off. He was visibly shaken by the furore. When the van arrived at the hotel Lias jumped out and declared he was quitting the band, and, if not that, he would at least take the train to the next gigs. He was sick and tired of the drama. Saul fled into the Reeperbahn's dark alleyways as soon as he was unleashed. Lias and Pete retired to a smoky bar with a tray of stiff drinks, attempting to comprehend what had just occurred.

'We can't have him attacking you like that,' Pete said. 'You know what, I have an idea . . .'

'A bodyguard?' Lias laughed.

'No. A taser.'

There was a pause. Then Lias swirled the Martini around in its glass before necking the contents in one go.

'Where would we get one?'

'The local gun shop. I looked it up.'

Within minutes they had both grabbed their jackets and were back out on the street, following Pete's directions on his phone. Much to their disappointment, the shop refused to sell them a taser, but they did leave with a pocket of high-grade mace pepper gel, two cans for ten euros.

They met up with Nathan at a nearby café where he was sat in the window waiting for them, folding a serviette into an origami bird.

'So how do we use this?' Lias asked Pete, as he fondled the can of SABRE Red, holding it close to the light to read its instructions.

'The guy said it's ideal to use in a contained space, like a tour van. So instead of spray that would contaminate all of us, the gel burns the skin, but doesn't affect anyone else. If Saul attacks you again, I'll launch this in his face. If this stuff gets on his eyes or cheeks it will drop him, I have no doubt about that.'

'Can I have a go with it?' Nathan asked.

'No, Nathan, you cannot *have a go* with it,' Pete replied.

He looked into Pete's eyes and broke a smile, flashing his disarmingly brilliant white teeth.

'Where did all this come from?' Nathan said. 'I don't understand it, Lias. Look at us now, we've bought a Saul defence weapon. Don't know why you can't just knock him out, like me . . . It always works. He's a pussy really. You shouldn't let him wind you up like that.'

Lias shrugged and rolled the mace across the table.

'I'm definitely getting the train tomorrow,' he sighed. 'It's gone too far.'

☪

When Lias stepped out onto the stage in Australia at Splendour in the Grass, he held up his fist in absent-minded defiance to the tent's welcoming audience. There was a peculiar intensity to the day already. Jetlag had fogged their collective brains into thinking it was 4 a.m. when, in reality, it was the middle of the afternoon.

Beforehand, Pete had warned them about the Gold Coast, and the conservative attitudes of its local residents.

'I'm not fucking about here; they will arrest you over any indiscretion. Don't be fooled by your British opinions of laidback Aussies. It's not the case at all.'

The band half-listened in the dressing room as Pete recalled his previous tours with various grisly bands, but they were more concerned about the stinginess of the rider: a handful of drinks tokens equating to one half pint of lager per ticket. Having travelled thousands of miles to play, they were greeted not with a crate of beer and bottles of spirits, but a gift hamper of organic hair conditioner, tea tree oil moisturiser and scented candles.

The cauldron of disdain boiled for a minute or two before Nathan's voice grew louder and he started to lose control, becoming belligerent with the staff who were trying to resolve the situation.

'Where's the tequila?' he moaned. 'I can't go on without it.'

'I've asked them to sort it out,' Pete snapped. 'I have to check the monitors and backline and we only have ten minutes until stagetime. Stop fucking whining.'

Fat White Family were the inaugural act on the inaugural festival stage programmed by the Go-Betweens. Aidan, an old friend of Pete's from Melbourne, was Saul's replacement. When they landed in Sydney, the band had had two hours' sleep, and three hours rehearsing with their new guitarist before catching a flight to the Gold Coast.

There was an ominous charge in the dressing room as Lias extinguished his cigarette and walked out towards the stage. The music faded and the lights dimmed as the band picked up their instruments. The audience was receptive and things seemed to be going well. Then, in the dying seconds of 'Heaven on Earth', Lias dropped his trousers, stumbled across to the drum kit, bent over, then stuck two fingers up his arsehole in full view of the tent.

After the show, his old friend Shannon, who Lias hadn't seen since Berlin, appeared backstage. When their other friend Rory walked into the dressing room, pupils like pinpricks, he gave the Saoudis a huge smile, only to reveal that all of his teeth had fallen out. After several years on narcotics, the pair had descended into the deep realms of physical dilapidation.

The reunion went well that day, until Shannon passed out on the dressing room steps, rolling and groaning in public view, where he was spotted by security. They took one look at him and decided he was a junkie, and that he – and by association the whole band too – had to be immediately ejected.

The fuming band were thrown out of the site and headed back to Sydney to play another show, before travelling to Melbourne where they eventually landed in a decent hotel.

After seeing a particularly vicious blog post about the event, Lias vented his rage on Facebook from his laptop. He tapped away at a rant for ten minutes, then pressed post.

Most of this article consists of sensationalist nonsense and ill-informed half-truths. Nobody's nose was broken, there was no violence or blood, we didn't trash and raid anybody's dressing room and police were involved only because a dear friend of ours was found, heaven forbid at a music festival, inebriated to the point of being asleep in our backstage room. There was nudity, but what of it? If you take your clothes off at the Serpentine, it's 'performance art', if you do it onstage you're a perverse, gimmicky shock-merchant. This kind of shit should be as bog-standard a part of the vocabulary of alternative music as big muff guitar pedals and Sonic Youth T-shirts by now. The idea of anyone finding it offensive is offensive; these people wish to inhabit the dullest of all possible worlds. I only bother to write this because outside our experience at Splendour, playing in Australia for the first time has been fucking phenomenal, the venues, the crowds, the way we have been treated along the way, it's been as good a time as one can have doing this job. Australian fans are the only ones out there that give Glaswegians a run for their money, and for that we salute you!

Lias was pleased with his response. He leaned back onto freshly laundered sheets, letting a deep breath out as he awaited the chorus of likes. He gazed across the city from the fourteenth floor of the hotel, before checking in again on his post. There was a threatening reply from a muscle-bound bogan sporting a lumberjack shirt and a leathery tan.

Red blotches rose through Lias's neck for a minute or two, and then he replied.

If you want to say that to my face, then here's my address and hotel room.

An hour later reception called his room.

'Mr Saoudi? Hey, it's Claudia downstairs. We have a gentleman here who wants to speak to you. Shall I send him up? What does he look like? Oh, he's about six foot five. Large build. Lumberjack shirt. He appears to be quite angry about something.'

Lias winced. As with all potentially violent situations, his response was to duck for cover and call Pete, who was quickly dispatched.

Many months later, after he had fled England to live on a beach and listen to eden ahbez through a Bluetooth speaker for three months, Lias checked his Facebook inbox from a beach hut in Koh Rong Samloem in Cambodia. Out of sheer boredom he began leafing through the messages sent from unverified 'non-friend' accounts, desperately in search of a little titillation. What he discovered instead was a series of messages from Byron Bay Local Court informing him that the Royal Constabulary of New South Wales were charging him with obscene exposure and summoning him to appear in court. Having read a sensationalist account of the gig online, they decided to press charges of public indecency. He spent long hours each day in the island's solitary internet café poring over the details of the case with two Australian lawyers on video chat, lawyers that would cost him the remaining half of his music publishing advance. They explained that there hadn't been any complaints from the public, it was just that New South Wales was a particularly conservative state, and that the powers that be in that jurisdiction despised the festival and were constantly looking for ways to get it shut down or moved elsewhere. Lias was their current scapegoat.

The core of his defence consisted mainly of the fact that it was common knowledge that he regularly performed naked, long before the festival organisers had booked him for the show. That and an in-depth exploration of nudity in art. Lias prepared a statement in his notebook that drew on every last line of performance art theory he could remember from the Slade: that the stage was a space for performance art, not just rock, pop and punk. What he was attempting, he wrote, was something akin to *live sculpture*. He wanted to be an Egon Schiele painting brought to life. Thankfully, his old professor from the Slade assisted him, and replied to his panicked email by supporting his defence with an essay on the importance of the naked human form where the history of art is concerned. By combining it with every celebrity endorsement he could harness, along with his completely clean criminal record, the Australian lawyers managed to get the charges dropped.

However, unbeknownst to the local constabulary, Australia wasn't the first time Lias had been arrested for lewd behaviour in front of an audience. Playing in Sicily, at Ypsigrock Festival the year before, in front of a thousand people in the ruins of a medieval castle, he stripped himself naked and writhed onstage.

As they launched into the closing song of their set, Adam, who was wearing a sombrero that night, knelt down in front of the amps, released a wave of feedback from his amplifier, and then proceeded to fellate Lias in the grand style of Mick Ronson and David Bowie.

Lias had been prowling the stage bollock naked after four songs. Faced with the prospect of kissing the lead singer's fag, fear and beer breath or putting his sweaty genitals in his mouth,

Adam opted for the lesser of the two evils. Lias was delighted, as were the rapturous audience, who erupted into a wave of cheers and screams as the bouncers attempted to crawl over the crowd barrier and halt the gig. As the scene straight from the days of Sodom and Gomorrah played out in front of him, Pete was grabbed by the collar by the local constabulary. He refused to shut the show down, so the lighting man did it instead, which, in turn, inadvertently switched on all the house lights so that every person in the audience that night could see their absurd affections in the floodlights.

Pete was immediately arrested, and when Lias came off the stage, he was also handcuffed and thrown into the back of the van where Pete was sitting waiting for him.

'Why is this fair?' Lias said. 'He sucked me off! How come Adam didn't get arrested?'

Pete shook his head and started to laugh.

'Because we always get nicked, that's why.'

'I'm exhausted. Totally done in. My lungs hurt.'

'They've arrested me for obstruction of justice, because I wouldn't shut the show down.'

'Oh, great, well that's just what we need.'

'And to think I was smuggling Saul's heroin under my ball sack on Ryanair just this morning . . . and now I'm getting arrested for this?'

The doors to the van opened, and the two men were led inside the police station and placed in a cell for the night. Pete frantically tried to contact their booking agent, who wasn't picking up his phone, so they were left for hours to sweat it out.

When they were finally released later that night, after several hours of questioning and a divine intervention from the festival's lawyer, the pair arrived at the hotel where the rest of the band were still partying.

They walked into Saul's room where music was playing to be greeted by him and Adam, both junked out of their minds. Saul was naked aside from tinfoil wrapped around his putz, a pair of white sport socks, a cowboy hat, and a holster filled with crushed Coca-Cola cans around his waist. In his hand was a belt, which was tied around Adam's neck; he was on all fours in his tight underpants, drooling onto the bed.

'What's been keeping you, gentlemen?' quipped Saul, as he reclined suggestively onto the mattress.

A few weeks after arriving back in England, the band played a show at Ramsgate Music Hall. It was Adam's birthday that night, and in the van on the way through Kent, Saul gave him a present; *The R. Crumb Handbook* in hardback. Together they pored over the pages, laughing at Crumb's images of hallucinogenic meltdowns, big-boned women, priapic longing and autobiographical confessions. Saul had turned up for the ride bare-chested and sporting a pair of long military shorts with braces, jackboots, a neckerchief and a Totenkopf-badged hat. It was a high-camp androgynous Hitler Youth look that he had been perfecting for days. Adam and Saul tucked into the birthday crack from earlier on, and both were blasted by the time they arrived at the venue for soundcheck.

The uncle of the band's administrative helper, Gemma, had died recently and her family couldn't afford a proper funeral service. The band had stepped in to help her and played a fund-raising show at the Windmill which paid for his burial. Adding to their long list of charitable gigs, it was not out of character for them, yet Saul didn't bother to turn up to that show at all. The good deed was left to the rest of the band to perform.

When Gemma's father appeared at the Ramsgate show, he thanked the band personally for all they had done. 'I really appreciate you guys. That show you did for my brother, I will never forget that.'

Saul smiled at him, took another blast of his crack pipe and replied: 'Yeah. I mean, you've just got to do what you can really, you know? Every little bit helps.'

Prior to the show Lias had called up an eighteen-year-old superfan, Angus Knight, to come and stand in reserve for Saul, who had said he wasn't going to be playing some of the upcoming shows, opting instead to stay with friends on the coast for rest and recuperation, which by that point was frequently a necessity. He was, once again, back in the depths of serious addiction and was attempting to find a new way of existing in the band, one that worked for everyone and wouldn't put him under unnecessary pressure. He had enough self-awareness about his current state to at least attempt to safeguard his bandmates. Saul knew he was unreliable, knew that he couldn't force himself to play when he was in the abyss and was therefore open to some level of compromise.

Angus was one of numerous replacement Sauls now scattered across the globe. There was a Sydney Saul, a Melbourne Saul, a West Coast Saul and a European Saul. Angus was drafted to play the Holland show, and potentially Ramsgate that night, which was still up in the air. Saul was coming along, though no one could predict how it would pan out. It was an internship of sorts, but Angus already knew every B-side and rarities even the band had forgotten existed. Out of laziness, the band employed him so that they didn't have to go through rehearsals with another player. It was easier to get Angus in than spend a whole day practising with someone else.

Three songs into the set, Saul had an issue with his guitar pedal, gesticulated at Pete on the mixing desk, then slammed his instrument down on the stage and stormed off. Lias leaned forward towards his microphone, searching in the audience, and said, 'Angus, you're up!'

Angus climbed up onto the stage, picked up Saul's guitar and started playing. The audience of five hundred fans started clapping. They thought Angus was just a random selection from the crowd. The band continued to play until midway through 'Touch the Leather', when the mains electricity cut out and the entire venue was plunged into darkness.

'What the fuck's going on?' Nathan shouted. He ran offstage and into the dressing room where the venue's power supply was kept, only to see Saul standing next to the fusebox, smiling sweetly. After seeing the audience's reaction to Angus, he had decided to sabotage the gig.

'He's fucking terrible!' Saul shouted. 'What did you expect? Have you lost your minds? I'm doing you a favour.'

The venue staff quickly fixed the power supply, and within minutes the gig was resumed.

Angus started playing again, but began doing something else, too. He would strike down on the strings then curl up his lip, extend his arm and then stick his finger up at the crowd, holding that pose. Adam shook his head out of embarrassment at the bottom-dollar histrionics in front of him. Performing like that was not acceptable. But the show had to continue, and the band needed to get paid.

As the audience started to cheer and screamed for an encore, Adam took off his guitar, gently leaned it against the amplifier and walked off the stage fuming with quiet anger, straight into the bar next door. He was joined by the rest of the band who were all avoiding Saul, who by that point was tearing up and down the street outside, scowling in the wind. All of the crack had been smoked. The epic crash of paranoia, exhaustion and aggression started to kick in.

When he stepped outside for a cigarette Adam spoke to a friend about what had just occurred. His friend sympathised, saying how annoying it must be to see Saul cherry-picking shows like that.

'Yeah,' Adam replied. 'It's obviously better with him there, so it's a bit of a let-down when he's not around.'

He huddled over his lighter and inhaled the smoke before Saul interrupted. He had been behind them the whole time, listening in to the conversation.

'What was that?' he said. 'Have you got something to say to me?'

Adam turned around and shrugged his shoulders.

'Man, I was just saying . . .'

Saul turned his back and started to walk away. Then he stopped, turned back, and taunted Adam under his breath.

'Just FUCK OFF!' Adam said. He had been pushed too far that night.

'What are you gonna do?' Saul sneered. 'Hit me?'

Without warning, the usually placid Adam, who had tolerated all manner of bullying over the years, exploded in flames and cracked Saul so hard in the face that he recoiled in shock. It was a blow that had been brewing for the best part of a decade.

In retaliation Saul picked up a glass tankard, ready to batter him from behind as Adam turned his back and quickstepped over the road, but he spotted Saul's reflection in a window of a florist's shop, his hand raised, the vessel held aloft behind him. Saul hurled the tankard at the back of Adam's skull, missed, and the jug flew straight through the florist's window, its shards landing in a display of fresh roses.

When Lias walked outside he trampled over the mess, shaking his head. The police had been called and were taking statements.

'What the fuck did you do that for?' he said. 'We'll have to pay for that.'

That night's events truly represented a step too far; it was the *final, final* straw. From that moment on Saul was excommunicated. He was no longer a member of the Fat White Family, both in name and in law.

Lost in the Garden of the Numb

In a place beyond patience, where curiosity goes to die quietly and alone, we would stake a final claim. Madness had begun to catch up with us in every way; Nathan's mind had begun to foam. A power vacuum had arisen at the centre of the group; I was acutely aware of having bitten off more than I could chew. The streets of Attercliffe were a place where Yorkshiremen came to bury their aspirations: right there opposite the studio, in City Sauna. The whores had made themselves a little shack attached to the side of the brothel so they could cop a fag without fully submitting themselves to the eternal northern drizzle, their bulging hides shrouded in the skin of artificial leopards, their ravaged features puffed and sated beneath absurd shocks of platinum-blonde hair; this now was our frontline, and this tender school of harlotry – known locally as the 'theatre of dreams' – our only neighbour.

We had come to Sheffield to replenish our connection with reality, to try and reform our group without our lead songwriter on a barren crop of industrial wasteland. We had marvelled at the cheap rent and the price of a pint here, and we had decided to make our bed in the North, a homecoming of sorts, although neither Nathan nor myself grew up here; all the same, everybody sounded just like Mother.

I couldn't work out exactly what it was I was trying to hold onto anymore, all I knew was that the fun and games were over. I had walked out onto the stage to finish our last tour at Brixton Academy six months previously with a head full of speed, MDMA, acid, mushrooms, heroin and liquor. We'd reached the summit, finally. I asked my mum in the backstage bar if she was proud of me; she said she was. Then I spent ten hours locked away in a room at the back of the afterparty huffing crack and rattling tinfoil, avoiding human life like the plague. When I re-emerged briefly and took a seat with my dear old friend and literary degenerate Lewis Parker, all he had to say was, 'Well that's the end of that then, what are you going to do now?' I cursed him from the bitterest depths of my heart, then returned to the security of my crack hovel. There is nothing out there but doubt, lies, cynicism, jealousy, out-and-out hatred and obsession. Eyes on the pipe, always on the pipe. When I finally managed to clear the bunker the next day it was to have sex with an almost stranger at the Britannia Hotel in Camden. In attempting to make a success of myself, I had all but ruined my life. It was around then that the exodus to Sheffield and the idea of erecting some kind of geographical defence against our drug problems took form. In London we were a danger unto ourselves and unto others. Things, evidently, had got a little out of hand. I collected my publishing advance and disappeared to Asia for three months to claw back some sanity. Upon my return it was to a little red-brick terrace in Sheffield where I made my way.

☪

Nathan tossed and turned in his bed, sweating through a fever dream set in the Barrio Bravo of Mexico City. Santa Muerte shrines of skulls and votive candles were tucked away down shrouded alleyways; incense and fresh gardenias hung in the air. He passed a line of young men with defeated expressions, those who had seen too much violence, and further down the road, at Plaza Garibaldi, he heard the faint sound of a mariachi band. 'Don't look in their eyes,' he told his girlfriend, but like Lot's wife she stared straight into the darkness of their sockets.

Nathan was back in the forbidden street, walking through the nest of market stalls with his Korean-American girlfriend who, no matter how much he tried to persuade her otherwise, would not stop using her iPhone in public, flashing it about to take photos or use social media as they bounced past the shops. After a week of smoking crack in the Love Hotel she moved them to another posada and here they had landed, in Tepito, the most dangerous area of Mexico City, where gangsters, dealers, hoodlums and crooks peered out from each doorway. They ate crunchy taco soup with coriander leaves from a stall and drank pulque through a straw, before catching a taxi to their hotel room on a busy crossroad junction. After seven drivers rejected their journey on Uber, one eventually turned up, shaking his head at the gringos.

'What the fuck are you guys doing staying here?' he laughed. 'Nobody goes in there because nobody comes here. Even the police don't come here. Are you crazy, man?'

The driver shook his head and lit a cigarette from his top pocket before driving off into the dusk's dimming light. Mangy cats wandered across the pavement in front of tenement blocks draped with clean washing: white vests, lace pants and shirts fluttered in the warm Mexican breeze. A full moon rose above the rooftops, lipstick was applied in pocket mirrors beneath streetlamps, the impudent rage of youth erupting in the clear night sky. Torn boxing posters hung from the walls, and the stench of urine filtered from drains as they walked through the hotel reception doors.

'We've got to get out of here,' Nathan said to his girlfriend. 'I've got a bad feeling about this.'

All night he sat up writing new keyboard lines, listening to the grunts and moans of prostitution in the adjacent rooms. He composed a melody in an Arabic scale as the sun pushed its rich morning rays through the blinds. Together they packed their bags and wandered out into the foyer where an old man sat on a stool selling newspapers; his face had the pallor of wax slowly melting with age. They stood and waited for a taxi. It was 10 a.m. And then it happened. A quick flash from behind them. A boy in a hood with a handgun. He pulled it out and Nathan held his Yamaha keyboard up. His girlfriend was chattering on her phone.

'Put it down,' Nathan said, 'put your fucking phone down.' The gun was under Nathan's chin, pointing up from his chest. The boy cocked the pistol and Nathan turned grey with fear, emptying his pockets and saying, 'Have it! Por favor! Por favor! Por favor!' When his girlfriend continued to clutch her phone, the boy pointed the gun at her and Nathan looked up to the sky, thinking this might be their last breath. She was visibly shaking as she finally handed over her purse and jewellery to the boy with a pierced brow and trouble in his eyes, then the keyboard caught his attention. In that brief moment it was as if Nathan was protected and Sandalphon had intervened, waving his wings over the pavement of Penitenciaria.

Beneath his duvet, Nathan could feel and taste and see each second of the event, as if his mind were replaying it in slow motion, again and again and again. It was the third time he had experienced the dream that week. As he emerged from the narcoleptic haze, the colours and sounds of Mexico City were still fresh in his mind. Within seconds the intensity had vanished and the slow, grey sepia shade of Sheffield in November had started to permeate his vision. In his bedroom the air was cold enough to reveal plumes of morning breath, pools of condensation gathered in the rotting window frames of this small terraced house, the new residence of the Saoudi brothers and the place where Fat White Family would attempt their resurrection, free of heroin and distraction throughout the grim Yorkshire winter.

☪

With Saul legally extricated from the group, Nathan and Lias found themselves in breach of their record contract. The label had signed Lias and Saul as a songwriting pair, and with Saul removed from the situation they were forced to renegotiate their record deal based on what they now thought the group was worth. The band had been signed at the peak of their hype, when it looked like they might just become *the next big thing*. Since then, the group had embarked upon a public descent into heroin and crack addiction, had recorded a deliberately unsaleable second album and then fired its chief melodist and musical director. There had been a revolving cast of twenty-six members of the band already, with only Lias, Nathan and Adam remaining. That the label boss put anything on the table at all was testament to a sympathetic streak in his character. It was a hopeless sum and could not support the band to record their next album, or even cover the rent for a cheap terraced house in the North. Upon hearing of the band's predicament, Laurence Bell, the head of Domino Records, stepped into the ring and met the Saoudis for lunch, where they informed him about their Sheffield scheme.

Domino had chased the band around for years, and already held their publishing rights. The night of Brixton Academy, Laurence was in the audience with a group of his friends. He was unequivocal that Fat White Family would be his next signing.

'We've got ideas' Lias said. 'But there's no way the band can function in our current state. We're going to build a smack fortress in Sheffield and drag everyone up there to clean up.'

Around the same time, Saul reappeared from the shadows. He had moved back to New York and was living with Sean Lennon in the East Village. Despite how sour things had become between him and Lias, Saul asked him to become the lyricist on his record with his new band, Insecure Men. What they worked on together in the studio symbolised the beginning of the pair making peace. Convening in Sean's studio with Nathan on keyboards and Ben Romans-Hopcraft on guitar, drums and bass, they recorded the album over a two-week period, except this time, Lias was not on the microphone and instead sat in a separate room with a pile of notes and reference material, slipping handwritten notes into the recording booth, including what would become the song he was most proud of writing, 'Ulster'. They had finally found a way to work with each other that didn't cause the stress, pain or commotion that was part and parcel of life in Fat White Family. Insecure Men represented a new beginning for Saul, one where the pressure to perform live was removed, and he could concentrate on working in the studio, the only place that truly felt like home.

☪

Throughout their first bleak Yorkshire winter, as Saul created his album of end-of-the-pier exotica in New York, Lias and Nathan spent their days in Sheffield huffing cartloads of ketamine to pass the time. Sitting in front of the large TV that Bashir had donated, and toasting his feet against the gas fire, Lias scrolled through his phone one evening and read out an article Lou Reed had written about Kanye West's album *Yeezus*, proclaiming its era-defining greatness. 'It's a dare. It's braggadocio . . . "I Am a God" – I mean, with a song title like that, he's just *begging* people to attack him . . .'

Initially, Lias baulked at the thought of Kanye having any artistic merit due to his celebrity, but he plugged speakers into his laptop and played it at full volume for Nathan, who was sprawled out staring at patterns on the Artex ceiling.

'I accept the King of New York's argument,' he said, as the chemical slowly drained through the back of his eyes, leaving a blank but devoted expression as the opening bars of 'Guilt Trip' permeated the room. Blu-tacked above his head, a vinyl copy of the Commodores' *Nightshift* was stuck to the woodchip walls. Beneath his feet, a mountain of discarded Red Stripe tins had started to spill from the wastepaper bin, and on the table in front of him, an ashtray overflowed from the previous week's roll-ups and the occasional hard knot of chewing gum wrapped in a rolling paper.

Lias reached over once more for an unsold, shrink-wrapped vinyl edition of *Mothers* and caught a glimpse of his own contorted reflection. *Finally . . . I'm putting the music to good use*, Lias thought, as he racked out several gleaming caterpillars of horse tranquiliser. He snorted a line and walked towards the bay window, his legs buckling slightly, then scratched his balls for an extended minute, opened a gap in the net curtains, and peered out onto the street outside, tracing his finger up the grimy glass before wiping a gap to expose the daylight. Nathan lay behind him, his legs propped up against the sofa, arms splayed out across the patterned brown carpet. The sky outside had long forgotten how to bear sunshine and hung over the two narcotic refugees like a coffin lid, sealing them in until spring broke.

For months, the band had dressed almost exclusively in their own merchandise, which was stacked in cardboard boxes around the house. It was a permanent reminder of their lack of commercial viability, although they designed a money-making scheme one night to sell Fat White T-shirts worn by the band, complete with original odours, on eBay. Nathan was overjoyed when he made a profit of £1,000, using the proceeds to buy studio kit, an ounce of weed and a delivery of high-quality ketamine.

A stand-up piano was acquired for the house, and over the next year, the youngest Saoudi brother would tear himself away from it only to smoke skunk, roast joints of stolen meat and occasionally masturbate. With Saul now absent, a power vacuum emerged. Nathan seized the opportunity and stepped up in his place. Now in a desperate lull, Lias was grateful for his brother's energy and commitment as his own will to create floundered. Nathan flourished in Yorkshire, and he fully embraced the hi-fi realm; listening to jazz, nu-soul and eighties disco, while developing a peculiar fixation with 'Blue (Armed with Love)', the Wham! B-side to 'Club Tropicana'.

As much as he liked the idea of DIY as a concept, Nathan took umbrage with the lo-fi sound. For him, lo-fi was a bourgeois choice.

'Middle-class people make it to sound like they are penniless. They are emulating the sound of people who can't afford studios. Working-class people want music to sound polished and elegant,' he would say on his daily exposition on the piano stool. 'Cheap noise doesn't happen in hip hop or grime. It is slick and futuristic. That's the record I want to make.'

It was ketamine theorising. Nathan began inventing maxims from his meshugas that only ever made sense to him, although he was always certain that his dictates were solid rules for progression. In his mind, the riddles made perfect sense. He was a soothsayer of some description, although when ketamine was mixed with hydroponically grown skunk, his dead-end limericks became a type of madness, one that eventually made his brain capitulate.

☾

As the band began to write songs in Sheffield, subsisting on next to nothing, Saul had once again landed on his feet, and true to form came up smelling of roses. He was now living in the

Marais with his delectable new Parisian girlfriend, next door to Vanessa Paradis. Relatively clean, and now released from the relentless drama of life on the road with his equally dysfunctional bandmates, he had settled into an existence of calm. Insecure Men's album, which featured artwork rendered in the style of Kim Jong-un's WPK propaganda, had received excellent reviews, far better than any of his former band, and a new confidence had washed through him. He could finally stand on his own two feet as a producer, arranger and songwriter, without being forced out on the road. This, in turn, created less pressure. Even so, Saul still didn't have access to a bank account, barely owned a phone for longer than a week, was not to be trusted with a passport under any circumstances and habitually turned up to his own shows without a guitar.

When Lias flew out on a press trip for a side project he had been working on, he rendezvoused with his former bandmate and spent an hour bemoaning the Sisyphean misery of the post-Saul Fat Whites landscape. After six months of living in Steel City's Sharrow district, all they had to show for the effort was a vast collection of low-rent charity shop furniture and an even more fragmentary and oblique amalgam of song parts; a backing track here, a chorus line there. Song ideas came thick and fast, but cohesion was thin on the ground.

'I've started to feel like Garth in *Wayne's World*, when Wayne fucks off,' he laughed.

'How are things in Yorkshire anyway? You made it out to be some sort of utopia when we last spoke.'

'The northern weather is fucking awful. And it's as if all the attractive women fuck off to London or Manchester at the first opportunity . . . or at least Leeds. I'm stuck in the drought.'

'How *awful* for you,' Saul replied sardonically.

The two men sat quietly at a window table in the Chair de Poule bar watching a car mechanic wrestle with a blown-out tyre in the garage opposite. Lias lit up a Gauloise with a Fat White

Family lighter he had kept from their tour, and pulled the glass of red wine towards him, letting the intense flavour roll down the back of his throat.

Saul smiled and rubbed sleep from the corner of his eye.

'What do you reckon then?' Lias said, as his face made the resigned expression of a man being led to the gallows. 'Nathan's coming up with loads of good shit, but his *eccentricities* are getting out of hand. Adam can spend an hour fucking around with his guitar pedal before he makes a note. We could replicate the Insecure Men sessions in Sheffield. This time smack-free, of course. Surely it's not beyond reach?'

☪

As if by synchronicity, when Fat White Family were invited to join John Cale's band and perform 'Heroin' onstage at Liverpool Sound City (where half the audience unwittingly mistook Lias for a besuited Richard Ashcroft in shades), once again the drug had wormed its way into the 'smack fortress'. Sheffield was supposed to offer an escape, yet even before Saul arrived, Adam was on a methadone script. He had been warned about using in the house; nevertheless, he started picking up again in a moment of weakness.

One afternoon he walked the band's resident saxophone player to the train station and embarked on a long conversation about drugs as they drifted through the streets. Adam waved goodbye to Alex as he boarded the train to Euston. On his way out of the station, he clocked a homeless man begging for change down a side alley. He crouched down next to him and asked if he knew where he could buy heroin. Within a matter of minutes, the homeless man had scored a bag for the pair of them, and they spent the rest of the day smoking it behind a bush in the city centre. When night started to close in, the man offered Adam a spot to sleep. It took an awkward lie to wriggle himself from the situation. Later that night Adam waited outside the house in the hope he could sneak into his room without Lias seeing the state he was in, with a small bag of brown powder tucked inside his wallet.

What began as a one-off quickly transformed into a habit when Adam was stopped on the street by a man asking him if he wanted to buy weed. In the man's top pocket was a piece of gauze which Adam immediately spotted as material for a crack pipe. He declined the man's offer and smiled back at him.

'No, I don't want weed,' he said. 'But I don't suppose you could sell me some crack?'

The man nodded back at him and gestured towards a house just up the road, a few doors along from the Fat White Family's.

From that moment on, Adam knew exactly where to score heroin and crack, at whatever time he needed it. And although he attempted to be disciplined, using only on weekends or whenever Lias was away, he quickly obtained a habit, using daily just to keep himself 'straight', whatever that might mean.

When Adam moved up from Hackney, he packed up his entire life and possessions and travelled to Sheffield at the band's behest. Once there, he began locking himself away in his room, where he had built a small studio and was earnestly recording demos that the band never managed to bring to fruition. Adam lived nocturnally, often leaving the house at three in the morning, always asking guiltily as he went out to score at that ungodly hour if Lias or Nathan needed anything from the shop.

Even through the haze of skunk and ketamine, it was obvious to Lias what was going on and he decided to bring the shoddy gavel down. Adam was given his marching orders a day after the John Cale show. It was the bitterest chord in their relationship and one from which they never completely recovered. Adam didn't expect his brother-in-arms to behave in such a merciless manner, and he was bemused at the way he had been treated.

Although aware of his serious drug problem, he begged for a few extra days to sort out his script. Lias, despite being an occasional piper himself, refused to let him return.

'I know I've fucked up, but can we handle this?' he asked. 'I just need to arrange it with the doctor. Then I'll go back to London.'

'No,' Lias snapped. 'You were warned a multitude of times, man. We can't have you back in the house. I'm sorry. Heroin just fucks everything up.'

Adam was evicted for using heroin but couldn't leave Sheffield until his methadone script was transferred back to London, a problem that would take a week to resolve. He was barred from entering the house again, even to collect his bags, so for the next few days he slept in the Attercliffe studio, knowing he would be kicked out as soon as the band returned. Nathan, who had had his own battle with heroin addiction over the years, became strangely militant and told Adam he had to give up everything, including methadone, which was impossible for him at the time as he was more likely to use without it. A month withdrawing from methadone in the house was not an easy task.

On the bank holiday weekend, with no funds for accommodation, Adam spent the last of his cash on a tent, which he pitched in the graveyard at the end of the road. In an act of cruel injustice, as he slept in his tent in Sheffield, zipped up and shivering without even a sleeping bag, Saul lay in his comfortable bed just up the road with his bedroom door locked and secretly smoked heroin before falling asleep listening to the gentle sound of Nether Edge's trees rustling in the cold October wind.

Although he professed to be clean, unlike Adam, Saul was much better at hiding it. So it was hard for him to agree to Adam's eviction, knowing he was just as guilty of the same transgression. In Adam's world there were no days, just moments to score and snapshots to use and hours to gouch before scoring again. The cycle repeated, ad infinitum.

Previously, when Adam was met by an intervention after returning from a gig in Vienna, it was pot-kettle-black in extremis. Nathan had paid Adam £5 to smuggle a wrap of heroin up his back passage on the plane out there, remarking, 'Where there's problems, there's profit!' Lias and Pete had dabbled with heroin on tour, but they didn't consider their usage to be problematic, merely 'touristic', therefore they took the moral high ground. They followed Adam into his hovel from the airport taxi, then sat him down and informed him if he didn't go to rehab the next day, his position in the band was in question. Adam shook his head as he sucked on a pipe, saying: 'This is unbelievable.'

'The thing is, the rehab clinic is in LA,' Pete said. 'So I'm going to drive you to Heathrow, and you're going to clean up before the next tour kicks in.'

'Why can't I do it here?'

'Because it's safer to get you out of the country.'

Within hours, at the behest of their LA-based manager, Adam was loaded onto another flight without food or money in his pocket, and sent to a rehab centre used by musicians and celebrities in California.

It was like a boot camp – he was forced to rise at 6 a.m. to clean toilets to earn the privilege of phoning home. One woman in the clinic turned tricks on Hollywood Boulevard, another was a *Valley of the Dolls* housewife with a mother's-little-helper habit, but the one who impressed him the most was an ex-hood biker gang member in her fifties, a grandmother still digging the vein.

'I'm still coming to these things,' she told him one day. 'Don't be my age and still fucking around with it. It's no way to live, believe me.'

The enforced 12-step programme had no impact on Adam during his short stay. Therapists repeated the daily doctrine, cult-like in their sense of belief, and he nodded along feeling like a traitor when he heard the testimonials from residents who were trying to kick their habits, counting down the days before he could leave. Unable to stand another night trapped in the clinic, with eight days of purity under his belt he checked himself out, and flew back to London clean and serene, before capitulating to the poppy within a month of landing back on damp English soil.

☪

Cancel fever! What a way to end the party! I don't think I'll ever shake off this case of banishment syndrome! Perhaps the worst thing about rotating back around to reality, having spent the best part of a decade in tour van stasis, was the emergence of this cultural scourge, this new-born quest for purification on the 'progressive' side of the political spectrum . . . the side you were used to thinking of as your own. Suddenly it felt like you were living through the middle of a great purge, that at any moment the pittance you'd earned for yourself making art could be ripped away from you for reasons unknowable. While we'd been busy bravely obliterating our minds with drugs in a Portakabin somewhere, purveyors of the new social justice faith had set about inverting the meaning of the word solidarity. *What constituted 'the struggle' now seemed to amount to little more than the righteous online condemnation of anyone failing to live up to the latest fad in identity politics, anyone not up to speed with whatever moral orthodoxy some elite US campus had thrown up just last week or the week before.*

A shapeshifting, one-size-fits-all 'trickle-down morality' then, an unquestioning subscription which allowed you to feel like less of a power-fixated narcissist, which – sadly – all of us inevitably are in the late-capitalist West. How does one negate the latticework of exploitation now engulfing the soul? How does one negate the abstraction of contemporary slavery? How do you get around the cobalt in your smartphone? Illusory collective action and industrial quantities of shame, that's how. It didn't matter that it completely alienated working-class people like my own family. It didn't matter that it rendered the left about as seductive as bowel cancer, because it wasn't about building consensus, it was about propagating as much guilt as humanly possible. In this shitty, infinite world of self-flagellation, your best shot at innocence, if that's your bag, is self-immolation. What was that old yarn about socialists being little more than Christians in drag?

Just as bourgeois city dwellers could avoid the aesthetic poverty of a hyper-corporate high street that the rest of us proles have to endure, and instead create for themselves a nostalgic dreamworld of the boutique, bespoke, homemade and 'human', the same methodology could be applied to elaborating fantasy versions of their political lives. The cultivation of a theatre of authenticity from which they hoped to salvage some sense of selfhood, a sense of 'decency' from the lurid cataclysm of consumer nihilism. At once omnipotent and utterly helpless before their hot little screens, consistency of thought began crumbling into a puerile obsession with 'self-help' and the individual's moral standing. Indeed, a socio-political identity became in effect just more 'stuff', just another acquisition with which to fill the screaming void. Activism became the zeitgeist, the ultimate fashion accessory, a form of tokenism that often lasted no longer than a good shit.

Artists who were willing to demonstrate fealty to this atomising double bind of moronic sentimentality and cold-blooded commercialism would be rewarded, anyone calling it into question risked being labelled a racist, a misogynist or worse. That the artist is not their art might well be the only rule of art-making; it's what grants permission to march across the borders and look back at your position in the universe with fresh perspective, it's what lends it critical power. Having thrown metaphor and humour into the trash, this new breed of hyper-literal thought-police gave up trying to separate evisceration from endorsement. Too much risk involved. God knows who it might offend? In these heady days what was required was safety art; the antithesis of the band we had created.

After a brief foray out into the light, Fat White Family had wound up in exactly the same place it had started: the wrong side of history.

I remember the first time I heard the expression 'woke'.

It was in Saul's girlfriend's flat, around 2016. He'd been dating a radical feminist for some time, so was slightly more clued up on the 'new morality' being imported from the States. He casually informed me that I was finished. That I was a chauvinistic dinosaur. That the kids were all into this woke shit now. Apparently singing songs about rapists and fascists while playing with your cock on stage was out, way out. It was something to do with privilege. Who had it, who should have it, blah, blah, blah . . . I didn't give it much in the way of thought, another dreary hipster fad no doubt, what do they want? Art without violence or perversion? Don't be ridiculous.

Then came the Pitchfork *debacle.*

I'd been sat up smoking draw and drinking alone one evening in Sheffield, having a bit of a scroll. Up popped a story about Libya. Conservative foreign secretary and future prime minister Boris Johnson had said that all we needed to do was get rid of the bodies and it'd be the new Dubai. According to him, it was an economic miracle waiting to happen. I became sentimental about this. It managed to pierce my armour of disaffection. Half drunk, I kept picturing my family back in Algeria who, in the grand scheme of things, had done nothing to hurt anyone. 'Only a peppering of sand-nigger carcasses to sweep up, and we'll have ourselves a new Dubai! Onwards gentlemen!' I typed into Facebook. Messages began trickling in denouncing my abhorrent racism. I began responding to a few, then cut my losses and deleted the post. Fuck sitting there all night, wrestling with shadows. There's no point. To bed I went, thinking nothing more of it.

The next day, I was rattled awake by the phone, that horrible little slab of dread . . .

'Morning Sarah, how's it going?'

'Eh, well, not too good actually . . .'

My manager proceeded to inform me that Pitchfork, *the biggest music blog in the US, had posted an article with the headline 'Fat White Family post racist slur'. On hearing this I was incensed. Then I read the article in question. In it, the 'journalist' had noted our left-wing credentials, the fact we'd raised money for Palestine, supported Corbyn and the fact that some of us are North African. It didn't make any sense. They say Americans struggle with satire, but this was beyond the* pale. Grief from the right-wing media you come to expect, almost take a little pride in, but these people were apparently on the 'left'. To what end were they attempting to savage our reputation? The writer of the article was of course white . . . white with a long hipster beard. What was his goal? What gave him or that magazine cause to publish such a headline, clickbait aside? Wasn't it perfectly obvious we were on the same side, so to speak?

These things always occur on a bastard of a hangover. Of that much you can be certain. They never come knocking when you're clear of mind, always through a thick fog of paranoia, when your ability to process the outrage being hurled back at you is chronically impaired.

Months later, I recall the endless vibrating of my telephone under my mattress early one afternoon, in one of those tour-bus coffins, parked up in Hamburg somewhere. Slowly coming to terms with consciousness again after the previous night's indulgences, I find thirteen missed calls on the thing. Thirteen. Christ, it must be bad. Before you've pulled that little curtain aside, before you've had time to fondle yourself or contemplate how you managed to get life so strangely wrong, you're on call with the manager trying to work out what's going down . . .

'Fucking hell, I've been trying to call you all morning. So that thing in the Sunday Times has come out . . .'

'Hang on a minute, Sarah, what thing? What are you talking about?'

'You know I mentioned the other day they're running a story about Glastonbury, that they were being a bit cagey about the whole thing . . .'

'Eh, oh yeah, yeah, sure, of course . . . what about it?'

'Well they've run it, and . . .'

'And what?'

'Well, it's not great.'

'How not great?'

'They've quoted you on a load of really old Facebook posts. Do you remember writing . . . "death is too good for George Osborne, he should be made to suffer first – in front of his kids . . ."?'

It was pre-election, and the newspaper was attacking Labour leader Jeremy Corbyn, trying to brand him an extremist by way of his affiliation *with the festival, which coincidentally we were booked to play that summer so, of course, we were being held up as a prime example.*

'Right. Fuck. Are Glastonbury dropping us then? Send me a photo . . .'

When I opened my messages, there I was splashed across the pages, a photo of me wielding a sledgehammer, shirtless, with a quote about executing leading austerity politicians on page four. I was the edgelord's edgelord! I had been hijacked by my former self! Just as I was attempting to cut a slightly more reasonable figure in the culture, the fear of having to hobble into middle age trapped in penury rapping at my non-existent front door . . .

Suddenly every paper in the country was covering the 'story'. They were having round tables on LBC about free speech. It was on the evening news.

Another band were mentioned in the article, a rave band nobody had ever heard of called Killdren. They had a number called 'Kill Tory Scum'. In the end a consensus seemed to emerge across the media – seeing as our comments pre-dated the murder of Jo Cox, we were off the hook, so to speak. This other band got the chop. Outrage flared up in the Fat White camp. We should drop out in solidarity! No, we should let them open for us as a part of our set! Smuggle them on!

Eventually one of us bothered actually listening to their forbidden anthem and the idea evaporated as quickly as it had sprung to mind. Glastonbury was too much of a laugh, all of our London friends were there, so were all the drugs, and our mums could watch us on the telly. A corporate ghost of its former self it may well be, but then what wasn't these days?

☪

Quietly but vehemently suspicious of Saul's involvement from the get-go, when it came to wrapping up a track he had obsessively worked on for months, Nathan resorted to a policy beyond zero-compromise. After falling out with Saul over a Sebley-related non-incident, one that Saul was being blamed for, Nathan decided between one day and the next that he was no longer going to collaborate with him on the record.

Unable to acknowledge that Saul had shaped the sessions, transforming random ideas and demos into a fully fledged releasable album, Fat White Family's drama triangle finally came to blows over the making of 'Feet'. Smoking skunk each day and overloading with ketamine had sent Nathan into a level of visionary madness: he was fixated on timescales and devils and mathematical frameworks. It was akin to Lee 'Scratch' Perry's Black Ark psychosis, where the studio walls became a trigger for psychic interference, paranoid delusions and disinhibition.

In a bizarre turn of events, Michelle became deeply embroiled in her sons' toxic inter-band politics. Sarah, the band's manager, had asked her to intervene, so Michelle flew over from Dungannon to look after Nathan in Sheffield after he stormed out of the house and threatened to leave the band. In the heat of the moment, Nathan had been given an ultimatum by Lias that if he didn't leave the city it was all over for him. Even though the band had always been a collection of unresolved conflicts that eventually resolved into a record, the edits made to his recordings had tipped Nathan into a whirlwind of serious paranoia.

On the day before they were due to start officially recording the third album the situation had reached its climax: the two brothers and Michelle were all standing outside in the horizontal Attercliffe rain. Nathan was refusing to go inside the studio in case his bandmate was waiting inside.

'He's not here, is he?' Michelle shouted. 'He says he's not coming in if Saul's here, he's had enough.'

Lias pulled his jacket over his head as rainwater trickled down his face.

'No, I left him up at the house. But he hasn't done anything. I don't understand why Nathan's being like this.'

'You're kicking your own brother out, are you? It's Nathan's house too. Nathan built this studio, didn't he?'

'He's not getting *kicked out*. We just have to get this done. And we can't do it with Nathan in this state. Look at him.'

The worst thing about the unholy mess was that Lias understood how his mother had arrived at her conclusion. For years she'd listened to Lias agonise over how much of a bastard Saul was being, how they needed rid of him, how he was the devil incarnate. When he finally left the band, Lias and Nathan began the whole writing process from scratch in Yorkshire, and suddenly – in Michelle's eyes – Saul was not just back on the scene but was cunningly supplanting her youngest at the last minute.

Their mother was furious at the situation her sons were in. She didn't have to hold Nathan's hand on the way back into the studio, but that might as well have been the case. Now in their early thirties, they were still relying on her to salvage the situation, one that she could only understand through the prism of her son's current distress.

Lias, as usual, was expecting to broker a peace deal, or inject a dash of rationale into the works, but this time he was way off course. It was a desperate situation; Nathan had declared that he couldn't risk so much as a chance encounter with Saul in the same room. In his delusional state he believed his bandmate was plotting to kill him. Only a week before they'd been laughing and joking together.

A storm of nervous anguish, Nathan could barely sit still when they entered the studio. Lias began asking him how they should resolve it, or in management speak, how they might *all get back onto the same page*. Nathan had always operated at his own frequency, with his older brother believing he was born strange, but this time it was different. It was as though the trauma of the last ten years was flowing through him all at once.

At the onset of recording, Saul and Nathan had a tiff that started with a Facebook thread gone awry. Saul had been tarred with the old brush, but in this case was innocent of charges. Even though he had salvaged the recording session, he was in the firing line once again. It was easier to blame their lead guitarist than be personally accountable. Since then, the situation had escalated.

'Fuck you both,' Nathan said. 'Because I've been here demoing this record, making it, while Saul's been swanning around and you've just been hanging out with your Hollywood girlfriend. You do fuck all. It's like this, Lias: he goes, or I go. He's going to destroy us all . . .'

'That doesn't make any sense,' Lias replied, as he put his head in his hands. 'I know as well as anyone he's been a cunt in the past, but he's actually trying to mend things . . . we've been working on this together for months now. Come on, let's at least give it a go? What's changed since this time last week? Give it a chance, bro . . .'

'WE DON'T NEED HIM. He's controlling you. Saul's in your head . . .'

Lias took this personally. He always did. Acknowledging it was emasculating. It was true that he had scant confidence in his own ideas and a tendency to defer to Saul on all creative matters. But in contrast to the Saoudis, Saul had turned a corner by this point in time. He was being encouraging, supportive, not the bully he'd once been out on the road or while recording *Mothers*. He had a deep affection for Nathan and loved him like a brother. But even though it was acknowledged that skunk psychosis had much to do with the current crisis, the paranoia and violent resentment that had flared up inside of Nathan were not born out of thin air.

Lias believed doggedly that it was not about the band *needing* Saul; it was more a case of making the best record possible. If that made him look like a traitor in the face of his own family then it was a price he was willing to pay.

Nathan paced up and down the studio as Michelle attempted

to calm him down. The argument between the brothers started to boil.

'He's going to kill you! He's going to kill you!' Nathan shouted. 'I've always had your back. He's nuts, Lias! The guy's a psychopath. Why don't you see this?'

Nathan went into overdrive, enumerating every way in which Saul had crossed them and the group, or had come up short as a human being in the previous decade. Michelle interjected occasionally to verify the claims that spilled from her youngest son's mouth and shook her head in exasperation. Her sons had resorted to arguing in an explosive way reminiscent of her former husband.

Aside from the obvious, one of the oddest things about Nathan's behaviour during this period was that Lias believed it resembled Saul's at his very worst; he was a mess, and a manipulative mess at that. After lighting a cigarette in the cold damp air, Lias started to scream that Nathan had Michelle eating out of the palm of his hand.

'The guy's a mentally ill heroin addict, same as Nathan, what do you expect me to do, Mum, just wash my hands of him? If he was carrying on in the same old way he wouldn't be here.'

The argument circled as they sat in the disused garage adjacent to the studio, but the more Lias demonstrated his immovability on the prospect of sacking Saul at the last minute, the more enraged and panic-stricken Nathan became. He kept proclaiming how he was in league with Kanye and the Beatles, how he didn't want to make another indie record, how he wanted to change music and the world, before reaching his hand out to Lias and saying 'brothers' – as in 'join me now, blood is thicker than water, you know where your loyalties truly lie . . .'

By this point Lias had reach the proverbial cliff edge. 'Look, we don't have the time or the money, and I don't have the slightest inclination to suddenly reshape this whole thing at the last minute without Saul in the frame. Are you seriously doing this? You're seriously gonna force me to choose between the two of you right here right now? In front of our mum?'

'I'm not working with him and that's the end of it. We don't need him, he's poison, he fucks with your head, he fucks with everybody's heads. It's either he goes, or I go . . .'

'I'm not going to be dictated to by you.'

Nathan grabbed hold of his head with both hands, leaned back in the office chair, and began crying and manically repeating the word 'no'; his eyes were almost popping out of his head as he stared up at the ceiling. Lias had never seen his brother behave like that. He wanted to solve the situation, but couldn't. His mother's disgust was palpable. She couldn't understand the behaviour of either of her sons.

'Isn't it all just a load of music?' she said in exasperation. 'What's the point in falling out over it?'

Michelle took hold of her son and walked him away from the studio, towards her Premier Inn guestroom, where she stayed with him until he calmed down. The next morning, she walked him to the hospital for emergency mental health treatment and was passed from pillar to post. No matter how hard she tried, she could not get any help for her son, even in his most desperate state.

Lias had never fallen out with his mother, not even as a depressed teenager. For the first time in their lives, they had entered a period in which they were at loggerheads. Throughout all of the misery that had occurred in Fat White Family, nothing hit Lias harder than watching Nathan sitting in his spinning office chair in Sheffield, pulling his own hair out. He was sure he was doing the right thing, but felt like he'd broken his own brother's mind in the process.

The first indication anyone heard about the mental collapse their frontman was facing came from Pete. Seemingly unable to cope with the situation that had escalated from the recording of the album, and his desperate infatuation with his Hollywood heiress, Lias was now not only at war with his brother, but also his mother. But the biggest battle was with his own mind. For months he had contained his anxiety over the situation, until one afternoon, sat alone in his girlfriend's Notting Hill flat, he decided to make a final gesture of *felo de se* to end his torment. It was a whimper for help.

Staring at a row of Sabatier knives lined up on the granite kitchen surface, Lias rolled up his sleeves, knowing that in an hour his girlfriend would return to find his body in the bathtub. He was loath to stain her white wooden floor. Life had become so intolerable that he could no longer face living it. Caught in a whirlwind of catastrophising, each rumination became a hell he had to relive each day. The future represented only misery, solitude and confrontation. Death seemed like a quick release.

Before walking into the bathroom he picked up his iPhone, unlocked the screen and sent the ever-faithful Pete a goodbye message: 'I think I'm going to kill myself.' They were supposed to meet up for lunch at Pain Quotidien an hour later, so the least he could do out of courtesy was to explain the reason for his no-show.

When he read the text message Pete replied immediately, but Lias didn't respond. He wanted his pound of sympathy. Within minutes a panicked Nathan called his brother, then Saul rang his phone. All went to voicemail.

After speaking to Pete, Nathan had called Saul to tell him that he thought Lias had killed himself, then hung up as he ran onto the Tube to West London. Saul was distraught, and fled towards Victoria on the Overground train, his stomach churning with upset as he imagined the scene he was about to find.

When he eventually arrived in Notting Hill, Saul ran up to the flat and rang the doorbell repeatedly. Lias's girlfriend's face appeared at the window, and she opened the door only for Saul to find a red-eyed Lias curled up smoking a cigarette with Nathan hectoring him. Saul was confused, unable to work out what had just happened.

He could hear Nathan shouting: 'If you kill yourself, I'm going as well! That makes two of us dead. That means only Tam left! Just CONSIDER what that will do to Mum. Don't even think that I won't do it if you do it.'

'Both of you, just calm down,' Saul said to the brothers. 'Nothing's going to happen. Let it settle.'

He sat down on the sofa and let out a sigh.

'Come on, it's going to be alright.'

In a remarkable change of dynamics, and one that his band members could never have predicted, Saul had become the unlikely voice of reason.

Sketching Ruins in the Dark

Dale, I had ignored your imminent death the first time I could make sense of it. It flashed up on a Facebook feed. You always hated social media; if you could see what we've been reduced to maybe you'd feel a little better about your relocation. The name of the disease you died from was in an alien tongue, one you had learnt fluently by the end, all that medical jargon you and Laura were forced to enrich yourselves with. I read the article about your terminal struggle with cancer and hid from its implications at first. I convinced myself that somehow you would be fine as you were the guy that wrote 'Where Is my Knife?' and smiled up at me after I played you that rough version of 'I Am Mark E. Smith' on a crappy little keyboard in the upstairs of that dive in Birmingham.

We hadn't spoken in a little while, months I'm guessing it might have been. I'd seen you and Laura doing your new thing at the Social in Sheffield, just down the road from where me and Nathan were crawling the walls at the time. I was really critical of your show, I told you that you were giving too much free rein to the new musicians you had up alongside you, that you were nothing if not a definitive frontman. I was telling you what I wished I could convince myself of at the time, but I stand by it. We were both adrift in different ways at that point, not lost at sea but certainly between ports. You'd started a new life in Berlin with Laura and had founded a new posse that didn't carry the burden of the crap you were tired of back in Glasgow; the sycophants, the imitators, the try-hards, folks that felt they had a place in this world giving you grief because they'd seen you in a few magazines.

My mother was staying with us in Sheffield when I finally plucked up the courage to pick up the phone and suss out what was actually going on. I can't remember whether it was days or hours between first reading that article and calling. You answered and you were full of beans as always, no shortage of fighting talk. You were the first one to go because you were the only one strong enough to go. I told you I'd make my way up to see you and Laura as soon as possible. By this time, I had googled the thing eating away at the inside of your skull; I had some grasp of the desperation but was wholly taken in by your self-belief. I didn't dare ask for the prognosis.

I boarded the train to Glasgow and spent the journey listening to unmixed versions of songs off my forthcoming record, staring out at an east coast bathed in the tired golden light of a late summer's afternoon. I'm not sure what I expected to find at the other end, but whatever it was it certainly didn't have me down. I was looking forward to seeing you, wondering if you were still able to have a drink or not. You met me at the station wearing a long black trench coat, cowboy hat and some far-out wraparound shades. The kind of sunglasses they give you to protect from any kind of excess radiation, a bit like the ones they give blind people but darker.

Your face broke out into the usual mirth upon meeting. You took off your hat and showed me your completely bald head. We jumped into a cab; I started relating the goings on of my own life and you explained that it was all or nothing now, that you were in the fight of yours. It was the same fuck-'em-all attitude you had with everything and everyone else that didn't add up in this life, that didn't make sense, anything that seemed like a wash-out that simply had to be routed from the day to day. 'If you stop, you die' was what you always used to say to me about the music.

Your illness had become apparent mid-tour in Germany quite a while ago, when you'd had a seizure on the road. This sparked off a series of events that led you back to Glasgow, inevitably. Your apartment in the west end was up four flights of stairs, a bit of a fucker to climb but bright and airy once you were up. You and Laura had prepared a big meal for me, all kinds of health food going on, I swear there were pine nuts involved. I had a glass of wine, but you were off the sauce now permanently. The way you looked at me over that dinner still breaks my heart. Pure warmth.

Me and Laura made our way through the best part of a bottle of wine and we all got royally stoned on the vape pens you'd bought to stave off putting any more garbage into your lungs. You had what I think was cannabis oil of some sort, this thick, bitter, tar-black elixir you insisted was a killer of cancer. Every so often you'd squeeze a shot of it out of the pipette into my gob. We were slinging it low, hitting the tunes and aside from your bald skull everything seemed pretty much like it did after a show back in the day. It seemed to me that despite Laura's somewhat shocked pallor, despite the boundless agony hiding just behind the smile, things might just be alright somehow. I bought into the hope you two were holding onto wholesale. I excitedly showed you the record we were working on in Sheffield, you sat there on the couch with your head thrusting away, every now and then exclaiming how you felt about this or that part of it, then asking me to flick through the Dropbox and play the next track. You were clearly buzzing, which left me buzzing in turn.

With headphones still in your ears, the rhythm of you gently rocking to the music slowly mutated into an upright posture as you stood up from your chair. This turned into an agitated stumble and then broke down into an unceasing cascade of muscular turbulence; your face became suddenly unrecognisable, as if your features were now in the possession of some demonic force. You collapsed to the ground before I could even realise what was going on; I had never seen anything like this before. Laura exclaimed that you were having a brain seizure, and without any hesitation whatsoever had cleared a space for you on the ground so your head wouldn't slam against any of the furniture. I called 999 and stared down into your face. I'd never seen such agony, your jaw repeatedly clenching upon itself, your eyes like two great white boulders, much too heavy for a frame now shot through with the hideous lightning of pure mania.

I think it took several minutes for you to come through the worst of it, although you were still in a complete daze, you didn't say a word.

By this time Laura was on the phone to the emergency services; I heard the words 'one year' as she explained the situation on the phone. I finally knew the prognosis then. Within ten minutes you were fit enough for us to help you up and take you to the toilet, I think you needed to be sick. You asked to be left alone in there, me and Laura waited in the lounge. You hadn't had a seizure for a great many months, which was a big reason for the high spirits that'd been on display; I had been the first visitor you'd had to stay at the flat, a sign of how well you thought things were going. When you finally re-emerged from the toilet you were completely yourself again but had absolutely no clue as to what had just happened, you couldn't understand why me and Laura were standing there deathly white with shock, obviously holding back the tears, just staring at you. When we told you, your face broke down all over again, this time with utter disappointment. The emergency services arrived, and you were put into bed where they conducted a series of tests. They thought it was possible you might have had a small heart attack. They stayed and monitored your vitals for forty minutes, and you started cracking jokes about it all again. 'That new record's killer,' I think I heard you say.

You had a show booked the following night at Broadcast on Sauchiehall Street, your old stomping ground. From the seizure onwards it became Laura's and my mission to prevent you from doing it. We agreed behind your back to work a double team on you, slowly grind you down so you wouldn't put yourself in harm's way, a ridiculous proposition in retrospect but at the time, immediately after watching you have a brain seizure, it made a fair bit of sense. This mission of ours dragged on a whole day. You had battered your shoulder during the fall, and it was clearly a struggle for you to be up and about. We agreed to go for a walk to try and assess your fitness. I remember ambling through the botanical gardens which were nearby, and it was one of those rare days of pure Scottish sunshine, and a bank holiday, so life was in its fullest force. I wonder if I will ever understand the pain of that stroll. We had mince and tatties and even stopped in a bar on the way home; I wanted/needed a whisky and you were keen to at least soak up the scent of one. 'I used to live for it, Lias,' you told me. You had to have a rest once we'd arrived home. The gig that night was still up in the air. I don't think a doctor alive would have prescribed you heading out to play music like that less than twenty-four hours after a brain seizure, but what did I know. Our nagging eventually became too much for you and you turned to me and said: 'Lias, I've got fucking brain cancer, would YOU go do the gig?' End of debate.

For the last ever time I watched you play a whole set that night, dressed in your black leather trench coat, cowboy hat and shades. I watched you perform and stood half-amazed, half-terrified by the side of the stage. It was the most 'Dale Barclay' thing humanly imaginable. Your face was as aglow backstage as I'd ever seen it, feeding on the atmosphere you'd just conjured up out of thin air, at your altitude for a moment we were all capable of sheer defiance, we all had your guts of steel. The next morning you struggled to make eye contact with me, you didn't want to burden me with any sadness, and you certainly didn't want to go through the dry run of a final goodbye. Which it wasn't, as it turns out, but near enough.

☪

Dale Barclay, the man who always heeded the call of duty and plunged into chaos without hesitation, died from cancer at the age of thirty-two just one week after his latest bout of surgery. As the formidable frontman of And Yet It Moves and the Amazing Snakeheads, and occasional live guitarist with Fat White Family, his reputation and natural musical ability was cruelly cut short in his fourth decade. Alongside the numerous tributes from the music world, a minute's silence was held at Glasgow's Ibrox Stadium, at the football ground where his mother worked on the turnstiles.

Dale's passing was devastating for Lias and Nathan, who once referred to their experience of being in the band as a form of survival, one akin to Vietnam. After Dale died, their own problems paled into insignificance. Now in their early thirties, it was the first time they had experienced the death of a close friend.

Although a tragic loss, it gave them a sense of perspective. When their third album *Serfs Up!* was released the following spring, the band were still living in the shadow of his passing. The record was dedicated to his life and memory: the sleeve notes read 'There is no why!', a motto of sorts for Dale.

Seven years into a career defined by collapsing masculinity, pound-shop shamanism, provocation, wanton violence, radical empathy, narcissism, hog-like indulgence, personality defects and a fondness for both extreme left- and right-wing aesthetics, Fat White Family returned to the stage, still bickering and, although wavering, still on their feet. The album, which had been recorded under desperate circumstances, received more recognition than any of their previous output, making it onto that year's 'best of' lists with positive and frequently gleaming critical reviews, even in the broadsheets.

Always a drug band with a rock problem, it appeared that the promise and potential invested in them was about to materialise into some twisted form of 'success' after all. For once, Lias was optimistic about the future. The impossible had been achieved: a semblance of stability.

The band's hidden strengths had only ever been truly glimpsed at their legendary live shows – part exorcism, part violent bacchanalian assault on the senses. No two nights were ever the same. But harnessing that energy in the studio or getting the band contained in one space to record had reached *Fitzcarraldo*-like levels of endurance. Would the boat ever be pushed over the mountain?

With the smoke now clearing they re-emerged from Sheffield with a record that invited the listener in rather than repelling them through wilful abrasion. Where once they soundtracked a grubby Britain of vape shops, Fray Bentos dinners and blackened tinfoil, a crepuscular comedown realm stalked by Shipman, Goebbels and Mark E. Smith, Fat White Family were now in danger of breaching the top ten for ten whole minutes.

Basking in the glory of a sold-out tour, a long list of festival dates, a line of European shows and another batch of UK gigs booked for the year's end, after a decade of trying the band were a stone's throw from being able to afford to live like actual human beings, without having to latch onto others in a neverending cycle of vampiric self-interest. Even with dwindling online streaming incomes, at least they could always depend on the money earned from live touring. At long last, all they had worked towards was coming to fruition. They agreed to book a large international tour for February 2020, taking in Asia, Australia, Europe and potentially a return to America. Tickets were placed on sale, flights were booked and visas were applied for. A large pot of the band's savings was invested in the 'Miracle of Failure' tour. It would surely be the making of them.

☪

Huddled in his moth-eaten wool coat, Lias walked past the Stephen Joseph Theatre in Scarborough with his mother's black and tan cocker spaniel, Jarvis, pulling on the lead. On his way into town, the dog stopped then curled over like a question mark and took a runny shit on a pensioner's front doorstep, which Lias deemed far too revolting to pick up. He looked from left to right then quickly ran off, leaving the dogshit for somebody else to deal with.

In the bright light of day, he wandered down Westborough and stopped at a corner café, ordering a tea with almond milk to settle his stomach. His IBS had been flaring up once again.

Michelle hobbled across towards him from Poundland and waved. After leaving County Tyrone and buying a small terraced house with Leslie in North Bay, she had finally returned to Yorkshire and would look out across the sea at the setting sun each night, the same view she had often stared across as a child. The place where her dreams began.

'My hip's bloody killing,' she said as she hunched over a seat and steadied herself into it. 'What a day . . .'

'Have you been standing for hours?' Lias asked.

Michelle zipped up her fleece and rubbed her hands together. 'As usual. I'll have a tea please . . . yes, just milk, no sugar.'

'Jarvis shat on someone's doorstep.'

'Did you pick it up? I left you some bags.'

Lias turned his nose up and avoided her gaze.

'You didn't, did you? Lias! You'll get me into bother.'

'I draw the line at picking up shit.'

The March wind whipped along the street towards the beach. Michelle started to shuffle in her chair.

'They've told me I've to wait another six months before I can get this hip sorted out. It's so painful. Even driving hurts, but I still have to stand on the self-service all bloomin' day for eight hours. They won't even let me sit down. I mean, all I need is a chair. It's not like I can sign off sick either . . .'

'Can't you ask for lower hours? I mean, that's a solution, isn't it?'

'No chance!' she laughed. 'It's zero hours. I have to take what's offered or I lose the job . . .'

She rustled around in her handbag and fed a biscuit to the dog, whose curly coat had started to resemble Lias's erratic haircut. That afternoon, the streets were quiet. An ominous feeling hung in the air. Even the seagulls were few and far between.

'Eh, it's a shame you didn't get to China in the end . . . you've landed in Scarborough instead. Can't complain.'

The news that week had featured a slew of stories about a virus from a wet market in Wuhan that had locked down half of the Far East. It was another source of concern for Lias: all of the band's Asia dates had been postponed.

'I should be in Japan right now watching the cherry blossom. Instead I'm here, watching chip wrappers floating in the shitty breeze. And for what? Pangolin soup?'

Michelle slurped the dregs of her tea and pushed the last morsel of chocolate muffin into her mouth.

'You'll get there in the end. Don't worry. It'll all clear up. They'll fix it and you'll reschedule. Oh, look at them fellas over there. See the one with the brown anorak on? He comes in and shoplifts, you know. But he's homeless. And he's starving. So I turn a blind eye . . .'

'You're too kind to the junkies.'

'Yeah, I know that. Because I wonder how much their mothers worry about them . . .'

'The bliss of heroin doesn't look so bad right now. Christ, when I think of the money we've flushed down the drain on that tour. It's almost bankrupted us again. The coffers are empty once more.'

Lias picked up his phone and started to check the news updates. For a moment, his face resembled a discarded dishcloth as he grimaced at the reports; it was only a matter of time before the virus came to the UK.

'I've to get back to work,' Michelle said. 'But look, I brought you a bottle of this. Hand sanitiser. Everyone's buying them in bulk. Five hundred bottles this morning.'

Leaning forward, she emptied a squirt into her son's hands and he smeared them with glistening gel. A wave of antiseptic rose through his nostrils, the first of many thousands that year, unbeknownst to him.

Later that night, he wandered down to the harbour front to watch the full moon rise over the calm North Sea. Pausing outside a Unionist pub, Lias stared through the window to see a bar decorated with St George's flags. Paintings of Orange marches and Glasgow Rangers insignia hung on the walls. Loyalist Weekend posters celebrating the 'Sash Bash' were pinned to the doors. Even in Yorkshire, there was no escaping sectarianism. The red right hand of Ulster was all seeing, all knowing.

He turned his back and crossed the street, noticing the Merchant Irish Bar's open mic night over the way that was picking up steam. Lias's face lit up as he walked through the door, spotted the open fire and shelves of liquor behind the till. He decided it was an opportune moment to sing a rendition of 'Straight Banana', an old chestnut from the Saudis era that he delivered in full Chas & Dave style. The bar started to empty as he attempted to hit the high notes.

To the thinnest round of applause known to man, he put down his guitar, marched over to the bar and valiantly knocked back two tequilas. Perched on an unsteady stool he listened intently to a flat-capped middle-aged skater who played a convincing and relatively soulful rendition of Neil Young's 'Harvest Moon'. Lias watched the silent streets outside as a portentous gale ripped through the castle. In Scarborough nobody, aside from Michelle, cared about Lias Saoudi.

As last orders were called, he picked up his coat and stumbled up the cobbled snickleway. He made his weary retreat back to the bosom of his mother, lighting the dregs of his roll-up in the wind.

Curtains, Carpets, Walls and Ceilings

'South London is a fucking dead end, man. I can't wait to be shot of this place. How long am I going to be living at your parents' house? It's fucking pathetic . . . I'm a thirty-three-year-old man. I've contributed. I've toiled. Some days I just want to lay around in my underwear masturbating in front of the telly, you can't do that here, not in someone else's family household, it's poor form . . . perpetual nomads, that's where we're at . . . no books, no records, no flat . . . your whole world is your laptop and your phone . . . no wonder young people are turning into fucking cyborgs, inhuman moralists . . . adulthood is forbidden, it's haram! Stability is haram! Unless of course you inherit it, if not, you're just a disgruntled twenty-something forever, except your body starts to wither, it gets more and more pricey to cane your way out of the deadlock, hangovers start cross-pollinating at a freakish rate, your consciousness becomes muck . . . They've even managed to gentrify squatting! Global Guardians? Suckle my grundle! You want me to pay? To be an ultra low-level security guard?! Kids running around south London like, oh yeah, wicked, sick man, I'm living in a disused mental hospital on Old Kent Road, next to a padded fucking room, and it's only five-hundred quid a month! A steal boyo! They managed to corporatise THAT! I almost admire them, whoever THEY are . . . that's London, in a nutshell, you even pay to squat!'

'Spare me the hyperbole, please . . . you could rent a place. I mean, I agree with you, but it's not as if you're flat broke are you now?'

Saul, sprawled across the kitchen table in the basement of his father's house in Peckham, unfolded his head and entangled arms to pour the dregs from a can of Guinness into a glass. It was 4 a.m. and the sun was starting to rise over Warwick Gardens. I had spent the previous month sleeping in the spare room, unable to find a permanent place to stay, and had once again become part of the furniture. A large tabby cat jumped up onto the sideboard, made a growling noise and proceeded to hack up a furball onto the floor.

'I could Saul, I could, it's true . . . some cupboard room in a shared house, £750 a month to live submerged in other people's issues on the Deptford–Lewisham borders. I would have fucked off to Paris or Spain as well if I knew all our shows were going to get canned. I resent spending my precious dollar on London rent. Paris is pricey as well but at least it looks like Paris. What did Matthew Johnson call London again?'

'A two-storey backwater,' Saul groaned.

'A two-storey backwater! That's exactly right! London is just a world bank with an endless, murderously overpriced cul-de-sac attached. There are no Lou Reedian boulevards! There's no Haussmann! You don't even feel like you're in a city! What's the fucking point?'

I took hold of my Nationwide card and began crushing down the final crumbs of chisel under a twenty-pound note. We'd settled on one last blowout after conquering the Algerian embassy. A plan that'd been ten years in the making was finally coming to fruition . . .

'You reckon in Algeria we'll become free men then?' said Saul. 'Maybe we'll end up setting up a little colony out there? Lurk around the bath houses, a gaggle of young boys following us around everywhere . . . can you get opium? Burroughs and all that lot went out there, right?'

'No, that was Morocco. Timothy Leary and the Black Panthers were out in Algiers for a bit, but that was fucking ages ago. They're a bit more hardcore on the old Islam now. Bit less tolerant. I'm not sure about opium, I never went looking . . . shall we finish that? Two small ones or one big one?'

Saul rubbed on his eyes and rocked his head from side to side.

'Four in the morning. One big one I reckon. My flight's at midday.'

I racked out the final line of cocaine for my comrade to help ease in the unflinching dawn that was spreading through the streets of Peckham. The small hours had not been kind: we were starting to look more than our age.

'Rough tings. You got Valium?' I said.

'Got a few, yeah . . .'

'Chuck us one then. Might as well start drifting down now. So, you've got your visa, you've got your flights, Fiona's gonna drop you off at the airport, right, in Barcelona?'

'Yeah, it's all sorted. Global pandemic aside . . .'

'It'll be fine, man. Algeria only has seventeen cases, no deaths. There's fuck all tourism, really young population, warm climate . . . safest place to be.'

It had always meant a lot to me, the idea of getting the Fat Whites out to North Africa. The concept of a bunch of recovering junkies living in that heat, surrounded by the children of Allah, clucking hard, trying to riff their way out of the total alienation that suddenly surrounded them. Even if a bunch of tunes didn't come out of it, as an anthropological curiosity it still held water . . . a kind of monument to displacement.

The last time me and Nathan had brought a group out there we could barely string two notes together, and it'd still been off the hook. With the wunderkind in tow and his capacity to soak up whatever music he was surrounded by, we might actually be able to get some interesting collaborations going.

Saul had been staying in Cadaqués with his girlfriend all winter, subsisting on rabbit stew, red wine and the occasional dark web parcel that made its way through the letterbox. He'd recently spent a month in Ibiza as part of a rehab programme, where he joined a parade of sinister criminal characters who gave him advice on how to dig untraceable graves in the woods as they attempted the 12-step programme. Despite our best efforts, the last stretch of touring had left most of us, yet again, chemically derailed. There was no bad blood though. The hatchets of yore seemed to have been buried. For a decade I'd been banging on about the return

309

to Algeria – I had a hackneyed vision of it as some kind of miracle cure. The Muslim world is, in a way, a giant rehab facility, I had told Saul. You might feel like you're going mad the first three weeks, but once you've settled into the absence of pace a pure sort of peace descends . . . Now was the time.

I watched the news intently. It was around that period footage of dolphins swimming through the suddenly crystal-blue waters of Venetian canals emerged online. I cast this hideous omen far from my mind. The virus had already robbed us of our Asia/Australia tour, and with it most of our funds. Surely there was a limit to this cruelty? Algeria's numbers did look promising. Seventeen cases, no reported deaths. Warm weather and a young population . . . they were dodging this bullet, for sure. And if it did swing into full lockdown? If we got stranded out there? Well, wasn't getting stuck up in the mountains for months sort of the plan anyway?

Saul made his way back to Spain. Nathan and I would rendezvous with him and Alex White in Algiers a week later. Alex's ex-girlfriend, the half-Algerian conceptual artist Lydia Ourahmane, was living out there. She'd found us an apartment right around the corner from hers, near the shoreline. It was through Lydia – who knew the language – that we hoped to sniff out other musicians in Algiers, maybe Oran as well, where she was from. We'd made up our minds to hang out with her for the first two weeks instead of heading straight to Kabylia to meet my family. There were too many old people back in the village, and we were wary of accidentally killing our grandmother.

I rode an anxious, jam-packed Tube up to the West End the day before my flight and purchased a new guitar, a boom mic for field recordings, a new suitcase, around two kilos' worth of wet wipes and six boxes of Solpadeine . . . was the back of my throat drying out? Was the heating up a little at high chez Adamczewski? Did I feel more tired than usual, lethargic, spaced out? My sense of smell seemed fine. It was probably nothing . . .

The strangest thing about our arrival was how much more Covid-ready the Algerians seemed to be, at least at the airport. Every single member of staff at Algiers wore a face mask. Not a single person at Gatwick did. They were taking everyone's temperature at the arrival gate, a feature we would find still lacking in the UK upon our return a week later, once the crisis had made itself excruciatingly apparent.

We were met at the airport by the husband of my stepmother's daughter, Adoul, and – unexpectedly – my cousin Djallel. Adoul and his wife lived on the outskirts of Algiers, and we were staying with them the first night before making our way to Lydia's. Djallel was having none of it; he wanted to drive us three hours straight down to Maillot and then to see Grandma. I mentioned the virus but both Djallel and Adoul laughed it off. It meant less than nothing to them. In Algeria trust in the media and the government is at rock bottom; as far they were concerned the whole thing was just a ploy to thwart the now one-year-strong youth-led protest movement, the Hirak. Even the preparedness of staff at the airport was some sort of ruse, according to them.

We stood firm and stayed put with Adoul on the outskirts of the city. I couldn't get out of bed until one the next day, which was unusual for me in my later years. I'd sweated the sheets through during the night. It was hard to tell whether I was getting ill or if it was all just in my head. Hypochondria has always come naturally to me; an unknown plague spreading across the continents was bound to aggravate that somewhat.

Adoul took us out for lunch and a stroll around his neck of the woods. Every café had a television on, upon which you would frequently spy Emmanuel Macron's shiny little head, full of po-faced concern, addressing . . . nobody. It wasn't of any real interest to the local populace yet.

I made contact with Lydia. She told me we had to get down into the city as soon as possible; there was a gig that night that she didn't want us to miss. It was at an arts club, a Tuareg desert band were playing. Nathan and I jumped into an Uber and made our way into town just as the sun started to set. Upon realising he had two (half) foreigners in the back of his car, the driver started weaving in and out of traffic like a little Arab Schumacher. He couldn't have been more than eighteen and was intent on giving us a bit of a tour on the way. Algeria is bereft of tourists; when you do show up, they treat you like royalty. The outer city landscape *had scant aesthetic appeal, just a motorway, endless rudimentary concrete housing blocks shrouded in yellow dust, the odd patch of waste and scrub, litter everywhere, and an excess of beggars at whatever traffic light you happen to stop at.*

Once you hit the central district, you were suddenly in perhaps the most romantic city on earth. An architectural melting pot of oriental and colonial tendencies, you'd snatch a glimpse of the Mediterranean Sea's brilliant blue through the endlessly colonnaded gleaming white boulevards; minarets, mosques and cathedrals jostling for supremacy up on high. Palm trees sprouted around ornate fountains, and the streets were awash with every type of vendor – tea salesmen, haberdasheries, hookah chieftains and spice merchants – the scent of bougainvillea intermingled with fresh coffee and fig. It was no wonder the French wanted to keep hold of all this. Had it not been ravaged by war, by endless terrorist atrocities, one suspects every traveller on earth would be on their way.

A friend of mine, also Algerian, once told me the French architecture depressed her. She thought it the embodiment of the suffering and exploitation that occurred here: its militant, miraculous symmetry a derision of the notoriously intractable Casbah next door. For her, this wanton contradiction denoted a hegemonic attitude utterly devoid of sympathy, it was a fixation on power that was borderline surreal in its ruthlessness. I felt the opposite. These buildings filled me with pride. They were no longer French, after all.

Lydia lived right by Le Grande Poste, in an almost seafront colonial mansion for which she was paying roughly fuck-all a month. It was a comfort to see such a familiar face.

I'd never before encountered the Algeria I found at the gig that night. For a start, there were beautiful women everywhere, and they were dancing, which was bizarre, because it wasn't a wedding. There were other foreigners at this party. English was spoken well. People were fashionably dressed. I'd only ever spent time in the mountains, so this was another scene entirely . . . effete, cosmopolitan, ever-so-slightly decadent; I suppose between here and my family's hometown there was a cultural chasm, one about as wide as that which separated London from Cookstown.

The band were playing a form of reductive, melancholic Saharan blues. Everything seemed to hinge on the djembe drum. When that got kicking, the whole room exploded. I started chatting to some of the guys from the band afterwards. They told me of their studio in town, how they'd just travelled up from the desert and would be in Algiers for the next few weeks. We swapped numbers and he told me to bring my friends down so we could play together. There were a lot of musicians he'd like to introduce us to.

That turned out to be the last gig any of us would attend for a long time. The news from Europe was getting darker by the minute.

Ambling through the Casbah the next day one couldn't help but notice that suddenly the cafés were full of people glued to the television. Macron would flash up, then the head of the World Health Organisation, then some Algerian official, then Macron again; no one could avert their eyes, disaster was in the post . . .

The Hirak continued regardless. Through the broader thoroughfares the youngsters were still marching in their thousands. Momentum had been hard won. They weren't going to suddenly drop everything over the 'flu'. Draped in green, white and red, the mob rolled and seethed its way across town right beneath Lydia's balcony. Heading out with masks strapped across our faces to join the parade we bumped into a few of my cousins from Kabylia. They'd been coming up twice a week for months. They instantly went in for the traditional greeting of a kiss on either cheek: 'Why not come back with us to Maillot?! To Jida?!'

I was starting to feel rough. Psychosomatic or not, I felt like shit and was slowly convincing myself I had the virus. We were all sat around at Lydia's manically scrolling through our phones, attempting to get to the bottom of it all, trying like everyone else in the world at that moment in time to fathom the unprecedented. Borders were closing, airports were running to a standstill. I spoke with Alex on the phone – he told me he'd picked up a serious flu and thought it was the virus but couldn't get tested anywhere, even in London. He wasn't going to make it. He was scared of getting trapped out here. Then the news reported that Spain was going into lockdown, a day before Saul's flight was due to take off. I called him up . . .

'The Lord doesn't want it! Allah won't let it happen!' he answered.

'I know, fuck's sake . . . It's tragicomic . . . The great Algeria project, up in flames once again!'

'Looks like I'm going to be stuck here. For months, man . . .'

'What? With the sea right out your front door? In an old villa in Spain? Oh, the tragedy! Oh, the suffering!'

'It could get ugly. Just me and Fiona. We're fine at the moment, but shit could get a bit Overlook Hotel . . .'

'Fucking right it could,' I laughed. 'Next time I see you it'll be on the news. The authorities will have found you next spring, wandering around the hills of Catalunya wearing her uterus as a crown, covered in your own faeces, searching for a lighter or something.'

I heard the pair of them chuckling down the line; I must have been on loudspeaker.

314

'What about Alex?'

'He's out as well.'

'Fuck. You gonna stay? What's Nathan saying?'

'I don't know, man. It's up in the air. Don't know what to make of it. The airport could shut down any day. Morocco just shut down. Same thing with Tunis. If that happens, we're stuck here. Indefinitely. Nathan's dead set against going home. I don't blame him. I was out here a year ago, you know . . . he's not spent time with our family here in over a decade . . . I feel sorry for him. He's gutted.'

'Yeah, that fucking sucks. Tough call.'

'If we go home, we'll just be stuck at Dad's . . . can you imagine?'

'Lockdown with Bashir!' Saul shouted. 'Fuck that!'

'I know! From the Algerian odyssey to stuck at Bashir's! In just five days! When will the pain stop?'

Over the course of the next forty-eight hours the atmosphere in the city shifted dramatically; a cloud of foreboding descended everywhere, an eerie silence began filling up the streets. Torn between staying put and bailing, we continued trying to make the most of our time. We took a cab to the botanical gardens where, despite it obviously being open and peppered with visitors, we were barred entry. As we marched back towards the flat, we were heckled in the street. Twice. 'Corona! Corona!' they shouted from their speeding cars. Me and Nathan were wearing the same pair of shoes the Chinese had been forced to wear back in Europe – biological pariahs! You can spot a European from a mile off in Algiers by their clothing, giant Berber hook nose or not. These people had moved swiftly from indifference to animosity, they were about to watch all of their hopes and aspirations slip through their fingers all of a sudden, just like we were . . . and they were fucked off about it.

Sharing our apartment for a couple of nights was a friend of Lydia's called Assia, who'd just spent six weeks in the desert. Like us, she had also been planning on staying in the city for a while but had made up her mind to leave and booked herself a flight out. She wanted to get back to London, back to her girlfriend. 'That sounds great,' I recall thinking, 'back to your girlfriend . . . I wish I had one of those. Maybe this wouldn't feel like such a fucking nightmare?' Unless of course you were in that bitter final third of a relationship, where every fibre of mystique has evaporated and sex is a distant memory . . . where you're only still living together because it's too much of a hassle to move out. That was almost as short a straw as ending up at Bashir's, surely? It was impossible to know. I'd never bothered giving it a try.

Should we stay or should we go? Our conversation went around and around in circles, for hours. One of the guys from the Tuareg band came over with a lump of hash. Assia had been staying with him and his clan down in the Sahara. Aside from the music, he made his living doing tours in the region. People from all over the world wanted to hit the deep desert, and he made a solid dinar as a chaperone. He was due to take Lydia down there in two weeks' time. That his bread and butter was under threat simply hadn't occurred to him at all. We had to break it right down for him. There is no cure. No, no, you don't understand. Nobody even really knows what it is. It might kill millions of people, it might not. It was quite something watching the news finally sink in, once we'd managed to traverse the language barrier. Like he'd just noticed his house was on fire.

With Nathan's head full of angry heat, he'd made up his mind to stay. He wouldn't budge. I chatted over the rationale of that decision with Assia. The health facilities in Algeria were abysmal. If there was a plague, if it got really bad, you'd be praying you weren't here. Any Algerian would feel the same. It was no time for tourism. Of course, Nathan and I weren't exactly just tourists, but all the same, a burden was a burden as far as an overstretched healthcare system was concerned.

I couldn't make up my mind. There really was fuck all to go back for. No flat is one thing. But no pubs? No gigs? What about sex? Would there be soldiers on the streets? How long would it last? A few months? A few weeks? A few years?

I called my dad back in Cambridge. A week previous he'd been totally relaxed about us coming out here, but that had all changed quickly . . .

'What do you reckon? Looks bad, no?'

'I cannot believe it, Lias,' he replied. 'I've never seen anything like this. It's terrible. And still, this fucking arsehole Boris has refused to shut the pub! Typical fucking English! There is plague and still, all they bloody want to do is drink! I really think you should come home you know. The Middle East is shutting down. God knows when you'll be able to get back . . .'

'I'm kind of swinging that way myself, but Nathan's having none of it . . .'

'For Christ's sake, Lias! Algeria is a fucking shitty country! If you get sick you will have no chance! They barely have fucking hospitals, are you crazy!?'

'Yeah, I get that, I get that alright!' I pulled the phone away from my ear as the sound of my father shouting boomed from the speaker. 'Please, please, there's no need to howl down the phone. I was over here just a year ago, Nathan's not seen our family for ten years, it'll break his heart, what's he got back in England now? There won't even be any music . . .'

My father took a deep breath and changed tack.

'Look, this might sound awful, but the family are scared about you coming, your Auntie Zahara has been sick for a long time, your grandmother is a hundred years old . . . it's not safe, Lias . . .'

It was a tone I'd seldom heard. This kind of concern. It wasn't my old man's style. He tends to wander between enraged and utterly indifferent. I was quite sure he'd made this up about the family. Of course he'd made it up. We could take a car down there tomorrow and they'd welcome us, few questions asked. Family was everything in Algeria. He wanted me to reel Nathan in, and this was the way to do it.

Although he kicked and screamed against the decision, Nathan finally accepted we had to abort. We booked ourselves onto the same flight as Assia, which in the end turned out to be the very last flight back to London before the airport completely closed down.

We walked into what was for the most part a ghost terminal, a giant marble emptiness, the sound of Matoub Lounès – Le Rebelle – spilling *out of a crappy little stereo at the one remaining sandwich kiosk as we staged our retreat.*

'Another time, man. Another time. We'll be back, Nathan,' I told my brother. 'Trust me . . .'

ACKNOWLEDGEMENTS

The writing of this book would not have been possible without the teachings of Sathya Sai Baba and the extensive recollections of Saul Adamczewski and Nathan Saoudi. Adelle would like to thank the families of Fat White Family for their contributions, including Michelle Barnes-Kee, Bashir Saoudi, Tamlan Saoudi, Simon Adamczewski and Ruth Owen. Thanks also to the following interviewees who took time out during the plague year to discuss their memories of the band: Adam J. Harmer, Pete Hambly, Alex Sebley, Lou Smith, Beth Soan, Joseph Pancucci-Simpson, Dan Lyons, Liam May, Anna McDowell, Ben Romans-Hopcraft, Alex White, Andrew Stahl, Stuart Green, Jason Williamson, Mairead O'Connor and Adrian Flanagan.

Steve Phillips' press cuttings file played an essential part in compiling this story, as have the combined efforts of Sarah Brooksbank and Dan McEvoy.

Our editors Lee Brackstone, Rosie Pearce, Martha Sprackland and all at White Rabbit deserve our utmost thanks. To all who read this in its early stages: Matthew Hamilton, Benjamin Myers, Lisa Cradduck and Rob Doyle, we offer our deepest gratitude.

FURTHER READING

Fat White Family's videos are available on their YouTube channel, with their discography on Spotify. Vinyl, merchandise, gig tickets and upcoming tour dates can be purchased directly from fatwhitefamilymusic.com

There is an extensive archive of Fat White Family gigs on Lou Smith's YouTube channel from the band's first gig to the present day. A selection of his photographs and Fat White-related merchandise can be purchased in *Through the Lens of Lou Smith: Fat White Family Vol.1* or via Lou's website: https://capturedontherye.bigcartel.com

Sweating Tears with Fat White Family by Adelle Stripe and Lisa Cradduck can be found at http://roughtradebooks.com

Woo! Strange Happenings at the Windmill and Other Tangential Rants by Dave Thomson is available at https://peasantvitality.com

A Void magazine, Saul Adamczewski's Make Peckham Shit Again poster and other Fat Whites-related ephemera can be viewed and acquired via Morbid Books: https://morbidbooks.net

Niall Trask directed *Moonbathing in February*, a short fly-on-the-wall film set in Hastings with the band. Visit https://thekillshop.com for further info.

Andrew Zappin has directed the full-length tour documentary *Utter Bliss: Lost in America with the Fat White Family*, which is forthcoming in 2022. He is also editing a forthcoming collaborative book of Fat White photography with Duncan Stafford.

Bashir Saoudi and Michael J. Malone's novel based on Kaci Saoudi's life story, *The Guillotine Choice*, was published by Contraband in 2014.

Fat White Family Discography

Albums
Champagne Holocaust (Trashmouth, 2013)
Crippled B-Sides and Inconsequential Rarities (Self-released, 2014)
Songs for Our Mothers (Without Consent / [PIAS], 2016)
Serfs Up! (Domino, 2019)

Singles
'Auto Neutron' (Trashmouth, 2014)
'Touch the Leather' (Hate Hate Hate Records, 2014)
'I Am Mark E. Smith' (Without Consent, 2014)
'Breaking Into Aldi' (Without Consent, 2016)
'Whitest Boy on the Beach' (Without Consent, 2016)
'Tinfoil Deathstar' (Without Consent, 2016)
'Feet' (Domino, 2019)
'Tastes Good with the Money' (Domino, 2019)

Those Who Served

Lias Saoudi
Saul Adamczewski
Nathan Saoudi
Adam J. Harmer
Dan Lyons
Joe Pancucci-Simpson

TEN THOUSAND APOLOGIES

Jack Everett
Severin Black
Jak Payne
Taishi Nagasaka
Sam Toms
Alex White
Adam Brennan
Ciaran Hartnett
Mairead O'Connor
Chris O.C.
Dale Barclay
Martin Dean
Mike Brandon
Chris Taylor
Simek
Angus Knight
Aidan McMillan
L.A. Solano
Rob 'Bongo' Doyle

LIST OF IMAGES

Lias and his then-sweetheart Amy Smith; only by some metaphysical sleight of hand has Amy become a Cornish pasty.
Courtesy of Lias Saoudi

p. 83 The Saudis shortly before failing to arrive at any kind of prominence whatsoever.
Courtesy of Michelle Barnes-Kee

p. 98 One of Saul's drawings. Through the years these have often provided invaluable insight as to what is actually simmering away beneath the 'man of action' veneer.
Courtesy of Saul Adamczewski

p. 110 Could either of these two ever be photographed looking more content? Saul embraces Mohamed Al-Fayed while on a visit to his school.
Courtesy of Ruth Owen

p. 123 Saul and Nathan sometime in the late noughties. Bastard music is coming.
Courtesy of Michelle Barnes-Kee

p. 128 Bashir gave a fine speech at Lias's funeral. No one had ever seen him so animated, in fact.
Courtesy of Lias Saoudi

p. 133 The original line-up with Svengali-type first manager Robert Rubbish in the middle. The struggle begins . . .
Courtesy of Lou Smith

p. 143 Poster for the Fat Whites' first album launch and final ever gig at the Queen's Head.
Courtesy of Saul Adamczewski

p. 158 Battlestar gurnica on the Stockwell/Brixton borders.
Courtesy of Enzo Peccinotti

p. 163 The big break: Nathan's hole. Still from 'Touch the Leather' video by Roger Sargent, 2014.
Courtesy of Roger Sargent and Fat White Family